THE STORY OF
FOOTBALL

FOOTBALL.—Last evening a meeting of the captains or other representatives of the football clubs of the metropolis was held at the Freemasons' Tavern, Great Queen-street, Lincoln's Inn-fields. Mr. Pember, N. N. Kilburn Club, having been voted to the chair, observed that the adoption of a certain set of rules by all football players was greatly to be desired, and said that the meeting had been called to carry that object into effect as far as practicable. Mr. E. C. Morley (Barnes) moved, and Mr. Mackenzie (Forest Club, Leytonstone) seconded, the following resolution :—"That it is advisable that a football association should be formed for the purpose of settling a code of rules for the regulation of the game of football." Mr. B. F. Hartshorne said that though he felt it was most desirable that a definite set of rules for football should be generally adopted, yet, as the representative of the Charterhouse School, he could not pledge himself to any course of action without seeing more clearly what other schools would do in the matter. On the part of the Charterhouse he would willingly coalesce if other public schools would do the same. Probably, at a more advanced stage of the association, the opinion of the generality of the great schools would be obtained. The chairman said every association must have a beginning, and they would be very happy to have the co-operation of the last speaker at a future meeting. The resolution for the formation of the association was then put and carried. The officers were elected as follows :—Mr. A. Pember, President ; Mr. E. C. Morley (Barnes), Hon. Secretary; Mr. F. M. Campbell (Blackheath), Treasurer. The annual subscription was fixed at one guinea, all clubs being eligible if of one year's standing, and to be entitled to send two representatives to the yearly meeting, to be held in the last week in September, when the rules would be revised, and the general business arrangements carried out.

ST. GEORGE'S-IN-THE-EAST.—The arrangement which has been for some time past in progress for an ex-

THE STORY OF
FOOTBALL

Marshall Cavendish London & New York

Endpapers: Gerd Muller (right), the man who won the 1974 World Cup for West Germany, at home in the penalty area for Bayern Munich. Page 1: The report in The Times *from 27 October 1863 giving details of the foundation of the Football Association. Previous pages: West Ham's Mervyn Day and John McDowell outjump Burnley's Peter Noble in a 1975 First Division game at Upton Park. Above and right: Football through its organised years, from left to right: the Harrow School team in the 1860s; Southampton score against Queen's Park Rangers in a 1904 Southern League game; a thirsty crowd at Stamford Bridge during a heatwave in 1914; one of the first colour photographs taken at a League match showed Tommy Lawton during his Indian summer with Arsenal in 1954; the despondent fan is Fred Ball whose team, Stoke City, have just gone a goal down at Leeds; Pele, the greatest of them all, during his magnificent 1970 World Cup; a new England strip and problems for Scotland as Colin Bell celebrates one of his side's five goals at Wembley in 1975. Page 6: Bobby Moore and team-mate Martin Peters at Guadalajara during the 1–0 defeat of Czechoslovakia in 1970.*

House Editing: Isabel Moore and Phil Soar
Design: Jim Bamber
Artwork: Paul Buckle/Diagram
Published by Marshall Cavendish Publications Limited,
58 Old Compton Street, London W1V 5PA
© Marshall Cavendish Limited 1969, 1970, 1971, 1972, 1973, 1976
This volume first published 1976
Printed in Great Britain by Severn Valley Press Limited

ISBN 0 85685 177 9

Certain chapters of this book are partially
based on material originally published in
the partwork 'Book of Football'. The
publishers would particularly like to thank
Brian Glanville for his contributions to
sections covering the Jules Rimet Trophy.

FOREWORD by Martin Tyler

No book, of course, can be large enough to house football's complete story. Nor can any published record keep pace with day-by-day additions to the tale. But THE STORY OF FOOTBALL is a genuine attempt to provide a new and wider umbrella for the game's history—a game in which I have been happily emeshed since I could first kick a ball.

Like its subject matter, THE STORY OF FOOTBALL is the product of teamwork, and I would therefore like to thank those whose original efforts for the partwork 'Book of Football' provided the background information for some of the chapters here—Nick Mason, on the early history, Brian Glanville, on the World Cup, Ken Jones, John Ruck and Richard Widdows. I am also indebted to Maurice Golesworthy for his authentication of the earlier chapters.

I must also record my deepest appreciation of the help given to me by Phil Soar, who initiated the concept of THE STORY OF FOOTBALL and then with his enthusiasm, encouragement and expertise brought it to reality. His contribution to the final product has been immense. Finally, I thank Dianne Owen who, in the darkest hours, instilled self-belief.

INTRODUCTION by Bobby Moore

The Story of Football must be among the best football books ever written and one surely destined to become a true collector's item. It is an entertainingly written history of the game we all love and its many pictures illustrate and expand the text in a really unique way.

I would be less than honest if I did not confess that I found the parts of the book coinciding with my own time in football particularly interesting, but really the appeal of The Story of Football is universal.

Those with long memories will revel in the nostalgia of reliving great goals, games and glories, while younger readers will perhaps appreciate today's game more for understanding and knowing its past a little better. It certainly makes me feel proud to have been part of that history.

THE STORY O

F FOOTBALL

For Brian James

FROM THE MISTS OF TIME...
The Game before 1863

If Britain manufactured association football, it was a product for which the raw materials could have been drawn from all over the world. From the time when the invention of the wheel made man aware of the properties of a curved surface, every land has had its pastime in which some type of ball played a part. Britain's virtue lay only in formalising some of these earlier games into organised sport, and, having fashioned the article, in ultimately exporting it around the globe.

Exactly where the first ball was kicked is buried deep in history, and no single individual or society can be said to have 'invented' football. But it is certain that, in both the ancient cultures of Greece and Rome, organised games formed part of sporting spectacles, though the Athenian League remained a concept for English amateur football in the twentieth century and the contest performed between rival Roman legions probably had more in common with contemporary rugby league or

Below: *Street football, for centuries little more than a disorganised brawl or formless contest between local villages.*

Above: *A print purporting to represent football in Italy in the sixteenth century. A 26-a-side game certainly existed in Florence as early as 1530 and the rules were codified as* Discorsa Calcio *in 1580.*

American football than the game we now refer to as soccer.

In civilisations as distant as China and ancient Mexico, records point to competitions of high skill and technique which would be beyond many a professional footballer of later years. The Far East has always been the traditional home of the juggler and the early version of football in those lands encouraged such virtues; points were not scored via the traditional medium of 'goals' but were awarded when the performers directed the ball through holes in curtains, or, as in Mexico, through rings set up high in a wall. Heading and kicking were both permitted methods of propulsion. In the light of such a heritage the suppleness and the co-ordination shown by the North Koreans in the 1966 World Cup finals should have come as no surprise, and, indeed, in Japan a game is still played which rewards participants who can juggle and manipulate with their feet, heads, thighs and shoulders a ball made out of wickerwork.

Such dexterity held little place in the English ball games of the early Christian era. You risked your life if you took part in the violent skirmishes, often between neighbouring communities, which characterised the prototype sports of that time. Every Shrove Tuesday in Ashbourne, Derbyshire, remembrance is still paid to this type of sport with a contest between the two halves of the town; the goals are the gates of Ashbourne Hall and the parish church. Records suggest that the first of these trials of strength took place around AD 217, and they also refer to similar mass contests across open countryside in Cornwall, Cumberland and Brittany.

As the game in all its forms was later to do, these early versions of football provided a means for release of tension; a public brawl in the middle ages could end in death for any person blamed for the incident, so there was a healthy interest in playing a game in which even severe violence passed unpunished. And while football flourished, there was also a considerable increase in the numbers who suffered often permanent injury during this sprawling, brawling pastime which spread itself across the countryside like a hunt in full cry.

Inevitably its anti-social aspects attracted criticism. Both Scottish and English monarchs—among them Edward III, Richard II and Henry IV—became anxious about

the large number of supposedly fit young men who became unfit for army training as a result of damage sustained while playing football rather than at valuable pursuits such as archery. The game was banned by royal decree. Later the Puritans, alarmed that the participants in this rough sport might actually be enjoying themselves, spoke out against it. The game was banned by ecclesiastical decree.

Both types of order were sensibly ignored by the masses. And eventually royalty and academics realised the virtues of the game. By the turn of the seventeenth century the students of Cambridge University were allowed to broaden their bodies as well as their minds by playing football. Certain thinkers of the day found that the rough and tumble of this often thirty-a-side sport lacked sophistication and hived off their interest into an Italian hybrid game called *calcio*. History recalls *calcio* as a game which needed speed and balance as well as physical resolution but it does not record whether its Italian ancestors played with the defensive attitudes of their twentieth century descendants; it seems unlikely.

And so football prospered—but in a whole variety of forms and with such in-

consistency of rules (when there were any at all) that competition, except between local opponents, was impossible. Kicking the ball was always allowed, so was handling in varying styles; goals came in different sizes, and shapes; the playing area had diverse definitions; and above all no one could exactly agree what atrocities one player could commit on another. But whatever form prevailed in a locality it now engendered sufficient thrilling activity that not only was there no shortage of participants but those too old, too scared, or of the wrong sex to take part would attend as spectators.

But the game still had one more damp fuse to survive before it exploded into immense and eventually world-wide popularity. The advent of the Industrial Revolution disrupted the social climate, particularly the pattern of working that had allowed rural villagers the time to play. As Britain urbanised, farm labourers became factory workers—exploited labour forces who toiled long hours in oppressive conditions; on the few public holidays, those who had indulged in sporting activities rarely had the energy or inclination to organise or participate. As a game of the

Above: *An artist's impression of a street match in London during the fourteenth century.*

Above: *A soldiers' friendly, from a print dated 1827.*
Above right: *A school game from a little later, showing the sort of melées that developed in the 'dribbling' game. Handling and hacking were clearly allowed.*
Opposite left: *Ashbourne in Derbyshire, where a Shrove Tuesday game has reputedly been played since AD 217.*
Far right: *A letter which appeared in* The Times *on 5 October 1863 pleading for a single set of rules. The content of the letter was an excellent summary of the problem and helped lead to the formation of the FA later in the month.*

common people, football was in decline.

This trend was redressed by the more educated classes. The game of the public became the sport of the public (meaning private) schools. Increasingly the purpose of these establishments was to breed a succession of generations of responsible young gentlemen, and the headmasters of all believed in the dictum of a healthy body breeding a healthy mind; football in some form or another was always on the curriculum. As a game it was expedient, too, because facilities were much cheaper than the traditional pastimes of the young aristocrat —hunting, shooting and fishing.

But there still remained little uniformity. At Charterhouse, for example, the rules did not permit handling, the players all being skilled dribblers on the stony surface of the cloisters (where the game was played), and teams consisted of twenty players per side. At Harrow football was an eleven-a-side game on muddy terrain at the bottom of the school's hill. At Rugby, where radical change was imminent, boys could handle the ball but could not run with it in their hands. Meanwhile Eton fashioned a totally unique experience, the famed Wall Game with goals (one a small door, the other a tree) at either end of a wall which was 120 yards long; scrimmages were long and fierce and goals were very scarce, the pitch being only six yards wide. The goalscoring rate in all games at Eton this century has been approximately one every two years, not exactly the kind of attack-minded displays likely to threaten the spectator appeal of soccer. Westminster based its game of football on a similar pattern to that of Charterhouse, while the Winchester version of football existed without any goals at all, points being awarded when the ball was kicked over the goal-line.

It was hardly a situation conducive to competition between the schools. Each generation of schoolboys handed down the codes of practice at their particular estab-

lishment (largely determined by the physical layout of the games area) and even within the major schools formal rule-books were rare. When one participant improvised in any way condemnation was hard to substantiate. So it was at Rugby School in 1823. There, on the wide reaches of The Close, William Webb Ellis made the transition from anonymous schoolboy to immortal. Ignoring the custom of his school, he picked up the ball, clasped it in both hands and ran with it towards the opposing goal-line. Just how his fellows reacted to such behaviour is a matter of conjecture, but he had broken only convention, not a set of written rules; his rather obvious action constituted not a foul but a matter for debate. And within twenty years Webb Ellis's interpretation had become an accepted feature of the game of football played at Rugby.

But still there could be no inter-school matches, nor indeed could those who had left school participate in organised football. And it was the need of the latter group which finally stimulated the first serious attempts to create a set of unified regulations. In 1848 fourteen students at Cambridge University met for this purpose, among them a former pupil of Rugby School who had played his football in the post-Webb Ellis vein. The areas for argument were vast and the meeting stretched on and on, but in the final outcome the delegate from Rugby could not have received much support. The use of the hands was only permitted in arresting the flight of the ball and the rules outlawed the practice of running with it.

The first mould of what was to become association football had been cast. A goal could be scored by kicking the ball between two posts and under a piece of string which joined them; tripping, kicking or grabbing an opponent was to be penalised; the ball could be passed forwards as long as the receiver had three opponents between him

and the goal. Some common basis for competition had been laid down.

As football at Oxford and Cambridge blossomed under the new regulations, the game had re-emerged outside the playing fields of the academic institutions. The spread of industry had not simply perpetuated the polarisation of classes of feudal times; it had created a new breed, a middle-class of professional men who had the luxury of leisure time. Men such as these turned to football as a newly respectable outlet.

The industrial atmosphere of Sheffield gave birth to the first football club of modern definition, and in the mid-1850s matches were allowed to take place on the ground of the Sheffield Cricket Club at Bramall Lane, a site which, over a hundred years later, was to reverse the process and become solely devoted to the use of Sheffield United FC to the exclusion of Yorkshire cricket. The Sheffield club was almost certainly in existence in some form as early as 1854, but its first rulebook was not produced until 1857. The original players were from the Old Collegiate School in Sheffield, with a probable sprinkling of Old Etonians. Sheffield are the oldest club still in existence, having preceded the first of the London clubs (Hampstead Heathens and Forest, later Wanderers, were both probably formed in 1858) and their proud history contains one major honour—the Amateur Cup of 1904. At first they played to the basis of the Cambridge Rules, but the protagonists were allowed to hit the ball forwards with their hands; the practice of pushing away an opponent with the hands was also allowed. And there was no denying the spectator appeal; when Sheffield met their local rivals Hallam in 1861, 600 followers attended.

The experience of Sheffield typified the upsurge of interest in the game—and the still differing versions that were being played up and down a land in which the

FOOTBALL.

TO THE EDITOR OF THE TIMES.

Sir,—A letter having lately appeared in the columns of one of your contemporaries on the subject of football, and the inconvenience consequent upon there being no general and universally acknowledged rules of this game, I seize this opportunity of making a few remarks on a subject so fraught with interest for public schools. I am myself an Etonian, and the game of football as played by us differs essentially in most respects from that played at Westminster, Rugby, Harrow, and most of the London clubs. Now, this difference prevents matches being made or played between either school or club; and, furthermore, prevents a player from gaining the credit of playing well anywhere but among his own associates. For instance, an Etonian who attempts to play at the Rugby game finds himself quite unable to touch the ball at all, and so *vice versa*. The Etonians have now for two years played against the Westminsters in Vincent-square; the game is a kind of compromise between the two, more closely resembling the Westminster game than ours; the display is therefore below mediocrity—neither of the sides can practice any of their favourite "dodges" without infringing the rules of the other, and an advantage gained by one side is not lawful by the rules of the opposite party. The results of the two matches have been that in 1861, at the eleventh hour, we fluked a goal, and in 1862, at the eleventh hour, also, one of our best players was knocked over, and broke his arm in the fall; and, while I am on this subject, I think it but just to do what I am afraid has not been done before—viz., acknowledge on behalf of my school the great kindness and consideration, as well as courtesy, on the part of the Westminsters on this occasion, for which they were, I dare say, thanked individually, though not collectively.

Now, Sir, all these annoyances might be prevented by the framing of set rules for the game of football to be played everywhere. Say, let the captains of the football elevens at Eton, Westminster, and Rugby, and the presidents of one or two London clubs meet, with members of either University, and frame rules for one universal game.

The public schools would no doubt be very unwilling to give up their old game, and so they might very well keep it up among themselves, while the new rules might be observed at any match between schools or clubs, and, the advantages being thus equalized, football might then stand a chance of occupying, among other games, the rank which so healthy and manly a sport deserves to hold, while all the inconvenience consequent upon playing a game with no fixed rules would be avoided.

I would suggest, in conclusion, that the new rules should be framed before the match between Eton and Westminster, as, with the present state of things, to whichever side victory may incline, it brings with it no glory, but a great deal of dissatisfaction.

With apologies for thus trespassing on your valuable space,

Oct. 3.
I am, Sir, yours obediently,
ETONENSIS.

Cambridge Rules had not found universal acceptance. Within a few years of the founding of the first Sheffield teams, the area could boast as many as fifteen football clubs. Both players and onlookers were becoming aware of the extra thrills that competition stimulated; but though Sheffield had its code of laws, there was still a faltering step or two to be taken even before any small consensus could be achieved.

Not many miles south of Sheffield, Uppingham School in Rutland performed their variation on this theme. The Headmaster, Edward Thring, and his younger brother J C Thring, formalised their game in a set of rules entitled *The Simplest Game*; for the boys of their school there was no physical violence, no kicking of the ball when it was off the ground, no attacker allowed in front of the ball. If the regulations sounded a little unattractive there was surely no shortage of goals, for the Thrings decreed that the goal should stretch across the width of the pitch, defined by two sticks joined by a long piece of tape.

But all the minor variations and interpretations of football boiled down to one major division of opinion—should players be permitted to propel or carry the ball with their hands. If you had chosen to watch a contest in 1860 it might have fallen into one of two kinds of spectacle. Either foot or hand would dominate. In the former, you would witness a game of dribbling, in which there would be a succession of individual forays into the opposing territory, and when possession had been lost an opponent would set up his solo counter-attack. Passing was an art as yet unborn, and the swift runner who could manipulate the ball with his feet was the coveted player. In the latter instance the spectator would see a match of scrimmaging, of long punts from one end of the field to the other, of players running with the ball under their arms while opponents could push them off balance. Many local versions were really a combination of both handling and kicking though, interestingly, never heading. It must be stressed that there was no soccer or rugby at this stage—merely 'football', though, for the game as played at Rugby School, this was already a misnomer.

If, as history turned the corner into the 1860s, the situation seemed rife for a split between the two methods of propulsion, there was little indication as to which emphasis of play had more adherents. The social environment, rather than individuals, had created two prototypes of a product for which there was a great demand. But late in 1863 a selection was to be made, and the process of sophisticating the product was to begin.

The many faces of football and the major varieties that the game has spawned. Australian Rules (below) is the premier game in the State of Victoria. Football in North America is of a very different nature, in both American and (bottom) Canadian versions. Rugby broke from soccer as early as 1863, a formal Union being established in 1871; New Zealand's All Blacks (this page bottom left) remain prime exponents. Rugby later split into two varieties, union and (left) league. Gaelic football (opposite page bottom) is the individualistic Irish version. South Wales (far left) and Cornwall are the only parts of Great Britain where a version of football other than soccer is the principal game.

17

AN ASSOCIATION, AN INTERNATIONAL, A CUP
Britain 1863-1872

Below: *The 15-man Uppingham School team pose in front of one of their idiosyncratic pitch-wide goals at the Rutland school in the 1860s. The 'Simplest Game' had been codified there in 1862.*

Football changed from a game to a sport on 26 October 1863. Representatives of eleven clubs in the London area gathered that day at the Freemasons' Tavern in Holborn with the explicit intention of founding an association. Their reasons were essentially mundane. They were not seeking to spread their old school games to the far corners of the earth, nor to take the first step in a movement that was to develop into the world's premier sport. Rather they were simply trying to establish a uniform set of rules and so avoid the long debates which always preceded any game between teams which operated under different codes.

Most of the clubs involved had been founded by old boys from public schools— as a result they all played to the rules operating at their old schools, and this explains the continuing lack of uniformity among codes. Almost as significant, in a sense, as those who did attend were those who did

not. Notable absentees were any representatives from Cambridge University (where one of several revisions of the 1848 rules had just been drawn up), the major public schools (as distinct from their old boys), and anyone from the two major provincial centres of the game, Sheffield and Nottingham.

It was essentially a local meeting of ex-public schoolboys living in London. At the time there were no national ambitions—or, if there were, they remained unadmitted. Most of the clubs involved subscribed more or less to variations of the Harrow School and Cambridge Rules, several of the more prominent sides, such as Forest (nothing to do with Nottingham Forest) and Kilburn No Names, being comprised of Old Harrovians. There was also a sprinkling of Old Rugbeians, led by the Blackheath club, who were to disagree with the Harrow party almost at once. One A Pember of Kilburn

No Names was elected the first chairman, F M Campbell of Blackheath briefly became treasurer and E C Morley, of Barnes, secretary.

Some of the other clubs represented were: Crystal Palace, a short lived side (named after the Great Exhibition Hall of 1851 which had been moved to South London in 1854) having nothing to do with the present League team and playing in blue and white with blue serge knickerbockers; two Blackheath schools which were closely associated with the Old Rugbeian Blackheath Club; Kensington Grammar School, represented by their captain William Macintosh, which had not so much an undistinguished career as no career at all in the years to come; Morley and the club's secretary P D Gregory represented Barnes, who played 'in a field belonging to J Johnstone Esq near the White Hart'; the War Office, represented by E Wawn, and a selection of representatives of various other sides including Forest, the Crusaders, an observer from Charterhouse, several other observers from undisclosed clubs and, even at this stage, at least one member of the press. Few of these clubs have survived in any shape or form; only Blackheath still exist at any remotely senior level—and then playing rugby union!

Blackheath's Campbell and Barnes' Morley clashed almost immediately in the subsequent series of meetings arranged to draw up the all-important formal rules, and the two were to remain the figureheads of the soccer versus rugby clash. Draft rules nine and ten were the stumbling blocks. The former allowed a player to run with the ball '... if he makes a fair catch', a basic ingredient of the Rugby game since William Webb Ellis's day. Draft rule ten, however, was far more contentious. It would allow players to 'charge, hold, trip or hack (an opponent) ...' but generously allowed that '... no player shall be held and hacked at the same time.'

In the end the issue was black and white. Blackheath and the Rugbeians insisted on the inclusion of these rules, the rest on their exclusion. At a decisive meeting on 1 December 1863, Morley insisted that if hacking were allowed '... men of business would be unwilling to play football.' Campbell retorted that: 'Hacking is the true football game and if it is done away with all the pluck and courage of the game will be at an end.' Campbell did not help his cause with tactless remarks directed, among other things, at Morley's lack of a public school education, thus implying that he was scared of the rough and tumble of the games as played at these institutions as well as suggesting some sort of social inferiority.

FOOTBALL.—Last evening a meeting of the captains or other representatives of the football clubs of the metropolis was held at the Freemasons' Tavern, Great Queen-street, Lincoln's Inn-fields. Mr. Pember, N. N. Kilburn Club, having been voted to the chair, observed that the adoption of a certain set of rules by all football players was greatly to be desired, and said that the meeting had been called to carry that object into effect as far as practicable. Mr. E. C. Morley (Barnes) moved, and Mr. Mackenzie (Forest Club, Leytonstone) seconded, the following resolution :—"That it is advisable that a football association should be formed for the purpose of settling a code of rules for the regulation of the game of football." Mr. B. F. Hartshorne said that though he felt it was most desirable that a definite set of rules for football should be generally adopted, yet, as the representative of the Charterhouse School, he could not pledge himself to any course of action without seeing more clearly what other schools would do in the matter. On the part of the Charterhouse he would willingly coalesce if other public schools would do the same. Probably, at a more advanced stage of the association, the opinion of the generality of the great schools would be obtained. The chairman said every association must have a beginning, and they would be very happy to have the co-operation of the last speaker at a future meeting. The resolution for the formation of the association was then put and carried. The officers were elected as follows :—Mr. A. Pember, President ; Mr. E. C. Morley (Barnes), Hon. Secretary; Mr. F. M. Campbell (Blackheath), Treasurer. The annual subscription was fixed at one guinea, all clubs being eligible if of one year's standing, and to be entitled to send two representatives to the yearly meeting, to be held in the last week in September, when the rules would be revised, and the general business arrangements carried out.

ST. GEORGE'S-IN-THE-EAST.—The arrangement which has been for some time past in progress for an ex- ... lergyman in ...

It is unlikely that Campbell would have won the argument anyway, and the vote went so firmly against the Rugbeians that they immediately left the Association. The rival Rugby Union, in keeping with its history of loose and informal organisation, was not actually formed until 1871. It immediately outlawed hacking.

The major public schools themselves (from where, it was assumed, the majority of future players would come) had already been asked their opinions on a uniform code of rules. Harrow replied: 'We cling to our present rules and should be sorry to alter them in any respect.' Charterhouse's observer at the original meeting had replied similarly. The rest were non-commital.

By 8 December 1863 general agreement had been reached among the clubs and the new Association's first laws clearly followed those of Cambridge which 'embraced the true principles of the game' and had, in turn, derived much from Harrow. There

Above: Organised football arrives. Yet the foundation of the Football Association warranted just three column inches in The Times *of 27 October 1863 and was ignored by all other newspapers except* Bell's Life.

were still some local variations but it probably seemed that all would soon be standardised. In fact it was to be nearly twenty years before the whole country was playing to an accepted set of rules—and even as late as the 1884 Cup final there were bitter disputes over basic interpretations.

The rules as finally agreed were:

1. The maximum length of the ground shall be 200 yd.; the maximum breadth shall be 100 yd.; the length and breadth shall be marked off with flags; and the goals shall be defined by two upright posts, 8 yd. apart, without any tape or bar across them.

2. The winners of the toss shall have the choice of goals. The game shall be commenced by a place-kick from the centre of the ground by the side losing the toss. The other side shall not approach within 10 yd. of the ball until it is kicked off.

3. After a goal is won, the losing side shall kick off, and goals shall be changed.

4. A goal shall be won when the ball passes between the posts or over the space between the posts (at whatever height), not being thrown, knocked on, or carried.

5. When the ball is in touch, the first player who touches it shall throw it from the point on the boundary-line where it left the ground in a direction at right angles with the boundary-line, and it shall not be in play until it has touched the ground.

6. When a player has kicked the ball, any one of the same side who is nearer the opponents' goal-line is out of play, and may not touch the ball himself nor in any way whatever prevent any other player from doing so until the ball has been played; but no player is out of play when the ball is kicked from behind the goal-line.

7. In case the ball goes behind the goal-line, if a player on the same side to whom the goal belongs first touches the ball, one of his side shall be entitled to a free-kick from the goal-line at the point opposite the place where the ball shall be touched. If a player of the opposite side first touches the ball, one of his side shall be entitled to a free-kick (but at the goal only) from a point 15 yd. from the goal-line opposite the place where the ball is touched; the opposing side shall stand behind the goal-line until he has had his kick.

8. If a player makes a fair catch, he shall be entitled to a free-kick, provided he claims it by making a mark with his heel at once; and in order to take such a kick he may go as far back as he pleases, and no player on the opposite side shall advance beyond his mark until he has kicked.

9. No player shall carry the ball.

10. Neither tripping nor hacking shall be allowed, and no player shall use his hands to hold or push an adversary.

11. A player shall not throw the ball or pass it to another.

12. No player shall take the ball from the ground with his hands while it is in play under any pretence whatever.

13. A player shall be allowed to throw the ball or pass it to another if he made a fair catch or catches the ball on the first bounce.

14. No player shall be allowed to wear projecting nails, iron plates or gutta percha on the soles or heels of his boots.

Laws one to eight remain the basis of rugby union to the present day. As they imply, much was left unregulated and it is immediately noticeable that there is no reference to the size and shape of the ball, referees, goalkeepers, free-kicks for infringements, penalties or even the number of players! The laws were meant to lay down *basics* which were common to all matches—'additional' restrictions could still be agreed by captains before games began. Even today certain variations are still allowed—there is no directive on the precise size of the pitch or shape of goalposts for instance. The original offside law (number 6) is particularly interesting—it was thirty years before anyone noticed that

'kicking' does not include heading and changed the law to 'played' rather than 'kicked'.

The twenty-year lag before these laws became universally accepted was due largely to the lethargy of the new Association. It was not until 1866 that a truly representative game was arranged and, up to that time, the strong provincial groupings were effectively ignored. Sheffield had approached the newly founded Association as early as 1863 in an attempt to formalise a single code, but received absolutely no encouragement and barely even a formal reply. It is vital to remember that, at this time, the Football Association controlled only the handful of clubs in membership. Most provincial clubs bore no more allegiance to it than the Rugby League does to the Rugby Union today.

But on 31 March 1866 London (in reality the Football Association) did finally take on Sheffield at Battersea Park, winning easily by 2 goals and 4 touch-downs to nil (see law 7). During the match one Charles W Alcock had the distinction of being the first man ruled offside in an official Football Association fixture. The same year Alcock joined the FA Committee and things began to move ahead again.

Born in Sunderland but educated at Harrow, Alcock seems to have had a much wider, national, vision than his contemporaries. He may have been aware that the Association was already being overtaken in the provinces and was instrumental in bringing the first Yorkshire representative on to the FA Committee in 1868. Sheffield already had a thriving group of clubs and was about to establish its own association. If Alcock had hoped to forestall this rival he failed, which was probably for the good, as the local associations which were to come into being during the next decade had a vital administrative role to play and in no way ever threatened the ultimate control of the original body in London.

There was already an annual representative game between Sheffield and Nottingham, the other major centre, which had first been played on 2 January 1865 and won by the eighteen-man Sheffield side. The number of players, incidentally, was one of the biggest bones of contention between rival codes in the early years and obviously related to the size of the playing area. Notts County (often known as plain Nottingham before 1880) had been founded in 1862 and are the oldest of the surviving senior clubs. Second in genealogy, and founded in 1865, come rivals Nottingham Forest. The Nottingham clubs sprang from the County Cricket Club—then the strongest in England—and some 'shinney' (a form of hockey) players. Both used Trent Bridge as a venue for major matches until the end of the century and thus retained their original links with the Cricket Club. The suffix Forest came from a clearing to the north of Nottingham, once part of renowned Sherwood Forest, where some games were also played.

That was the venue of the Nottingham clubs' first clash (also the first between any two Football League clubs though in 1865 Sheffield had played County) in 1866 which ended in a 1–0 win for Nottingham Forest when, according to a guide of 1871, '. . . there was a sort of steeple chase across the goal-line and over the grandstand railings where W H Revis touched down. The place-kick, 15 yards at right-angles from the goal-line, was taken by the same player.' As can be deduced, the Nottingham game was a hybrid, relying on a mixture of Sheffield, Rugby and London rules with a few Nottingham perversions probably thrown in. Most codes required a try and goal (as in rugby union today) for a proper score until the end of the 1860s.

Elsewhere Chesterfield, midway between Sheffield and Nottingham, was founded in 1866. Stoke have long claimed to have been founded in 1863, but there is no satisfactory evidence of their existence before 1867 and they come next in the ranks of current League clubs (City was added in 1925). Other than Sheffield, the major local associations—such as the Scottish, Lancashire and Birmingham—were not founded until the 1870s and individual provincial clubs tended to vary their rules according to their opponents.

The contact between the FA and Sheffield in 1866 inevitably provoked further efforts to standardise laws throughout the country. The fair catch (and thus handling) was abolished and a tape was soon stretched between the posts (thus returning to the Cambridge Rules) after a goal had been scored at Reigate '. . . from a balloon kick which had passed quite 90 feet in the air between the posts' according to the FA Chairman. Sheffield wanted a bar, but this was not made obligatory until 1882. Free-kicks for infringements had been incorporated in the laws by the 1873–74 season; before this date the game had apparently functioned on the presumption that gentlemen did not commit fouls.

Other law changes gradually followed, although Sheffield continued to play to their own rules when at home until April 1877. Goal-kicks were introduced in 1869, corner-kicks in 1872, umpires in 1874. It was not until 1870 that all clubs accepted eleven-a-side as the norm and, in the same year, came what has been described as the law-makers' master stroke, the innovation of a goalkeeper who was governed by a largely different set of laws from other players. Before this date, whichever player was closest to the goal took the responsibility and, as penalty-kicks were still two decades away, tended to handle regularly.

Strangely, the change of law that was to affect the game most significantly in the next dozen years was not regarded as being of any great importance when it was approved in 1867 and, indeed, it did not affect

Below: The commercial side of a developing game; this advertisement is from the 1890s.

football materially for several years. This was the alteration of the offside law from the old Harrow (and current rugby) rule that, basically, a player was offside unless he was behind the ball. It was changed to the more relaxed Charterhouse, Westminster and Cambridge version under which an attacker was onside unless there were fewer than three defenders between himself and the goal.

For nearly a century the early English footballers have been criticised for their slavish devotion to the 'dribbling' game. This has often been seen as an ill-considered manifestation of the public school ethic of self-reliance—quite unfairly if viewed alongside the rules adhered to by most schools and the FA before 1866. Under this code a player really had few alternatives. He could either pass back or dribble forwards, and this very simple fact explains the existence of the dribbling game. Its persistence is probably attributable to the conservatism of the sport, in that English teams had developed tactics suited to the old offside law and prized good dribblers above all others. The best of them all, and the first 'Prince of Dribblers', was the Reverend Vidal, who played for Wanderers in the first FA Cup final and who once scored three goals without an opponent touching the ball. This was in a game where the local code had the side which scored kicking off and Vidal simply dribbled straight from the off three times running.

It was not until the English came into contact with Scotland's Queen's Park in 1872 that they began to question their outdated methods. Queen's Park, in determining their own laws, had never been influenced by a repressive history and, from the beginning, had played the more complex 'combination' short passing game. Queen's Park also suffered far less from the competition and influence of the Rugby game. That school was, after all, a long way from Glasgow although the relative success of soccer over its competitors in Scotland is more often put down to the fact that it can be played on literally any surface and, with a little imagination, on any shaped area. Rugby generally requires a soft landing and the Scottish central lowlands had precious few open grassy areas within its towns.

The game had had as distinguished a history in Scotland as in England (Sir Walter Scott was a particularly notable fan, writing in 1815: 'Then strip lads, and to it, though sharp be the weather, And if, by mischance you should happen to fall, There are worse things in life than a tumble on heather, And life is itself but a game of football!') but there had been no formal codification. The centres of population

were in the central lowlands, and in Glasgow the keenest players eventually gravitated to one of the three public parks —Queen's Park.

On 9 July 1867, together with some local YMCA members and, according to legend, caber-tossing Highlanders who also used the park, the Queen's Park Football Club was founded at number 3 Eglinton Terrace. To begin with, their interests did not extend outside their own domain, matches being arranged between their own members and recorded as 'North of the Clyde' versus 'South of the Clyde' and such like. But gradually outside opposition was discovered and games organised—the first on 1 August 1868 against Thistle (nothing to do with Partick Thistle). Later Queen's Park were to have an influence all pervading north of the border and quite important south of it, but, for the time being, it suffices to say that their interpretation of the rules automatically became the Scottish interpretation.

Back in England, the contacts with Sheffield had awakened the proselytizing spirit in the Football Association and, for the first time, serious efforts were made to recruit new members. The Sheffield club joined in 1867, with teams from as far afield as Hull, Lincolnshire and South Wales. In 1870 Charles Alcock became secretary (at the age of twenty-eight) and the next ten years were to become the most significant in the history of the game, just as Alcock is arguably the most important figure in that history.

Alcock was soon to turn his attention to formally competitive events rather than informally arranged friendlies—and his

Above: The Sheffield team which won the Amateur Cup final of 1904, beating Ealing 3–1 at Bradford. This is the only honour ever won by the world's oldest football club. Officially formed on 24 October 1857, Sheffield took no part in the creation of the wholly Southern original Association.

Left: *The Royal Engineers side which in 1872 lost the first ever Cup final to the Wanderers. Arguably the best side of their era, Engineers lost only three of their 86 games from 1871 to 1875. Sadly two of these were the 1872 and 1874 Cup finals. Captain and co-ordinator Major Marindin is standing in the middle of the back row.*

FOOTBALL MATCH,

WANDERERS, London, v. QUEEN'S PARK,

Played on Hampden Park, Mount Florida, Glasgow, on Saturday, 9th October, 1875.

H. W. CHAMBERS.
Goal Keeper

A. H. STRATFORD,
Back.

A. F. KINNAIRD,
Right X Half-back
Blue and white cap

W. S. RAWSON
Left X Half-back
Blue cap

J. TURNER,
Left X Wing.

W. D. GREIG,
Right X Wing
Blue stockings

B. L. GEAVES,
Centre X
Red and white cap

C. W. ALCOCK,
Captain X and Centre.
Cap— blue and white chequers.

H. S. OTTER,
X Centre.
Pink cap

HUBERT HERON,
Left X Wing
Grey stockings and orange, violet, and black cap

J. KENRICK,
Right X Wing
Cerise and French grey cap

UMPIRE—ROBERT GARDINER, CLYDESDALE CLUB.
REFEREE—THOMAS HASWELL, 3RD L R.V CLUB
UMPIRE—W. C MITCHELL, QUEEN'S PARK CLUB

HENRY M'NEILL,
Left X Front
Orange and black stockings.

W. MACKINNON,
Centre X Front
Red stockings

JAMES B. WEIR,
Right X Front
Red and white stockings.

M. M'NEIL,
Left X Back-up
Blue and white stockings.

C. HERRIOT,
Centre X Back-up
Black and white cap—no stocking.

THOMAS LAWRIE,
Right X Back-up.
White stockings

JAS. PHILIPS
Left X Half-back
Red and black stockings.

CHAS. CAMPBELL,
Right X Half-back
Red, white, and black stockings.

R. W. NEIL,
Left X Back
Heather mixture stockings

JOSEPH TAYLOR,
Captain and X Right Back
Black and white stockings.

JOHN DICKSON,
Goal Keeper.

Colours : Wanderers, White Jersey — Queen's Park, Black and White Stripe.
Play will begin at 3.30 p.m. and end at 6 p m

PLEASE DO NOT STRAIN THE ROPES.

immediate interest was attracted by the reputation of mighty Queen's Park, who had still not had a goal scored against them! They actually remained unbeaten until February 1876 when Wanderers (the club of which Alcock was secretary and with which he won a Cup winner's medal) finally despatched them in a friendly. However, back in 1870 they were attracting all Scotland's best players but had little contact with England or the Football Association.

On 3 November that year, Alcock wrote to the *Glasgow Herald* announcing that the FA intended to select teams of English and Scottish players to compete against one another at Kennington Oval on 19 November. He invited nominations, stating: 'In Scotland, once essentially the land of football, there should still be a spark left of the old fire and I confidently appeal to Scotsmen. . . .' Alcock did not expect this challenge to be ignored, nor was it. Queen's Park nominated Robert Smith, one of three brothers who were founder members of Queen's Park and who now lived in London, and he effectively represented Scotland in the capital over the next two years.

The team that eventually lost 1–0 at the Oval was hardly representative of Scotland. W H Gladstone, son of the Prime Minister, was a Member of Parliament himself, Quintin Hogg was father and grandfather of Lord Chancellors of the same name, Lord Kinnaird was later High Commissioner for the Church of Scotland. The whole team was comprised of Scots living in England, and in some cases with only very tenuous links with Scotland at all. Nonetheless, unofficial and unrepresentative though the game was, it was counted a success and three more followed. England won two, the other being drawn 1–1.

In the meantime, at Raeburn Place in Edinburgh, there had been an 'official' international football match—but at rugby, the defecting code. Provoked by this, Alcock and Kinnaird sought to arrange an official soccer equivalent. Wanderers teammates, they had already forged links with Queen's Park during the first FA Cup semi-final early in 1872, and the Glaswegians therefore organised everything from the Scottish side of the border. Their whole team was comprised of Queen's Park or ex-Queen's Park (two of the brothers Smith) men, adequately reflecting their standing in the game at the time.

The momentous event was arranged for 30 November 1872 at the West of Scotland Cricket Club in Partick, and the English went north intending to give the Scots an object lesson in the game. Nothing could have been further from reality. The Scots obviously had an understanding the English could not match, but neither side could score and the game ended in the last goalless draw in a peacetime match for ninety-eight years. Four thousand people turned up to watch, at one shilling a time, and Queen's Park immediately started to look for a larger ground.

Glasgow Corporation agreed to lend them Hampden Park, Mount Florida, which, although the exact location has moved twice, has remained the home of Queen's Park and, by and large, the Scots international team ever since.

As was briefly mentioned, the men of Queen's Park were not unfamiliar to many of the England side. Earlier in the year, they had travelled to London for a game which was (probably correctly) described as: 'the most remarkable event in modern football'. This was that first semi-final of the first ever Football Association Challenge Cup.

The Cup was another of Alcock's innovations and was unashamedly based on a similar competition between the school houses at Harrow (where Alcock had been a pupil between 1855 and 1859). There, the winners of a knock-out competition became 'Cock House'. He put a resolution that such a competition be established on 20 July 1871. It was enthusiastically agreed; the committee were nearly all ex-public school men and shared similar memories from their own schools—although their counterparts at the Rugby Union refused to institute such an idea for another century.

A Cup was purchased for £20 and entries were invited. There were only fifteen, of which two, Maidenhead and Marlow, have entered every year since. Most were home county clubs, but Donington School came from Lincolnshire (though they scratched, never entered again, and thus established the shortest Cup history on record) and the ubiquitous Queen's Park not only entered but also sent a guinea (reputedly one-sixth of their income that year) towards the cost of the trophy.

Queen's Park remained a more or less enthusiastic member of the Football Association for over a decade and the founding of the Scottish FA, the Scottish Cup, and the formal codification of the laws are all very closely linked to their regular contact with the Association in London.

The knock-out idea so familiar today was basically followed back in that first season, though in a rather pragmatic fashion. Despite the common belief, Queen's Park were not allowed any special concessions. However, they did receive a fortuitous bye in the first round, drew Donington School

Top: *The 'Tin Pot', as the first FA Cup was known. It was stolen in 1895.*
Centre: *The oldest existing ticket for an international football match—the first ever game between Scotland and England, appropriately on St Andrew's Day 1872. The match was scoreless, the last to end that way for 98 years. The game was not strictly the first international, as the two countries had played each other at rugby the previous year.*
Right: *Charles W Alcock, secretary of the Football Association, creator of the FA Cup, instigator of the first ever international, captain of the great Wanderers and arguably the single most influential figure in the history of football.*

in the second (the Lincolnshire side probably could not afford to travel to Glasgow for the game) and then were lucky enough to be the odd team of five in the quarter-final. Thus they arrived in the semi-final without having played a game.

For the first few years all semi-finals and finals had to be played in London, and Queen's Park therefore travelled to Surrey County Cricket Club's ground at Kennington Oval for their game against the Wanderers, the renamed Forest of 1863. Their opponents had also arrived by a less than strenuous route. In the first round opponents Harrow Chequers (an old boys club) had scratched, in the second they defeated Clapham Rovers 3–1, in the third they drew with Crystal Palace but both teams went through to provide four semi-finalists.

Thus, on 4 March 1872, Charles Alcock's Wanderers faced Queen's Park in the first ever semi-final—between them having won only one game to get there!

The match was something of an anti-climax—the dribbling Wanderers and the short passing Scotsmen effectively neutralising each other for a 0–0 draw. Queen's Park had to go home before the decider, could not afford to travel the 400 miles again, and Wanderers went through to the final. They had gone through four rounds by winning only one game, but history only remembers the victors and they won the one that mattered on 16 March 1872.

Their opponents in that first Cup final, of any competition, anywhere, were Royal Engineers, 7–4 favourites and probably the best team of their time. Engineers were unlucky in that Lieutenant Cresswell broke his collar bone in the first ten minutes and, though he played on, they could not equal Wanderers' one goal scored by M P Betts. Betts, for many years subsequently a member of the FA Committee, was down on the team sheet as A H Chequer, meaning that he had played for the same Harrow Chequers that had scratched to Wanderers in the first round.

Why Betts played under this pseudonym has never been established—but he has found a place in history under both names. The crowd was only 2000, who paid a shilling each and then, according to contemporary reports, went off to watch the Oxford-Cambridge boat-race. But the idea clearly had a future and its growth was to parallel that of the game in the next few years. For the very existence of the Cup was the major force for uniformity of rules. If clubs wanted to enter, they had to agree to abide by FA rules in Cup games—and these thus became the 'compromise' guide for provincial teams.

THE AGE OF THE AMATEUR
Britain 1873-1893

For the decade and a half after its foundation, the FA Cup was to act as a focus for both the growth of the game and for the aspirations of football clubs all over Great Britain. It was a period of remarkably rapid development, symbolised by several distinct but clearly related currents. The first was the gradual adoption of every club into the various county and national associations under standardised rules, the second a movement of the centre of gravity away from the ex-public schoolboys of the south to the working men of the north, the third, intimately bound up with the second and ultimately the most important, was the rise of professionalism.

It was also an era which saw the creation of most of the institutions which control the game in Britain today. Significantly, these did not develop independently; most were part of a single movement and it must be remembered that there was no great distinction between the games in England and Scotland until the mid-1880 s, paradoxically just the time that representatives of the separate associations finally standardised the laws.

For several years Queen's Park, basically the arbiters of the Scottish game, certainly regarded themselves as being more directly comparable with the better English clubs than with their Scots contemporaries. Queen's Park's interest in the first FA Cup competition and their subsequent appearance in the semi-final led directly to the first of the official internationals later that same year of 1872 (in many ways the international was the 'return' leg of the Queen's Park versus Wanderers semi-final). It was that international, the need to select genuinely national teams, and Queen's Park's desire to organise a similar cup competition north of the border that led to the formation of the Scottish FA in 1873.

The earliest known 'action' picture of a soccer match—the 1887 Cup final between Aston Villa and their local rivals West Bromwich Albion. Albion forward Bayliss heads for goal in front of 15,000 spectators at the Oval. Note the external shin-pads, lack of goal nets (not introduced until 1891) and the fact that the goalkeeper wears the same strip as his teammates. Villa won 2–0.

Above: *The Queen's Park team which won the first ever Scottish Cup final in 1874, beating Clydesdale 2–0.*

Its birth, therefore, could not have been more different from that of the English version ten years before. Scottish ambitions were on a far larger stage, and there was no discussion of fripperies such as rules—Queen's Park regulations were simply accepted by the seven other founder members—Clydesdale, Vale of Leven, Dumbreck, Third Lanark, Eastern, Granville and Kilmarnock.

Initially things did not go quite as smoothly as was probably envisaged. The very first game of the very first Scottish FA Cup competition was between Kilmarnock and Renton in October 1873. As the *Glasgow Evening News* reported: '. . . Kilmarnock were at a disadvantage through not being thoroughly conversant with Association rules, having formerly played the Rugby game and being a man short. . . . On account of this Renton kept the ball well up . . . and received several free-kicks in succession through some of the Auld Killie's men persistently using their hands. . . .' Renton won 3–0; there was clearly some way to go in Scotland before old habits could be conquered under the newly-uniform rules.

It is not possible to minimise, in both England and Scotland, the contribution of a very few men in the rapid development of these years. Principally, these were the senior members of two clubs, Queen's Park and Wanderers, particularly the latter's secretary Charles Alcock and his club colleague Arthur (later Lord) Kinnaird, who graduated from Cambridge in 1870 and shares much of the credit for forging the links between England and Scotland. In 1890 Kinnaird succeeded the third of the great founding fathers, Major Marindin, as President of the Football Association. Marindin, who refereed a record eight FA Cup finals, was the inspiration behind the

great Royal Engineers team which introduced the passing game into England and was also largely responsible for many of the protracted negotiations which eventually led to a uniform set of rules. He was, unlike Alcock, violently opposed to professionalism and was to regret its official blessing coming during his Presidency.

But, above all others, it was Alcock who took advantage of the interest shown in the Wanderers versus Queen's Park semi-final to organise the first official international. Over this vital period Alcock's influence was all-pervading—so much so that it is impossible to assess what course the game would have taken over the next hundred years had Alcock not been in a position to introduce such deceptively obvious innovations as the FA Cup. Rather as the World Cup in the twentieth century has reflected the ebbs and flows of international football power, so did the FA Cup, from its inception up to the founding of the English and Scottish Leagues, do the same for the game in Britain. After those dates the Cup was no less accurate a guide, but the Leagues were more so and, in a sense, the Cup became the secondary rather than the primary competition. For its first few years, however, it was not only pre-eminent but quite unchallenged.

During the 1870s the Cup was completely dominated by the gentlemanly clubs of the South, or, to be precise, a handful of those clubs. Old Etonians (six final appearances), Wanderers (five), Royal Engineers and Oxford University (four apiece) were the dominant teams in the period 1872–83. Only four other sides (Clapham Rovers, Old Carthusians and the two Blackburn sides, Rovers and Olympic) even appeared in the first dozen finals.

Honours were not exactly evenly shared among the 'big four'. Wanderers were unquestionably the dominant side—reaching and winning five Cup finals in seven years. Basically an Old Harrovian side, they had abandoned a ground at Snaresbrook (in Essex) and a name (Forest, after Epping) to do as their name suggests—play anywhere in the home counties. They repeated their opening success again in 1873—the only year that the 'Challenge' part of the FA Challenge Cup Competition has ever been observed. Wanderers, as holders, were excused until the final, when they were 'challenged' by the winners of the open competition. This turned out to be Oxford University, who had suffered a hard slog through the qualifying rounds in beating Crystal Palace, Clapham Rovers, Royal Engineers and Maidenhead before walking over Queen's Park in the semi-final. This was the year that the Scotsmen were given a bye to the semi-final, then failed to take advantage of it by being, as in 1872, unable to afford the fare to Kennington Oval.

Wanderers were also allowed to choose their own venue for the final. This would have been the only time in the Cup's history that a club had played the final at 'home' but Wanderers, of course, did not have a home ground. They chose Lillie Bridge, very near where Stamford Bridge stands today, and won 2–0. Oddly, the only other occasion when such an event almost happened was also at Stamford Bridge in 1920 —Chelsea losing in the semi-final with their ground already having been chosen for the final.

But back in 1873, Oxford chose to play without a goalkeeper after Kinnaird had put Wanderers in front, and thus allowed Wollaston to score a second with a very long shot. Both goalscorers went on to accumulate a record five winners' medals.

Wanderers later completed a hat-trick of victories between 1876 and 1878, then dramatically collapsed and faded away in quite unparalleled fashion. The old boys' clubs were getting much stronger and players began to automatically offer themselves to their old schools before clubs like Wanderers. Even Kinnaird preferred to play for Old Etonians in 1878–79 and, as fate would have it, the two teams were drawn against each other in the first round. Etonians won 7–2, then repeated their success, 3–1, in 1879–80. Wanderers failed to find a good enough side the following season and scratched, never to play a game of football again.

The Universities suffered from a similar drain of talent and withdrew the same year, though Oxford, in a last bold gesture, reached the final of the 1879–80 season. Wanderers demise was as sad as it was swift, but at least it served to emphasise their remarkable dominance in those early years. Nearly a hundred years after their disappearance only three clubs, Aston Villa, Newcastle United and Blackburn Rovers, had won the Cup more often and Wanderers retain one truly remarkable record in having won every semi-final and final in which they ever appeared.

They could have claimed the Cup as their own after the first of only two hat-tricks ever recorded, but Alcock, as secretary of the Wanderers, handed it back to Alcock, as secretary of the Football Association, with the proviso that it would never again be won outright. Only Blackburn Rovers, between 1884 and 1886, have ever lost out through this restriction.

Wanderers' main rivals in the 1870s were the magnificent Royal Engineers. Between 1871 and 1875 Engineers lost only three out of eighty-six matches, but two of those happened to be the 1872 and 1874 Cup finals. The side was moulded together at Chatham by the remarkable Major Marindin, who personally appeared in a record ten Cup finals, twice as a player and eight times as referee, but his absence from the 1875 winning team (Engineers' only Cup success) was not, as legend has it, because he could not decide whether to play for Engineers or Old Etonians, but because he had already been posted away from

Below: *The Darwen side photographed late in 1879, the year they had become the first Northern side to seriously threaten the Southern dominance of the FA Cup. The team which scored four times in the last 15 minutes of a quarter-final tie against Old Etonians also contained the first real professionals ever seen in London, James Love and Fergus Suter.*

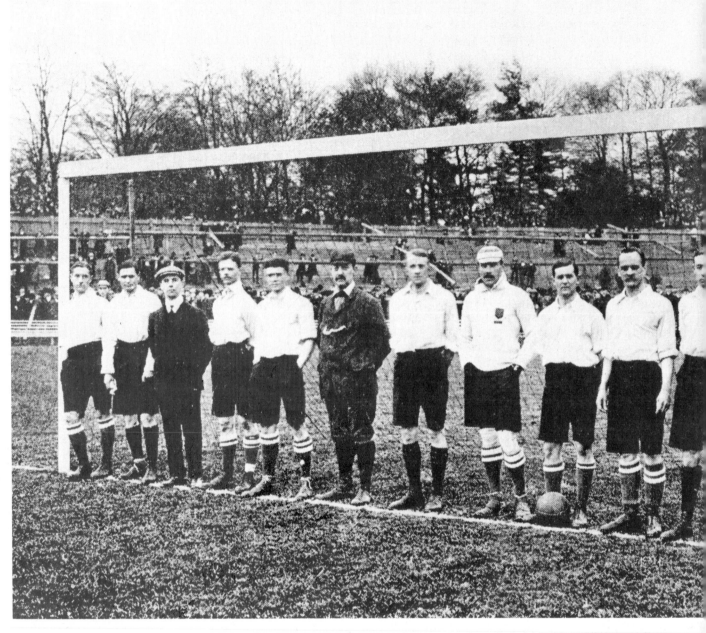

Chatham. The Engineers were probably the first English team to play in the 'combination' rather than individual style and included one Lieutenant Sim, reputedly the first player to develop heading as a deliberate rather than accidental skill.

The public schoolboys of the Home Counties retained undisputed control of the Cup until the last year of the 1870s. In the 1879 semi-final Old Etonians were lucky to defeat Nottingham Forest 2–1 before going on to win the final. Forest are the sole current League club to have reached the semi-final stage at their first attempt and it is interesting that they and their neighbours Notts County are the only clubs which can reasonably claim continual membership of the upper reaches of organised English football throughout its 110 plus year history. Virtually all the other notable clubs of the

age have faded away to oblivion or obscurity, including the shock side of that 1878–79 season, the Lancastrians Darwen. Having already suffered several tough games, including one in which they defeated neighbouring Eagley by the actually registered score of 'four goals and a disputed goal to one', they found themselves with just fifteen minutes left and 5–1 down to the same Old Etonians in the quarter-final at the Oval. Then, finding their feet, Darwen scored four times to level the scores, only for their exhausted opponents to refuse to play extra time. Public subscription, including handsome contributions from Etonians and the Football Association itself, brought Darwen back for a 2–2 draw, but they lost the third game 6–2.

Nevertheless their display, coupled with the fact that they had in their ranks the first

become a flood—so much so that the Lancashire FA banned further arrivals in 1881. (At one stage Bolton Wanderers had only one Englishman in their team.) The footballers did not come alone, rather as part of a widespread migration from the 'fringe' areas of the British Isles, particularly Scotland, to the booming textile towns of Lancashire and other parts of northern England in the 1870s. Newly arrived Scots surprised the Lancastrians with their skills, learned under the more open Queen's Park rules, and provoked a search by many clubs for their talented brothers who had remained in the Clyde basin. Suter, for instance, was first discovered by the Lancastrians during a friendly game between Partick Thistle and Blackburn Rovers in 1878.

By the time Darwen so nearly became the first northern side to reach a Cup final, the writing was firmly on the wall. Many of the underlying assumptions of the men who had founded the Football Association were really not appropriate for the working men of Lancashire and the north—there was not the same amount of leisure time, surplus energy or tradition of public school gentlemanly rivalry. Indeed, perhaps the most significant boost to the game in the 1870s was simply the introduction of the Saturday half-day, which had become the norm by the end of the decade. This had less of an effect on the players themselves than on club finances (there was now a much greater pool of potential support), games always being played on Saturday as Sunday remained inviolate.

Nonetheless a Lancashire working man at the top of his craft in those days might earn no more than £2 for a full six-day week, a labourer no more than 75p. Without some sort of financial inducement no working man could find the time necessary to develop his skills to a requisite level. The vital moment of decision was clearly approaching, though for the time being all chose to turn a blind eye to the resident professionals teaching the Lancastrians the 'combination' game.

And, for a time, appearances continued to deceive. Clapham Rovers won the 1880 final, Old Carthusians that of 1881. In 1882 a northern club finally appeared at the Oval when Blackburn Rovers were unlucky to lose 1–0. Interestingly, Blackburn's MP gave the team dinner afterwards, the first sign of the upper-classes thinking the game significant to constituents.

The defeat was Blackburn's first in thirty-five games, since they lost to Darwen in the first round of the 1880–81 Cup competition. This run of thirty-one wins and four draws is still recognised as the longest undefeated

two Scots professionals to appear in a major FA Cup game, James Love and Fergus Suter, ensured that the match became one of those rare games to acquire a significance well beyond the immediate. This was the first time that a northern side had shown itself equal to a southern (in the same round Nottingham Forest had defeated Oxford University 2–1, but the former were essentially a middle-class side in the southern tradition) and the first notable appearance of genuine but discreet professionals. Love and Suter were certainly not the first to be seen in the North; that distinction is claimed by one James J Lang who moved to Sheffield's Wednesday from Glasgow in 1876.

By the turn of the 1880s the flow of professionals (or 'professors' as they were called) from Scotland to Lancashire had

Opposite page: The Corinthians of 1905, a year after they had recorded their most famous victory—10–3 over reigning FA Cup holders Bury. At the time, it was normal to distinguish the goalkeeper solely by his wearing of a cap.

Above: *Major Marindin during his days as President of the Football Association. As well as appearing in two FA Cup finals (he never won a winner's medal) Marindin refereed eight more. Along with Kinnaird and Alcock, Marindin must be regarded as one of the three founding fathers of the English game.*
Right: *Lord Kinnaird, who succeeded Marindin as President of the FA. He appeared in nine of the first twelve FA Cup finals, captained the last amateur side to win the trophy, and accumulated a record five winner's medals.*

run of first-class games ever in English football; it included a 16–0 defeat of Preston in the latter's first ever professional game. Fergus Suter, recently transferred from Darwen, and three other Scots were in the Blackburn side. Lord Kinnaird, captain of the victorious Etonians, stood on his head in front of the pavilion after receiving the Cup. It was, in its way, a significant gesture, not only because it was made by Kinnaird, but because Old Etonians were the last amateur side ever to have their name inscribed on the trophy and were also the last southern club to win it that century. Anderson's solitary goal was really the last fling of the men who founded the Football

Association, controlled it for two decades and, in their way, created the game as we know it today.

The following season, 1882–83, was one of the most momentous in the history of football. On 6 December 1882 Major Marindin chaired a meeting of the representatives of the English, Scottish, Welsh and Irish Associations to standardise the laws finally. The Welsh and Irish were very much junior partners—in fact it is rather surprising they were there at all. The Welsh FA had been founded in 1876, the Irish version in 1880, though the latter did not actually play their first international until early in 1882.

As far as the laws were concerned, handling had already been restricted to the goalkeeper in 1870 and neutral referees (called on in cases of dispute between the umpires from each side) a year later. In 1878 the whistle was first used during a game between Nottingham Forest and Sheffield Norfolk. Before then the poor umpires had given decisions by waving a handkerchief. Referees with sole authority did not become the rule until 1891.

At the 1882 meeting the size of the ball was fixed and the crossbar finally replaced tapes. The English offside law was generally conceded to be the formal rule (though it was to cause problems as late as the 1884 Cup final), as was a modification of the Scots throw-in. This had been causing problems for several years. The Scots used the throw roughly as it is today, though at right angles rather like a rugby line-out, while the English preferred a single-armed hurl which could carry the ball almost the whole length of the pitch. Before the 1880 England versus Scotland international, the English refused to take the field unless the referee, a Mr Hamilton, agreed to let them take throws as they liked. He did, but as soon as the game started obviously suffered a kind of selective amnesia which led him to allow only the Scots version. The ultimate trade of the Scottish throw for the English offside rule was probably a 'behind the scenes' deal but, nearly twenty years after the founding of the Football Association, there was a uniformly accepted code of laws—even if, for good or evil, Old Rugbeians disagreed.

It was four years later, in 1886, that the official law making body, the International Board, was formally established. This comprised representatives from each of the four home countries and reigned supreme until 1946. Four members from FIFA were then added, plus one each from the home countries, thus maintaining the enormous (and many would say disproportionate) influence of the United Kingdom in the game to the mid-1970s.

The only really major addition to the basic laws which came after 1886 was the penalty-kick, which was to generate an astonishing amount of heat for the rest of the century. Matters came to a head during a 1890–91 FA Cup quarter-final between Notts County and Stoke at Trent Bridge when a shot was punched off the line by the County left-back Hendry with his goalkeeper Thraves well beaten. As the laws made no mention of penalties, Stoke had to take a free-kick on the goal-line which Thraves, needless to say, easily smothered. County won the match 1–0 and went on to the final. The incident provoked so much

comment that, largely as a result, penalties were finally introduced by the home associations from September 1891. This led to another controversial incident in which Stoke were also the sufferers the following season. They were losing 1–0 to Aston Villa when a penalty was awarded against Villa less than two minutes from time. The Villa keeper picked up the ball and booted it out of the ground. By the time it had been found the referee had blown for full-time. The law was soon changed to allow referees to add on time, specifically for the taking of penalties and generally for hold-ups during the game.

This was not the end as far as the penalty law was concerned. The law had to be changed again to prevent players touching the ball twice in succession—and hence dribbling into the net—and later still to stop penalty takers knocking the ball back to a colleague in a better position. It is still an offence, though little known, to kick the ball backwards at a penalty. Actually it was not until 1929 that the law as we know it today came into being; up to that date the goalkeeper could move about on his line, even rushing forward from the back of the net when the referee blew his whistle.

But way back in the traumatic season of 1882–83, another event was about to change the face of the game. That was a goal scored by a Lancashire cotton spinner, one Jimmy Costley, who volleyed home a cross from Dewhurst, his opposite winger in the Blackburn Olympic side, to win the 1883 Cup final. Olympic, a team comprising weavers, spinner Costley, a plumber, a metal-worker, an iron-moulder, a picture

Above and below: *William Gunn, the England and Notts County cricketer and footballer, whose one-armed hurls from one end of the pitch to the other forced a change in the throw-in law in favour of the Scottish two-handed version. Gunn's name is still remembered in the famous Gunn and Moore cricket bats.*

Top: *A typical sight at any of the Crystal Palace Cup finals.*
Above: *The final change in the penalty law did not come about until 1929, when goalkeepers were forced to keep still on their line until the kick was taken. This was the result of a protest by Chelsea after their 1927 quarter-final defeat by Cardiff in which the Welsh goalkeeper Farquharson had rushed out from the back of his net and saved a vital penalty. The FA decided that Farquharson's behaviour was 'against the spirit of the laws.' Cardiff went on to win the Cup.*

framer and one or two with no visible means of support except football thus defeated Old Etonians, the pride of southern England and real inheritors of the Wanderers tradition.

It would have been difficult to find more apposite opponents to represent the last of the old breed of football champions and the first of the new. The Old Etonians speak for themselves, gentlemen amateurs, representatives of all that was privileged in southern England at that time; Olympic, hailing from one of the world's most industrialised and dingy areas—the Lancashire weaving belt.

Olympic even had a player-manager, a talented half-back by the name of Jack Hunter who was well known for organising exhibition matches (and other entertainments) for profit. He had even taken Olympic away to Blackpool for a few days training prior to the match, most assuredly

a sign of things to come and clearly an idea that paid dividends. Hunter was, for his day, an astute tactician. Just as Queen's Park had first showed the English the advantages of short passing as opposed to dribbling, Hunter seems to have been the originator of the 'long passing' game. It was, at least, the first time that this tactic had been seen in a Cup final and it provided Olympic with the only goal when Dewhurst hit a long ball right across the field for left-winger Costley to score. It seems remarkable today to consider that such a pass could be considered revolutionary—but it must be recalled that football has taken many years to evolve and the tactics of the 1970s will probably seem humorously dated eventually. Remember, for instance, the trouble and surprise that Jackie Charlton first caused when, for Leeds United and England, he took to standing on the opposition goal-line at corners.

Blackburn Olympic, and the Cup, went north to a frantic reception, where a supporter is supposed to have yelled at Olympic captain Alf Warburton: 'Look at t'Cup, it's like a copper kettle. Still, it's welcome here and it'll never go back to London.' It never did, of course, being stolen from a Birmingham shop window in 1895 and lost forever. For a time it looked as if it would never even leave Blackburn, for Rovers were to win the next three finals and so that relatively small Lancashire town had a team in the final for five consecutive years—a record matched by nowhere since, although Manchester managed four years running between 1955 and 1958.

The pendulum had swung violently the other way. By the 1880s the great sides of the future were already finding their feet. In the west Midlands Aston Villa were formed in 1874, Small Heath (later Birmingham) in 1875, West Bromwich in 1879. In Lancashire Bolton in 1874, Blackburn Rovers in 1875, Everton in 1878 and the two Manchester clubs by 1880. The great days of the old boys' sides were at an end as the game swung away from the south, the amateurs, the upper classes and, in a sense, the administrators, to the north, the industrialist and small businessmen directors, the working classes and, in effect, the players—though this revolution was not to be confirmed until the formation of the Football League in 1888.

Far away from Lancashire, the southern gentlemen had played their part in the game and had created what was to become the world's major player and spectator sport. In customary fashion one of their members was even to give the game its alternative name. While in his room at

Oxford University one afternoon, Charles Wreford-Brown was asked if he would like a game of 'rugger'. No, he replied, playing on the word association, he preferred 'soccer'. So did the country and the world.

The theme of conflict between north and south has continued to the present day, perhaps reaching its height during Arsenal's great period during the depression years of the 1930s and being revived when they won the Double in 1971. Arthur Wise in his novel about a British civil war, *The Day the Queen flew North for the Grouse Shooting*, suggested the starting point of such a war to be an FA Cup final contested by Chelsea and Newcastle.

Blackburn Olympic's win was most obviously a manifestation of the swing of the pendulum from south to north. But, at the same time, this was barely distinguishable from amateurism's decline in the face of

paid professionals. Olympic, like all the major north western clubs, had their 'Scottish professors'. These clubs were run by local businessmen who were most unlikely to be impressed by the opinions and regulations of home counties amateur sportsmen.

The ex-public school men had, naturally enough, codified a game according to their own way of life, limited ambitions and interests. These had most assuredly not considered the competitiveness, finance and public support that had become the norm in Lancashire and the Midlands by the mid-1880s. What was important to the Old Etonians and Royal Engineers was generally not relevant to the mill-worker and miner and there is no reason why it should have been. It is significant that not until 1882 was a Cup semi-final played outside London (by order of the FA). Moreover, players were not allowed travelling ex-

Above left: Charles Wreford-Brown, Corinthians stalwart, member of the FA Committee and the man reputed to have invented the alternative name for football, soccer, as a play on the word Association.
Above: William McGregor, whose letter of 2 March 1888 led to the formation of the Football League.

Above: *The Scottish Cup.*
Top: *The Cup again in the possession of Vale of Leven, winners in 1877, 1878 and 1879. On their way to the first of that hat-trick they had become the first Scottish side to defeat Queen's Park. In 1879 they had drawn the final with Rangers, whose players refused to attend the replay because of a goal which had been disallowed. In the 1878 final Leven had beaten Third Lanark, whose ground (top right) Cathkin Park is now overgrown and used as a playground. Last of Queen's Park's co-founders of the Scottish FA to disappear, Third Lanark resigned from the League as recently as 1967. Cathkin was actually the second of the three Hampden Parks and the home of Queen's Park until the present Hampden was opened in 1903.*

penses until the following year, and then strictly for semi-finals and finals only.

The only really surprising thing about the clash over professionalism was that it was so long coming. The cause célèbre was to be a fourth round Cup tie between Upton Park and Preston North End on 19 January 1884. The match was drawn and Upton Park protested what everyone already knew —that the Lancastrians paid their players. William Sudell, a mill-owner who effectively owned Preston, disarmed his accusers by immediately admitting the charges—and going on to suggest that it was not only widespread but an advantage to the game.

The cat was among the pigeons. Upton Park were awarded the game and local associations took action quickly—Great Lever and Burnley joined Accrington in Lancashire, Walsall and Birmingham St George's in the Midlands and Hearts in Scotland in being banned for paying players. For the next eighteen months there was a tedious series of general meetings, defeated motions, and utter confusion. As a result most clubs simply played on as the danger of split grew greater. Sudell provoked matters further by proposing the formation of a British Football Association in October 1884. Twenty-six Lancastrian clubs plus Aston Villa and Sunderland supported him—a situation which was a forerunner of the conflict to face the Rugby Union in Huddersfield a decade later and lead to the formation of the breakaway Northern Union Rugby League.

Sudell was a good politician and it seems unlikely that he was trying to do any more than persuade the FA to concede the point. With Alcock in favour, they finally did so on 20 July 1885 and professionalism was legalised. Some minor restrictions (such as local residence qualifications) remained and were not lifted until 1889. Professionals were to be registered in a book kept by the Football Association (even today fees are

not strictly paid for players, but for the transfer of their registrations) and this, rather than freeing the game and its performers, was actually to lead to more rather than fewer restrictions. The strangest was to be the maximum wage, invariably set far below the better players' 'market value' and leading to massive abuse of Football League regulations before its disappearance in 1961. Interestingly other Leagues, such as the Southern and Scottish, paid little attention to restricting earnings, which led to situations such as John Charles finding himself being offered twice as much to play for Barry Town as for Leeds United. The persistence of the maximum wage through to the second half of the twentieth century does, however, show the remarkable durability of the ethics of those who established the game, detrimental to its health though they occasionally were.

After the debate was ended things quickly settled down in England, but not so in Scotland. In a fit of puritanism the Scottish FA, firmly led by Queen's Park and disagreeing with the English conclusions, banned sixty-eight Scots currently playing in England. The ritualistic process, each was individually named, effectively stopped them from performing in their native land again. The Scots also tried to prevent James Forrest, Blackburn's nineteen-year-old half-back, from becoming the first professional ever to play for England—failing for the simple reason that they had absolutely no power to do so. 'If the matter of professionalism is followed up,' commented the Scottish FA's annual report, 'the evil will be kept out of the Association.'

Tensions had been created between the two national associations which were eventually to boil over during a first round FA Cup match between the archetypal amateurs of Queen's Park and the original professional sinners, Preston North End, on 30 October 1886. Preston battered their way to a victory which can only be described as 'professional', causing a crowd invasion, and the worst offender (Scotsman Jimmy Ross) escaped only by being smuggled out of the ground. Opinions hardened.

That season seven Scots clubs had entered the FA Cup but this was to be their final year. After Rangers had lost the semi-final to Aston Villa at Crewe (chosen as the venue because of the convenient trains) the Scottish FA, on 10 May 1887, declared '. . . that clubs belonging to this Association shall not be members of any other national association . . .' Nor were they allowed to play in competitions organised by other associations.

This was something of a pity—the associations had, if anything, been coming together with larger crowds, more revenue and much easier travel from Glasgow to Lancashire and London. But, as long as Queen's Park's influence remained so strong, there was probably little chance of any Scots side joining the professionals' Football League in 1888 or the British League, which had been semi-seriously mooted in 1887.

Even when the Scottish League was formed in 1890, it was still supposedly strictly amateur. Queen's Park refused to become involved and there were immediate tensions between League and Association, the latter keeping a beady eye out for any hint of 'the evil'. As a result, Renton were thrown out after only five games for breach of regulations. Dumbarton and Rangers shared 29 points from 18 games, drew 2–2 in a play-off and, for the only time in the history of either League Championship, the trophy was shared.

Dumbarton won it again the following season to complete a brief period of glory and, a year later, even the Scottish FA bowed to the inevitability of professionalism when a motion from the 1893 champions Celtic was accepted. This rapid policy reversal probably owed less to any sincere conversion on the road to Parkhead than the string of defeats the national side had been suffering at the hands of the English (the Scots won only one game between 1888 and 1893). The good players were leaving almost automatically to join the professional clubs in England (who paid far more than a labourer's job in Glasgow) and the Scots, for a time, refused to have them back. The 4–1 defeat in Glasgow in 1892, followed by a 5–2 repeat at Richmond a year later, were particularly humiliating.

After the Scots acceptance of professionalism and a League, Queen's Park (who were still good enough to beat League champions Celtic in the 1893 Scottish Cup final) watched their fixtures fade away and, one supposes inevitably, joined the League in the last year of the nineteenth century. By then, however, their great days were over and they had become a club with a past rather than a future or even a present. Their's was a dramatic decline from a position of remarkable eminence and there is little doubt that, had they been pre-

Below: A newspaper drawing from March 1883 of a quarter-final tie between Dumbarton and Queen's Park. Dumbarton won 3–1 and went on to win their only Scottish Cup, after a replay, from Vale of Leven.

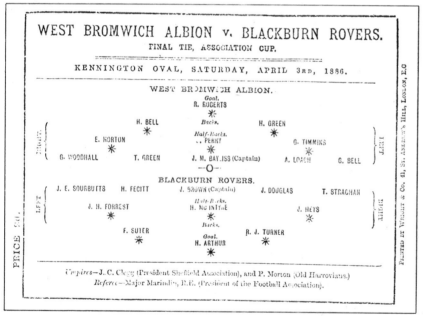

Top: *The Blackburn Rovers side which recorded the last ever hat-trick of Cup wins in 1886 and (above) the programme from the first game, which ended in a goalless draw. The replay, at Derby, was the first final held outside London and Blackburn captain Jimmy Brown became the only man to score in three successive finals.*

pared to embrace professionalism in the 1890s, the subsequent history of Scottish football would have been very different.

Perhaps Queen's Park believed that, after such a dominant twenty years, they could not go the same way as the Wanderers. The club that founded the Scottish Football Association and its annual Cup competition majestically maintained its strength through to the mid-1880s. Queen's Park had won the first three Cup competitions

(1874–76) and contributed greatly to the side that, at the end of the Association's first season, defeated the English for the very first time. Surprisingly, nearby Vale of Leven then managed to match Queen's Park's feat with another hat-trick of Cup wins becoming, on 30 December 1876, the first Scots side ever to defeat Queen's Park, by 2–1 in a quarter-final game. The latter retaliated with yet another hat-trick, this time between 1880 and 1882. Then, wanting to flex their muscles on a wider stage, Queen's Park entered the FA Cup in 1883, eleven years after their only previous appearance in the competition. Oddly, they had also entered in 1872–73, 1876–77 and 1877–78, been given byes on each occasion, but had always withdrawn before actually taking to the field.

The Glaswegians' new found confidence was also a reflection of Scotland's success in the annual international against England at this time. Of the first eleven games, the Scots 'combination' play defeated the Englishmen on no less than seven occasions, including a 7–2 win in 1878, 6–1 in 1881 and 5–1 in 1882, and they lost only twice (in 1873 and 1879). Not until 1888, when the strain of losing their best players to Lancashire finally took its toll, did the Scots lose again. Queen's Park remained largely responsible for the national side's success, providing most of the teams and much of the understanding which the English could never match.

It came as no surprise, then, when Queen's Park reached the FA Cup final in the 1883–84 season with considerable ease. In the semi-final they crushed the previous year's winners Blackburn Olympic 4–1 (thus asserting the power of the amateurs over the semi-professionals) and then came up against their fellow citizens, Blackburn Rovers, in the final. The game was, for once and perhaps the only time, a real championship of Britain—Queen's Park having already been awarded the Scottish Cup after Vale of Leven failed to turn up for the final, claiming that several of their players were ill.

This was also the infamous occasion when the *Pall Mall Gazette* referred to Rovers' supporters as '. . . a northern horde of uncouth garb and strange oaths,' likening them to '. . . a tribe of Sudanese Arabs let loose.' The *Gazette* also made the oft repeated error of describing them as 'up for the Cup'; no one from north of Watford ever goes 'up' to London, of course, it is always 'down'.

As a game, it was to go into the history books as one of the most contentious ever. Rovers won 2–1, but referee Major Marindin disallowed two Queen's Park goals which would have stood under the offside rules the Scotsmen still usually played to (it was still common in Scotland to apply 'two men including the goalkeeper' rather than the 'two men plus the goalkeeper' that had been theoretically conceded as the offside law by representatives of the home countries at the 1882 conference). According to Queen's Park's official history, Marindin visited the team the following day and told them that Rovers first goal was offside and that Queen's Park had not been awarded one perfectly good goal because, in both cases, they did not appeal. In England at this time, like cricket, the referee could only give decisions if appealed to and this remained the case until 1894. In fact, at this time many football regulations followed those of cricket. The games were closely linked, both using Kennington Oval for their most important events; Charles Alcock was also the secretary of Surrey County Cricket Club.

One major result of the 1884 Cup final was the residual bitterness which greatly contributed to the break between the associations later (a far more subtle series of differences than were superficially admitted), but Queen's Park put it behind them and were back the following year. On the way they defeated the Nottingham clubs (considered at the time second only to Blackburn in England) in the quarter

and semi-finals. The replayed semi-final against Nottingham Forest is the only one ever to have been contested outside England. It was staged at Merchiston Castle School in Edinburgh and it helped Forest set up their remarkable record of having been drawn to play Cup ties in all four home countries, though they never did contest a Cup game in Ireland. In the first round of the 1888–89 competition they drew 2–2 with Linfield and were on their way to Belfast for the replay when Linfield decided to scratch. Forest arrived anyway and played a friendly instead.

Back at the Oval, Queen's Park faced Blackburn Rovers again on the only occasion there has ever been a repeat final. It was also the last time an amateur club appeared in a final tie and this time there were no complaints when Blackburn won again, the only difference being the score, 2–0 rather than 2–1. Jimmy Brown and James Forrest scored in both games.

Blackburn went on to the second and, as yet, last hat-trick of Cup wins in a remarkable game at The Racecourse, Derby, in 1886, having drawn their first game with West Bromwich Albion at the Oval. This was the first time a Midland club had appeared in the final (though matters rapidly

changed and on only one occasion between 1886 and the end of the century were the Midlands not to be represented) and the first time that the Cup had been won outside London. That has happened only eight times since. But perhaps it is best remembered for the performance of the Blackburn captain Jimmy Brown who, in his last game for the club, dribbled the whole length of the field for one of the Cup's great goals and, in so doing, became the only man to score in three consecutive Cup final ties.

A shield, which still hangs in their board-room, was presented to Rovers. They were back again in 1890 and 1891 (James Forrest played in all five games) and remained undefeated in five finals over eight years. In the intervening period the west Midlands came into its own. Aston Villa produced the first of their record seven wins (by 1976) in 1887 when West Bromwich were the losers for the second consecutive year. It was the first of three finals between the Midlands pair in the space of only nine years, of which Villa won two and West Bromwich the other.

West Bromwich became the last of only four clubs to have ever appeared in three consecutive finals (Wanderers, Old Etonians and Blackburn Rovers are the others) in 1888, the famous occasion before which Preston are supposed to have asked to be photographed with the Cup, so confident were they and not wishing to appear muddy. West Bromwich won, of course, and the story is almost certainly apocryphal (referee Marindin never recalling his supposed comment: 'Had you not better win it first?'). West Bromwich then travelled to Scotland to play Scottish Cup winners Renton for the title 'Champions of the World'. The game was apparently played in a blinding thunderstorm, Renton winning 4–1. After which the champions of the world were suspended by the Scottish FA for professionalism, resigned from the Scottish Second Division in 1898 and disappeared.

While Queen's Park are remembered as the last amateur side to reach the FA Cup final, there was still a slim chance of another non-professional success as late as 1888. A year earlier Old Carthusians (they and Royal Engineers are the only two sides to have won both the FA and Amateur Cups) were defeated 2–1 by Preston in extra-time of a rough quarter-final. In the same round, incidentally, Darwen raised their troublesome heads again at Villa Park. Aston Villa, 3–0 up at half-time, opened and drank a celebratory bottle of champagne and, as a result, held on unsteadily just to squeeze through 3–2. The following year Old Carthusians, with a poorer side, again reached the quarter-final only to lose to eventual winners West Bromwich 4–2.

That was the last fling of the amateurs in the FA Cup. In later years the only competent amateur side, Corinthians, refused

to play in the Cup until it was really too late. As befitted a club formed in 1882 to combat the growing strength of Scottish football as evidenced in the annual international, fifty-one of the eighty-eight England caps awarded against Scotland between 1883 and 1890 went to Corinthians. While that fact probably says more about the prejudices of the international selectors than the abilities of individual Corinthians, they did have some excellent players including the definitive Charles Wreford-Brown and the England full-backs, A M and P M Walters, inevitably known as morning and afternoon.

Although England won only one of those games against Scotland between 1883 and 1890, the Corinthians were invited to form the whole England side against Wales in both 1894 and 1895—the only times a club has formed a whole international side. Corinthians won their first international 5–1 and drew the second 1–1, but neither compares with Corinthians' two most famous displays. These were defeats of the Cup holders by quite remarkable margins—Blackburn Rovers by 8–1 in 1884 and Bury (who had earlier

Left: *The Corinthians pose with founder 'Pa' Jackson on their Christmas tour of 1896. The previous two years the club had provided the whole England side for the internationals against Wales—the only time this has happened—while ten years earlier the 1886 England side which played Scotland contained nine Corinthians and two treble-winning Blackburn Rovers stars. Many later felt that the Corinthians' amateur ethic infected the halls of Lancaster Gate for too long, a view suggested (below) in this Bill Tidy cartoon. Certainly the age disparity between administrators and those they were supposed to be administering was to create tensions for many years.*

Below: *The highpoint of post-War amateur football came in 1951 when the Oxbridge combination Pegasus beat the greatest of the Northern amateur clubs, Bishop Auckland, in front of a packed Wembley. Pegasus won 2–1, their first goal headed home by left-winger Jimmy Potts.*

defeated Derby County by the record final score of 6–0 and had not conceded a goal in the 1902–03 tournament) by the astonishing 10–3. It is conjecture to guess what boost Corinthians might have given the amateur clubs had they entered the FA Cup at this time, but it is history that a century of uncompromising social forces slowly forced the decline of the amateur game and the whole basis for it.

The Amateur Cup had been founded in

1893, Old Carthusians winning the first competition at Richmond by defeating Casuals (later to combine with Corinthians) 2–1. Until its demise eighty years later, the Amateur Cup was dominated by the Northern League teams from Northumberland and Durham and the Isthmian and Athenian League sides from the home counties.

In 1907 an Amateur Football Association (later Alliance) had been formed and this pursued a semi-independent existence for seven decades. Amateur internationals never attracted much attention, and although Great Britain (oddly the Scots joined in the amateur teams) won the Olympic tournaments of 1908 and 1912, there was little success in later years. After the Second World War Olympic contests became a total sham, simply allowing the Communist bloc countries easy international victories and experience, and genuinely interesting only in how long the International Olympic Committee would allow the farce to continue. Had it not been for the significant gate money that soccer provided the movement (out of all proportion to the international interest), no doubt it would have been removed from the Olympic programme soon after the Second World War.

Amateur football actually staged a brief and romantic revival in England just after that War, culminating in the classic 1951 Amateur Cup final between Durham's Bishop Auckland, record ten times winners in eighteen finals, and Pegasus, a newly formed combination of the Oxford and Cambridge University teams. Pegasus were really the inheritors of the Corinthians' tradition (many went on to join the newly formed Corinthian-Casuals) and flowered briefly with a 2–1 win over Bishop Auckland before 100,000 at Wembley in 1951 and a 6–0 exhibition over Harwich and Parkeston two years later. But by 1960, internal divisions had weakened Pegasus and they ceased to compete in the competition. From this point onwards the amateur game suffered a dramatic decline—both in terms of interest at the gate and in its standards regarding non-payment.

In 1971 reigning Cup holders Skelmersdale United were fined £1500 and had their chairman suspended for illegal payments and no one was surprised or shocked. In 1974 the Football Association finally abolished the distinction (by now effectively meaningless) between professionals and amateurs. The Amateur Cup final that year was the last (unlikely Bishops Stortford won it by defeating Ilford); after nearly 100 years of debate there was no more hypocrisy or accusation—only 'players'.

COMING OF AGE
England 1888-1919

'Every year it is becoming more and more difficult for football clubs of any standing to meet their friendly engagements and even arrange friendly matches. The consequence is that at the last moment, through Cup tie interference, clubs are compelled to take on teams who will not attract the public. I beg to tender the following suggestion as a means of getting over the difficulty— that ten or twelve of the most prominent clubs in England combine to arrange home and away fixtures each season . . .'

Those words belonged to one William McGregor, a director of Aston Villa. They were written on 2 March 1888 in the form of a circular letter to the football clubs Blackburn Rovers, Bolton Wanderers, Preston and West Bromwich, as well as to the secretary of his own. And the acceptance of his sentiments led very quickly to the founding of the Football League.

McGregor, a Scot from Perthshire who had moved into the drapery business in Birmingham, had established a reputation as a man of integrity. He had been a forceful spokesman in favour of the legalisation of professionalism, and when he sent his letter he received an immediate response. In a postscript he had suggested that the representatives of the five clubs met for a

Below: *The 'khaki final' of 1915, so called because of the number of soldiers in the crowd. It was played at Old Trafford, the only time this century that a Cup final has been initially contested outside London, and Sheffield United defeated a sombre Chelsea 3–0.*

friendly conference on 23 March, the eve of the Cup final, at Anderton's Hotel in London. The five clubs were also asked to consider which other clubs should be invited to join such an alliance.

In the event ten clubs were represented at Anderton's Hotel where McGregor's format was agreed in principle, and where the liveliest area for debate concerned the titling of the new organisation. McGregor's original letter had suggested that . . . this combination might be known as the Association Football Union, but the body of the meeting feared a confusion with the Rugby Football Union. In the end the term Football League was adopted despite McGregor's own objection on the grounds that League had become an unpopular word because of its associations with the extreme political opinion and activities of such groups as the Irish National and Land Leagues.

There is no record of how long those present at Anderton's Hotel continued their discussions, but at the end of the evening there was much unfinished business; a further conference was called for 17 April at Manchester's Royal Hotel, a more convenient venue since the entire block of membership applications came from the professional clubs of the Midlands and the north; amateurism still prevailed in the south.

At this second convening, it was agreed that twelve clubs should be elected into the initial Football League—a figure determined by an investigation into the number of available Saturdays during the season; the number arrived at was twenty-two. The five clubs who had been originally circularised by McGregor were duly voted in, along with Accrington, Burnley, Derby County, Everton, Notts County, Stoke and Wolverhampton Wanderers; Nottingham Forest and Sheffield's The Wednesday, among several others, had their claims rejected. Of the final twelve five came from the Midlands, six from the north, and Stoke from the no-man's land between. This regional bias is still reflected in the contemporary siting of the headquarters of the Football League at Lytham St Anne's in Lancashire. McGregor's foresight and endeavour were rewarded by his appointment as the first president of the new conglomerate.

Though baseball in the United States was already being run on a League basis, the Football League became the first such organisation for soccer, a format later to be copied all over the world. It was to become a body with its own autonomy which existed under the umbrella of the Football Association but which instituted its own matches and to a large extent went its own

Opposite page: *In 1902 the pitch markings were changed, as these two pictures from an identical spot during Cup finals at the Crystal Palace show. In the upper picture Sheffield United goalkeeper Billy Foulke fishes the ball out of the net after Sandy Brown's first goal for Tottenham in the 1901 final. In the lower picture, Harry Hampton scores Aston Villa's first goal against Newcastle United in the 1905 game.*
Above: *Hampton's second goal in the same game—Newcastle's keeper Lawrence has just stopped a shot from Hall but Hampton follows up to get his second. As the hoarding shows, this goal was scored at the other end of the pitch.*

Above: *Preston's double-winning side of 1888–89, the only team to go through either an English or Scottish season undefeated in both Cup and League. William Sudell is standing third from the right.*

table with just twelve points from their programme of matches. Those humble beginnings, though, were built on strong foundations. At the start of the 1975–76 season, six of the founder members, Aston Villa, Wolverhampton Wanderers, Everton, Burnley, Derby County and Stoke City were in the First Division; four more were in Division Two, and a not-so-proud Preston were in the Third; only Accrington had disappeared into oblivion, and they had lasted more than seventy years, most of them within the Football League, before they went bankrupt in 1962.

Though Preston retained their League title in 1890, their supremacy was being challenged as the competition grew in popularity and expanded. In 1891, the twelve clubs became fourteen and twelve months later League membership was doubled by the introduction of a Second Division. Another competition, the Football Alliance, had been in existence since 1889 to cater for the needs of clubs who had not achieved full Football League status. A side representing the Alliance had exhibited the quality of its players by drawing with a star-studded team from the League and the Alliance was shortly afterwards taken under the League umbrella; the First Division was enlarged to sixteen clubs while twelve more constituted the Second.

Automatic promotion and relegation did not follow until five years later; instead the bottom clubs in Division One played the top clubs in the Second Division in what were known as 'Test Matches' to establish which should play in the top class the following season. It was a system which appeared to work until, in 1898, Stoke played Burnley knowing that a draw would ensure both clubs of First Division status the following season. The result, 0–0, smacked of collusion, and, though no charges were brought against the participants, the system of test matches was abolished and automatic promotion and relegation took its place. But at the outset of the Second Division the monopoly of the north and Midlands remained; not until 1893 did the south have a League club when Royal Arsenal were elected.

As Preston's star declined those of two other clubs moved into the ascendant, Aston Villa and Sunderland. Villa, no doubt to the delight of the League president, were champions of the Football League five times between 1892 and 1905, and during that period they also contested four Cup finals winning three of them. In 1897 they matched Preston's achievement by doing the Double, the last for sixty-four years, sprinting away with the League, won by an unsurpassed eleven points, and beat Everton

way. The very wording of McGregor's letter, which implied that there was Cup tie interference, emphasised that there would be areas of conflict between the two bodies, rivalries that had only marginally improved eighty years after the founding of the League.

On the 8 September 1888 the first series of matches between the twelve clubs took place, and the season was duly completed to specification, with all the teams playing each other home and away, twenty-two matches each, though the system of two points for a win and one for a draw was not finally given its assent until well into the November of that year. It was a season dominated by Preston North End, whose exceptional playing record justified their nicknames of Proud Preston and the Old Invincibles. Invincible they certainly were for their team of gifted Scotsmen plus England's centre-forward, John Goodall, went through the season unbeaten, a feat which has never been repeated by a British club in both League and Cup. They won the League by winning eighteen of their games and drawing the other four, scoring seventy-four goals and conceding just fifteen along the way, and they won the Cup without conceding a goal; the first Double-winners.

Aston Villa finished second, eleven points adrift, while Stoke propped up the

3–2 at Crystal Palace in a thrilling Cup final, all the goals coming in a spell of twenty-five minutes before half-time.

Their 1–0 win over West Bromwich Albion two years earlier in Crystal Palace's first final had been less exciting but sensation followed later. For, having won the Cup, Villa then proceeded to lose it. It was given to a football outfitter, William Shillcock, for display in his shop window in Newtown Row, Birmingham. From there, on the night of 11 September 1895, it was stolen, and never recovered. Villa were fined £25, most of which went towards paying for a new trophy. In 1958 a Sunday newspaper published a confession from eighty-three year old Harry Burge who claimed that he stole the Cup and melted it down to make half-crowns, but the validity of his admission was never established.

Sunderland, who were admitted to the League in 1890, contested Villa's supremacy throughout the decade, though their initial season was marred by a deduction of two points and a fine of £50 for fielding an ineligible player because he had not been registered for the required length of time. He was a goalkeeper, Ned Doig, a Scot who made the short journey south of the border, from Arbroath, and who cost the aspiring club little more than a signing-on fee. But the extra expense incurred by Doig was soon recovered; he became the key figure in a water-tight defence, and in seven seasons they were beaten just once at home. Their skilled all-round play earned them the title of the team of all the talents, and

Above: *The Aston Villa side which equalled Preston's feat by taking both Cup and League eight years later, in 1897.*
Left: *Two years earlier Villa had won and lost the Cup in quick succession when it was stolen from the window of a Birmingham boot and shoe manufacturer.*

they were champions in 1892, 1893, 1895 and again in 1902.

Sunderland were still a fine side in 1913, based on a formidable half-back line of Cuggy, Thomson and Low, and an attack which owed much to the legendary Charlie Buchan, who played at inside-right and combined brilliantly with his winger Mordue and the right-half Cuggy. Sunderland were champions that year, winning by four points from their old rivals Villa, and Eng-

land's two leading clubs battled through to contest the Cup final, which thus gave Sunderland the chance of emulating Villa's double of sixteen years earlier, while Villa were all the more keen to protect the exclusivity of a record which belonged solely to Preston and themselves. It remains the only occasion when the League's two leading clubs have met in the Cup final.

In a quiet moment during the early minutes of the Final, Villa's Clem Stephenson imparted to Buchan the substance of a dream he had experienced the previous night; that Villa would win 1–0 and that the goal would be scored by Tom Barber, the Villa right-half, with a header. Early in the game Villa's right-winger Charlie Wallace was to miss a penalty (the only one not converted in a Cup final) but Stephenson's vision came to pass with total accuracy. Barber did indeed score the only goal of the match—with his head. Not until 1937 were Sunderland to win the FA Cup and Buchan, to his undying regret, never won a Cup winners medal though he did play in another final, for Arsenal against Cardiff, fourteen years later.

By then Wembley was the established scene for finals, but in the late years of the nineteenth century there was still some changing of venues. The popularity of the game was beginning to embarrass officials of the Surrey County Cricket Club which had staged the final, with one exception, since the inception of the competition; in 1889 the crowd had swelled to the 22,000 who watched Preston claim the second leg of their double. In 1892 that number had reached 25,000 for West Bromwich's win over Villa, and at that point the Cricket Club cried enough.

The 1893 game was placed at Fallowfield in Manchester. Wolverhampton Wanderers met Everton and the officers of the Football Association felt sure that the large stadium would more than meet the demands of the situation. But in fact the ground did not possess much of the steep terracing of more modern stadia; only about 15,000 could have any real view of the proceedings, though the official attendance figure is three times that amount and the actual number who forced their way into the ground was probably twice as large again. The result was chaos, spectators who could see nothing of the action showing their discontent by surging forward and hurling missiles at those in front of them. People continued to spill onto the playing area, and Everton appeared to be greatly distracted; they lost 1–0, though their reserve team had beaten Wolves 4–2 in a League match the previous week.

Fallowfield was summarily rejected as a satisfactory venue and the 1894 final took place at Goodison Park, 37,000 fans watching Notts County beating Bolton 4–1 and becoming the first Second Division winners of the trophy. The following year the final was returned to the south, to the natural amphitheatre of Crystal Palace, where Londoners stood curiously watching the city being invaded once a year by supporters

Above: *The programme for Villa's double-winning final against Everton on 10 April 1897; Villa had already secured the League, eventually winning it by a record 11 points from Sheffield United. Campbell, Devey and Crabtree scored for Villa, Bell and Hartley for Everton, all five goals coming in the 25 minutes before half-time. On the following Saturday, 17 April, Villa played their first game at the new Villa Park, beating Blackburn 3–0.*

from the north. But, at the turn of the century, the south finally had a representative in the final though there was still no southern representative in the First Division. Unromantically, Southampton were put firmly in their place by Bury by four clear goals.

But the following year London had a winner. Totally against the odds Tottenham Hotspur, who carried out their weekly business in the Southern League, beat Sheffield United. The interest in the capital was enormous and responsible for a record attendance of 114,815 at Crystal Palace, and there was pandemonium when United were awarded a second goal when Clawley, the Spurs goalkeeper, was adjudged to have carried the ball over his own line. But the north London side earned a draw, and had to travel into the heart of League football, to Bolton, for the replay. There they won 3–1 and became the only non-League club (after 1888) ever to win the competition, much to the delight of those southerners who happily chose to ignore the fact that not one native born Londoner played in the winning side.

While Spurs were doing their bit for the capital, Arsenal were still the only London side actually in the League, in the Second Division. They had been founded in 1886 in Woolwich and they played on Plumstead Common in south-east London under the name of Dial Square; the name was altered first to Royal Arsenal, then Woolwich Arsenal, under which banner they turned professional and entered the League, then, in 1913, The Arsenal, and finally, simply, Arsenal. In 1904 they became London's first First Division side when they finished second in Division Two and were promoted along with Preston. And still based south of the River Thames they maintained a respectable position in the upper echelons until a disastrous season 1912–13 when they took just eighteen points out of a possible seventy-six, finished bottom and returned whence they came. It proved a blessing in disguise for Henry Norris, chairman of Second Division Fulham, decided to give the club a helping hand.

Norris recognised that a club situated as far out of town as Plumstead was, in those days, living with a continual threat of financial disaster. 'Supposing there was a place only ten minutes from Piccadilly where one could go and see a first-rate football match?' said Norris and answered his own question by securing a site at Highbury and persuading the Arsenal club officials to pull up their roots and move north. This they did to the annoyance of Tottenham who had no wish of a competitor moving in on their own doorstep. The Woolwich was

dropped from the club name and, in September 1913, the new Arsenal club beat Leicester Fosse 2–1 to celebrate the opening of their Highbury stadium. Nor had Norris finished acting for the club. When,

FOOTBALL.

THE FIRST
GENERAL MEETING
OF THE
GOLDTHORN
FOOTBALL CLUB

Will (by the kind permission of the Vicar) be
ST. LUKE'S SCHOOL,
BLAKENHALL,
ON
Friday next, November 10, 1876,
AT 7·30 P.M.

Any Gentleman interested in the game is
invited to attend

Barford & Webb, Steam Printers, Queen street Wolverhampton.

and were chosen above some with better claims, among them Tottenham. Chelsea, for whom a giant stadium had been built in 1905 before they even had a team, were the other fortunate club.

While Arsenal were growing up, and moving towards a series of events which were to earn them the tag of 'Lucky Arsenal', Derby County were labouring against misfortune. They had established their headquarters on a plot of land that was formerly a gipsy encampment, and folklore laid down that there was a witch's curse on the club. Certainly the events of the period 1896 to 1904 do not help those who argue that black magic has no substance. For Derby who had arguably the best centre-forward in the country in Steve Bloomer, who scored 352 League goals, and 28 for his country, could never quite win either the League or Cup. In those nine seasons they lost three Cup finals, among them the record 6–0 beating at the hands of Bury in 1903 and four times they were beaten in the semi-finals. Indeed when Derby reached the first final after the Second World War, in 1946, their captain was taken to a gipsy who lifted the curse before the match; Derby won 4–1.

at the end of the First World War, the League announced that they were extending the First Division by two clubs, Arsenal, sixth in the Second Division, profitted from some back-room promotion from Norris

Another side of great talent which remained on the fringe of total achievement was Newcastle United. Between 1905 and 1911 they could have broken all records with a side which owed much to two of the great tacticians of the times, Billy Mc-Cracken, the Irish full-back who learned to play opponents offside with the cleanness of the whistle that inevitably followed his moves, and Peter McWilliam, the stylish Scottish international left-half. How Newcastle did not achieve the double during this period remains a mystery. In 1905 they won the First Division only to lose the Cup final at Crystal Palace to two goals from Aston Villa's buccaneering centre-forward Harry Hampton; the following year they finished fourth in the League but again fell at the final FA Cup hurdle, this time to Everton. In 1907 the League title was Newcastle's again, though they went out of the Cup against non-League opposition in the first round; in 1908 fourth again in the League and another Cup final defeat, 3–1 to Wolverhampton Wanderers. In 1909 again League Champions, but more Cup

Far left: *Part of the crowd at the 1901 Cup final, recorded the following day as 114,815 and surpassed at an English football match only by the 1913 and 1923 finals. The interest stemmed from the appearance of a London club for the first time since amateur days—and Tottenham's resulting victory remains the only time a non-League club has lifted the Cup.*
Above: *Southern League Tottenham owed much of their success to Sandy Brown, who scored 15 goals in the competition (a record which still stands) and became the first man to score in every single game, including two in the first, drawn, tie and another in the replay at Burnden Park, Bolton. Brown is in the front row with the ball between his knees.*
Left above: *Discomfort but no doubt worth it for fans who had never seen a professional London victory.*

disaster, a semi-final defeat by Manchester United. But in 1910 they finally won the Cup, beating lowly Barnsley at Goodison Park after drawing at Crystal Palace, but the following season they lost the final once more, again after a replay against Bradford City.

In five finals at Crystal Palace Newcastle did not win one game, though they did draw twice—the theory being that they did not or could not adjust their accurate passing from the bare surface of St James' Park to the longer, thicker grass of Crystal Palace. The very thought of Crystal Palace obviously unnerved Newcastle. The name of that non-League side that beat them in 1907 was . . . Crystal Palace. Generations of their successors had less trouble with the thick pile of the Wembley turf for that ground was to become a lucky charm whereas Crystal Palace had been a hoodoo; Newcastle won Wembley finals in 1924, 1932, 1951, 1952 and 1955 before Liverpool broke the run by beating them in 1974.

The years leading immediately up to the First World War are remarkable for the

increasing democracy in a game no longer dominated by a handful of clubs. The First Division title was shared around, and unfashionable Oldham Athletic would have added their name to that particular scroll of honour had they won their last game of the 1914–15 season. The Cup continued, too, to throw up some surprise names. Bristol City, inspired by their 5ft 5in centre-half of solidly built Fatty Wedlock, who won twenty-six England caps, were losing finalists in 1909. Barnsley produced a team of resolute spirit, known as Battling Barnsley and reached the final in 1910 and won

it two years later; like Bristol City they had their own charismatic character, Tommy Boyle, a centre-half who never tipped the scales at more than 7 st 6 lbs. Boyle, who is reputed to have been (indeed must have been) remarkably strong for his size, played in the 1910 final and later moved on to Burnley whom he helped gain promotion in 1913 and win the Cup the following year. The story goes that he was one of the most talkative footballers of his day, and that, frustrated by his inability to communicate with Nesbitt, the Burnley outside-right who was stone deaf, he studied lip-reading so

A typically self-satisfied photographer's line-up of the period —the Derby County of 1905, 11th in the First Division and knocked out of the Cup in the first round at home by Preston North End. Of particular interest is the presence of England centre-forward Steve Bloomer (third from left) who scored 13 goals in 29 games for Derby that season and played in all three internationals. His record of five goals in a game (against Wales) for England still stands as a joint record, and it was not until the 1930s that William 'Dixie' Dean broke Bloomer's record of 352 League goals in 600 games. He retired just before the First World War aged 40 and spent the next four years in a prisoner of war camp, having gone to Germany on a coaching contract.

that he could pass on his instructions!

Bradford City were another unfashionable club to win the Cup, beating Newcastle after a replay in 1911. A succession of drawn finals at this time prompted the FA to introduce extra time in 1913, a move which proved particularly successful as no drawn final survived the extra period of play until Chelsea drew with Leeds in 1970.

These were times, too, when those who were engaged in the new occupation of professional football were battling for acceptance of their status. The Football League for many years fought against recognising the Football Players' and Trainers' Union, which had been formed early in 1898 and later accepted by the Federation of Trades Unions. Players who were known to take active part in the running of union matters earned for their efforts a bad reputation with football's authorities; Charlie Roberts, the redoubtable Manchester United centre-half, might well have played in more than the three internationals for which he was selected in 1905 if he had not been an overt union sympathiser.

Indeed Roberts played for his club

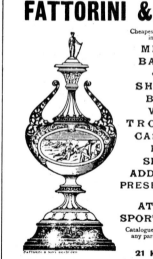

This page: In 1911 Bradford's Fattorini & Sons made a new FA Cup; strangely Bradford City won it that year, drawing (top) at Crystal Palace and then defeating Newcastle 1-0 at Old Trafford. Bradford's O'Rourke (right) distracted the keeper to allow a Spiers lob into the net.

against Newcastle United in 1908 in a challenge match, the proceeds of which were invested to form a provident fund for the still unrecognised FPTU. The following year the conflict came out into the open. Both the League and the FA spoke out against the Union's efforts to become affiliated to the Federation of Trades Unions, and suspended the chairman and

the secretary of the FPTU; the players, in retaliation, called a strike.

But two days before the commencement of the 1909–10 season the authorities bowed down and the strike was averted. The Union was recognised and the suspensions on union officials called off, but if the players now felt they had a powerful tool to improve their conditions it was a long time

before they brandished it. The concept of a maximum wage for a professional footballer had been accepted in 1901 but in the new climate the players made no attempt to alter the system. So, with occasional liftings of the ceiling to co-ordinate with rises in the cost of living, restrictions were placed on the pay packets of footballers for the next sixty years.

The advent of the First World War did little to help the players wages. It provided a social climate far from conducive to watching football, and the League devised a system to share out the money that was available. They collected a pool to be redistributed around the struggling clubs by taking fifteen per cent from the weekly earnings of each player. Though the major competitions of 1914–15 were allowed by the government to be completed the atmosphere was subdued and occasionally poisoned.

In April 1915 a match between Liverpool and Manchester United was fixed by players who felt the need to make some quick money from betting before their livelihood was taken away from them by the hostilities, although the result was allowed to stand. Nor was there much more joy about the last Cup final for five years, moved to Old Trafford, and contested by Sheffield

United and Chelsea. The London club, at the bottom of the First Division, played a centre-forward blind in one eye, lost by three goals and were solemnly watched by a crowd whose mood was out of keeping with the occasion but very much in tune with the times. The match goes into the history books as the 'Khaki Final' because it was witnessed by so many soldiers in uniform.

For the next four seasons organised football was restricted to regional competitions in and around London, Lancashire and the Midlands; but players were to receive no payment for participating in these games nor were any trophies presented to the winners of the regional tournaments. The Football Association, whose offices in Russell Square were taken over for military purposes, could not fail to be aware of the war effort and they permitted matches to take place only when they did not interfere with necessary production. Norwich City and Bradford City, for example, were ordered to play a replayed Cup tie at Lincoln behind locked doors because of the effect the match might otherwise have on production at a local armaments factory—thus establishing Britain's lowest first class attendance, technically nil.

Domestic football was, during the War,

Above: *Sheffield United's Cup winning side of 1902, which defeated Southampton at Crystal Palace after a drawn first game. Twenty-one-stone goalkeeper Billy Foulke (standing third from left) was the largest player ever to have appeared in League football and was to die sadly after catching pneumonia while saving shots for coppers on Blackpool beach. Alf Common, seated second from left, scored United's goal in the first game and was later to become the first player transferred for a four figure sum when Middlesbrough purchased him from Sunderland for £1000 in 1905.*

totally meaningless. Far more memorable in the history of the game are the records that in the midst of that mud-bound, disease-ridden, inhuman war football provided a common bond between the feuding sides. On Christmas Day in 1914, a totally unofficial truce brought a day of peace between a German unit and one from Britain. For that day, in the midst of all the conflict and bloodshed that was to prove futile, Briton and German talked together, ate together and played a game of football against each other.

When the slaughter was over, League football resumed, but not without a problem or two. Leeds City were expelled from the competition after playing eight games of the 1919–20 season following their refusal to open their books to the FA and the League, and Port Vale took over their fixtures. Illegal payments were suspected, though never proved, and manager Herbert Chapman was suspended for, allegedly, burning all relevant records. For that first post-War season both First and Second Dvision were increased to twenty-two clubs, and the following year a Third Division was introduced. The success of clubs from the Southern League had for several years prior to the War brought forth requests for membership of the Football League; now the Premier Division of the Southern League was taken en bloc as Division Three and all the clubs accorded the status of associate members.

Since all these new clubs came from the south, the west and East Anglia, there were strong protests from northern clubs on the fringe of Football League status; so, duly, in 1922 the Third Division had the postscript (South) added to its title while twenty northern clubs joined the alliance as the Third Division (North). And though several of these junior members could not in the end support full-time status and would disappear into the backwaters that they had sprung from, the basic structure of the Football League had been established. Doubtless William McGregor, who had died more than a decade earlier, was smiling down with satisfaction. The institution born by his astuteness had really come of age.

60

INTERNATIONAL GROWTH
AND THE FIRST WORLD CUPS
The World 1900-1939

While mania for the new sport of organised football was reaching epidemic proportions inside the British Isles, the disease began to spread abroad. The carriers were emigré Englishmen and around Europe and beyond their enthusiasm for this game, which had never before reached out beyond Britain in codified form, proved infectious. More than six decades later the work of these footballing envoys carried an ironic curse as the ambitions of Britain's top clubs, in an era of European competition, were thwarted by clubs from the continent which had been founded and nurtured by nomadic Englishmen of the previous century.

In 1973 it was no consolation to Leeds United that their conquerors in the final of the European Cup Winners Cup, AC

Below: *The England team gives its controversial salute in Berlin in May 1938. From left to right: Bastin, Robinson, Goulden, Sproston, Matthews, Welsh, Willingham, Young, Broome, Woodley and Hapgood. Some objected, others felt it unimportant.*

The first official international ever played by England against a foreign country was on 6 June 1908, against Austria in Vienna. England won 6–1. Arsenal followed up with a tour to the then Austro–Hungarian Empire during which (above) they defeated Slavia of Prague 5–1.

British mounted the winners rostrum by virtue of a superiority solely in the goal-scoring department.

By this time other nations had caught up with the development in Denmark. And again the British influence was patently clear. In Switzerland St Gallen FC began its life under the driving force of students who had learnt the game from their British counterparts. That was in 1879 and seven years later the more renowned Grasshopper Club in Zurich began on the same basis; the unusual name of the club is credited to an English student. Lausanne soon boasted a Football and Cricket Club, with a membership of many Britons, while yet another club, Old Boys of Basle, was started by ex-pupils of the High School in that city and stimulated the founding and titling of the Young Boys of Berne, which remains one of Switzerland's leading sides. By the time Denmark were contesting their Olympic final, there were more than a hundred Swiss clubs.

Similarly, in Germany, British students and businessmen provided an introduction to football. The archives record the founding of a football club in Bremen in 1880, and an Anglo-American Football Club in Berlin a few years later; Dresden was the home of the English FC, while a football club in Hamburg, one of the forerunners of the mighty Hamburg Sports Verrein, kept the minutes of its meetings in English for its first five years.

In the late nineteenth century Englishmen were plentiful in Paris, and a group of them met regularly in the Red Lion Bar in the centre of the city. There, probably while the wine was flowing freely, they agreed to start a football club. They called it Standard AC and it began its life in 1892. Other clubs sprang up in the capital around the same time, often the inspiration coming from Frenchmen who had fallen in love with the game while on a trip across the channel. Standard soon became the first French champions and they established such an illustrious reputation that their deeds were revered in Belgium; when a number of enthusiasts in the industrial city of Liege started their own football activities they copied the name and the famed Standard Liege came into being.

In Belgium, too, the initial impetus had come directly from Britain in the forming of a club in Antwerp as early as 1880; but the Belgians needed little encouragement, founded their own competition, and in 1895 their own Football Association. It was the same story in Austria where again the game began as an import from England. One of the country's premier teams, First Vienna, evolved from a desire for relaxa-

Milan, were a club of English descent, and that the official club name is Milan and not Milano (the city's Italian name) out of deference to those Englishmen who developed the game there. Nor did it help heal the wounds of their defeat two years later in the European Champions Cup final to know that Bayern Munich were similarly formed.

But the first seeds were sown in a country which did not develop into a challenger to the British supremacy at top professional level, Denmark. In 1879 the Danes needed just minimal prompting; football was a game which suited their temperament and they learned quickly and took the development of their clubs into their own hands. An organisation called the English Football Club was instituted in Copenhagen in 1879 but the rules of the game it played resembled the hotch-potch of those of England's public schools thirty years earlier. Nevertheless, within five years soccer in the form of the day was being played with gusto across Denmark.

The Kopenhagen Boldklub instituted a competition which boasted an entry of fifteen clubs and before the end of the decade Denmark had a Football Association of her own. Such an internal structure bred a strong national team, and by the time of the 1908 Olympic Games, held in London, Denmark was the only side really capable of challenging Great Britain. Coached by an Englishman, they swept their way to the final, destroying a French team en route by 17–1, and they might have beaten the hosts to the gold medal if their finishing had matched their elegant approach-play. Four years later, in nearby Stockholm, the Danes again mounted a realistic challenge but history repeated itself and again the

Left: *The original World Cup, more correctly called the Jules Rimet Trophy. Made of solid gold, it stands 32cms high and became Brazil's permanent property after they won their third tournament in 1970.*

tion on the part of the gardeners, many of them British, who worked for Baron Rothschild. Another expatriate, M D Nicholson, who had left his home to work in the Vienna branch of Thomas Cook's travel agency, had been in West Bromwich Albion's Cup winning team of 1892. He made such an impact on the Vienna sport-

Right: *A shot from right-winger Pablo Dorado gives Uruguay a twelfth minute lead against Argentina in the 1930 final.*
Below right: *Uruguay's fourth and final goal in the 1930 World Cup final, scored by Castro.*

ing scene that when the Austrian Football Association was instituted in 1900 he was elected its first president.

There was nothing in the Latin temperament which reacted against the playing of football when English businessmen helped form the Genoa Football and Cricket Club, and soon Italians were playing against and alongside the British for clubs like AC Torinesi and, of course, AC Milan. And one Italian, Vittorio Pozzo, took to the game like a new religion; his passion was to carry him to football's mecca, to many of the leading English professional clubs, where he formulated his own theories. From such grass roots as this, he was to twice coach the champions of the world. Others like him, from South America and Spain, were to catch this new bug which entered the bloodstreams of athletes all over the world. And well as the British taught, the pupils learned even better.

The first step towards unifying all these distant outposts took place as early as 1903 when visionaries in Germany, Holland, Spain, France and Belgium decided to form an international football association. They looked for guidance from England, and Robert Guerin, the first but not the last Frenchman to play a critical role in the growth of world football, visited the headquarters of the Football Association in London. There insularity prevailed, and the officials shilly-shallied for so long about taking up the offered option of starting the association themselves that Guerin and his committee, sadly disappointed with the British attitude, went ahead on their own. In 1904 they formed FIFA, and the Football Association, like an adult agreeing to play with a group of children in order to silence their clamouring, consented to becoming a founder member.

It was the first sign of a blinkered attitude,

the folly of which was to remain unexposed for nearly fifty years. Not until 1953, when Hungary were to come to London and shatter many an illusion, was the British-must-be-best snobbery to crack. Certainly in those early years in the twentieth century the longer experience of English clubs and their players were to make them unbeatable against those who were just learning the skills. England's first venture into Europe with a representative team, in 1908, brought ridiculously easy wins over Austria, 6–1 and 11–1, Hungary 7–0 and Bohemia 4–0— all this accomplished in seven days. But others were beginning to acquire that experience.

A diminutive Lancastrian, Jimmy Hogan, an undistinguished ex-professional from England, and a rich Austrian, Hugo Meisl, were two men of totally differing backgrounds who did more than most to improve standards in Europe. Both men believed in the kind of ball skills so often regarded in Britain as unproductive, even unmanly. But in Holland, Austria and Hungary Hogan preached the doctrine of skill and in Austria Meisl gave him the facilities to do so. While the English game did not progress from its reliance on strength and stamina, Hogan took an altogether more sophisticated and futuristic view; his players were encouraged to cultivate the ball, to work and live with it until it became another limb. England's professionals rarely saw a ball from one game to the next.

But though Hogan and others produced teams which gained success over British clubs they gained little prestige because they were out of the context of competition. The attitude of the Football Association made sure of that. Though they had paid lip-service to FIFA it had never been a happy marriage, and when a dispute over broken-time payments to players (compensation for loss of earnings) became an issue in 1928 the FA seemed glad of an excuse to pull out. It meant that when plans for a world championship were discussed neither England, Scotland, Wales nor Ireland would be taking part. Just how far the supremacy of Britain had been challenged could not now be put to the test in a competitive arena. But in 1929, just a year before the first World Cup, there was a definite pointer. England played a three-match end-of-season tour of Europe, and, though they beat France 4–1 and Belgium 5–1, they lost 3–4 to Spain in Madrid, their first ever defeat by a foreign country. The writing was on the wall—but no one who had any influence over the future of English international football would read it for many years.

Far, far away Uruguay, in 1930, were to achieve a pair of notable firsts—staging and eventually winning the first ever World Cup, the tournament that was to become the grand prix of football. But while it was the first, subsequent World Cups have shown the 1930 competition to have been the one least worthy of its important title, for defections and withdrawals by European countries killed it as a really meaningful competition.

Uruguay had a very fine team then; one which had already won the highly contested and virtually professional Olympic tournaments of 1924 and 1928, and which has since been enshrined in Uruguayan history as other nations enshrine their military heroes. These now elderly gentlemen are forever meeting and toasting in public on the occasion of the anniversaries of their various triumphs.

Across the River Plate, Argentina were another very strong proposition. They had been runners-up to Uruguay two years previously in a close and exciting Olympic final in Amsterdam, and though since then Juventus of Italy had stolen away their brilliant left-winger, Raimondo Orsi, many stars were left; among them the ruthless, attacking centre-half Luisito Monti ('The Man Who Strolls') of Boca Juniors. He too would later join Juventus and, with Orsi, win a World Cup winners' medal with Italy in the 1934 competition.

Uruguay, even at that remote date, had a so-called 'Iron Curtain'. It was the nickname given to their splendid half-back line of Jose Andrade, the little coloured right-half, Lorenzo Fernandez and Alvaro Gestido. It should be remembered that, at this time, the gospel, or possibly the contamination, of the third-back game had scarcely spread beyond Britain. Uruguay, indeed, were to remain immune from it for

Below: *Jules Rimet, President of FIFA, takes the chair at the first post-War meeting.*

1st WORLD CUP Uruguay, 1930

Group 1

France (3)4   Mexico (0)1
Laurent, Langiller,
Maschinot 2   Carreno

Argentina (0)1   France (0)0
Monti

Chile (1)3   Mexico (0)0
Vidal, Subiabre 2

Chile (0)1   France (0)0
Subiabre

Argentina (3)6   Mexico (0)3
Stabile 3, Varallo 2,   Lopez, Rosas (F),
Zumelzu   Rosas (M)

Argentina (2)3   Chile (1)1
Stabile 2, Evaristo (M)   Subiabre

	P	W	D	L	F	A	Pts
Argentina	3	3	0	0	10	4	6
Chile	3	2	0	1	5	3	4
France	3	1	0	2	4	3	2
Mexico	3	0	0	3	4	13	0

Group 2

Yugoslavia (2)2   Brazil (0)1
Tirnanic, Beck   Neto

Yugoslavia (0)4   Bolivia (0)0
Beck 2, Marianovic,
Vujadinovic

Brazil (1)4   Bolivia (0)0
Visintainer 2, Neto 2

	P	W	D	L	F	A	Pts
Yugoslavia	2	2	0	0	6	1	4
Brazil	2	1	0	1	5	2	2
Bolivia	2	0	0	2	0	8	0

Group 3

Romania (1)3   Peru (0)1
Staucin 2, Barbu   Souza

Uruguay (0)1   Peru (0)0
Castro

Uruguay (4)4   Romania (0)0
Dorado, Scarone,
Anselmo, Cea

	P	W	D	L	F	A	Pts
Uruguay	2	2	0	0	5	0	4
Romania	2	1	0	1	3	5	2
Peru	2	0	0	2	1	4	0

Group 4

USA (2)3   Belgium (0)0
McGhee 2, Patenaude

USA (2)3   Paraguay (0)0
Patenaude 2, Florie

Paraguay (1)1   Belgium (0)0
Pena

	P	W	D	L	F	A	Pts
USA	2	2	0	0	6	0	4
Paraguay	2	1	0	1	1	3	2
Belgium	2	0	0	2	0	4	0

Semi-finals

Argentina (1)6   USA (0)1
Monti, Scopelli,   Brown
Stabile 2, Peucelle 2

Uruguay (3)6   Yugoslavia (1)1
Cea 3, Anselmo 2,   Seculic
Iriarte

Final: Montevideo 30.7.30
Attendance 100,000

Uruguay (1)4   Argentina (2)2
Dorado, Cea, Iriarte,   Peucelle, Stabile
Castro

Uruguay: Ballesteros; Nasazzi (capt),
Mascheroni; Andrade, Fernandez, Gestido;
Dorado, Scarone, Castro, Cea, Iriarte

Argentina: Botasso; Della Torre,
Paternoster; Evaristo (J), Monti, Suarez;
Peucelle, Varallo, Stabile, Ferreira (capt),
Evaristo (M)

Refree: Langenus (Belgium)

Leading scorers: 8—Stabile (Argentina)
5—Cea (Uruguay)
4—Subiabre (Chile)

Above: *Argentina's Guillermo Stabile raises his arm in delight after putting Argentina 2–1 up in the first ever World Cup final. Uruguay, however, came back to win 4–2.*

over another quarter-century. Wing-halves were what we would now call attacking full-backs, practising what would now be called the overlap.

The European teams which did make the wearying journey to Uruguay—in those days you went by sea and took nearly three weeks—were a curious lot.

There was Rumania, whose young king, Carol, was chiefly responsible for their entry. It was strange, in view of the unpopularity of Carol among the Rumanian people at large, that he should have played such an exemplary role. As Prince Carol, he had founded the Federation of Rumanian Sports Societies. Now he went in person to the big oil company, an English concern, to ask for the release of those footballers whom they employed, and whom they had refused to let go under the threat of dismissal. Needless to say, Carol was successful in his plea.

There were the French, who were to surpass themselves, but who at that time were very far from being a European power. There were their near neighbours, the Belgians, who were without their best forward, a left-winger called, like his contemporary in the Arsenal team, Bastin.

The French, in fact, decided to come only a month before their boat was due to leave, after at first refusing. The Yugoslavs, scarcely a force in those days, and victims, like France, of Uruguay in the 1924 Olympiad, also accepted after indecision. And that was the extent of the European entry.

One can imagine how infuriated and slighted the Uruguayans were. It was, after all, the Centenary of their foundation as an independent nation, while they themselves bitterly pointed out that they had twice travelled to Europe to compete in and win the Olympic tournament. Now there was to be no entry from Britain which, though regretted, had been expected, even though it would gravely compromise the status of the championship. Other powers, such as Hungary, Austria, Germany, Italy, Czechoslovakia and Spain, who had become highly revered as the first European country to beat England, were also absent.

Still, Latin America entered in bulk. There were the Brazilians, whose football was improving and who had just beaten Chelsea in Rio. Mexico, who were to play with so little success in so many World Cups, were to be there. So were Bolivia, Paraguay, Chile and Peru, and the United States of America.

That the USA should ultimately and quite impressively reach the semi-finals of the competition was not quite as surprising as it might seem. In the early and middle 1920s, there had been one of those spora-

dic and doomed attempts to get the game going in that huge country. As a consequence, many fine footballers, especially Scots, like the young **Alex Jackson**, had been imported by such teams as Bethlehem Steel. Some, like Jackson, went back; others stayed, and these it was who formed the core of a large, muscular team whom the French whimsically nicknamed 'The Shotputters'.

As in 1950, when the second South American World Cup was staged, there were not enough teams to make up the requisite four pools of four winners going straight into a knock-out semi-final. Nor was there any nonsense about an academic third-place match.

The four teams seeded at the head of the pools were all from the Americas; and they included the United States, whose genuinely amateur and quite different 1928 Olympic team had been thrashed 11–2 by the Argentinians. The latter, Brazil and Uruguay were the other seeded teams.

As the opening day, 13 July, drew near—France would open the tournament in honour of 14 July, Bastille Day—the Centenary Stadium was still not finished. Nor would it be, due to heavy rain, until the competition was well under way. Early matches had thus to take place on the grounds either of Penarol or Nacional, the two leading and

eternally dominant Uruguayan clubs.

The Uruguayan discipline was professional in the extreme. Their players were monastically cloistered in an hotel in the Prado, Montevideo's huge park of 150,000 trees. When their lively and talented goalkeeper, Mazzali, an Olympic hero, sneaked in one night after curfew with his shoes in his hand, he was caught and sent home. Ballesteros of Rampla Juniors replaced him.

Other members of that fine side included the powerful full-back—or centre-back, as he would be today—Jose Nasazzi, the skipper, and two splendid strikers in the red-haired, slight Hector Scarone, a triumph of brain over brawn, and Pedro Petrone, a great schemer and finisher, but now somewhat past his best.

France's opening game, against Mexico, was won 4–1, even though a kick on the jaw put their brave and splendid goalkeeper Alex Thepot off the field with concussion after only ten minutes. Chantrel, their left-half, took over in goal, and was beaten only once. The roving centre-half was the elegant Marcel Pinel, a cultivated figure both on and off the field. The skipper and right-half, Alex Villaplane, was to die a sombre death; shot for collaborating with the Germans after the 1944 liberation of France.

Two days later, with Thepot magically

Above: *Jimmy Hampson, the Blackpool centre-forward who was to be tragically drowned in a fishing accident in 1938, scores England's first goal against Austria at Stamford Bridge in December 1932. The Austrians feared a heavy defeat, but their 'Wunderteam' exposed England's defensive failings and the home side were lucky to win 4–3. England held on to their undefeated home record for another twenty years.*

Above: *Another one goal defeat for Austria, this time in Milan in a 1934 World Cup semi-final: Guaita scrambles the ball over the line to give Italy a place in the final.*

recovered, France played Argentina in the key game of the group; and so very nearly won. It was a day on which Pinel was acquainted with the full menace of Monti. Later he was to say that he never went near the Argentinian centre-half without receiving a blow of some sort. Indeed, it was a tackle by Monti which hurt the ankle of Laurent, France's inside-left, early in the game. Pinel was in splendid form; later the famous Belgian referee, Jean Langenus, wrote that he put Monti into his pocket.

Yet Pinel had to take responsibility for the solitary goal which it took the strongly-fancied Argentinian side all of eighty-one minutes to score. Argentina were given a free kick a couple of yards outside the box. Monti put it down and took it quickly while the French were still organising. Pinel took a step to the right, unsighted Thepot, and the ball sped past him.

There was a weird moment, three minutes later, when the clever Langiller went dribbling through the Argentinian defence. Whereupon the Brazilian referee, Rego, blew for time, six minutes early.

Argentinian fans poured over the so-called safety netting on to the field to congratulate their idols, mounted police galloped on, order was restored, the French called back from the dressing-room, the Argentinians torn from their admirers and the final minutes played out. But by now the French morale was in pieces. The score stood as it was.

Two Uruguayan stars, Andrade and Nasazzi, gave it as their view that France deserved to win. As it was, the only European team to win its group turned out to be the Yugoslavs who did so at the expense of the fancied Brazilians.

Yugoslavia were much better balanced and went ahead through Tiranic and Beck after half-an-hour, and in a very hard-fought game had another goal disallowed for offside. Neto, the Brazilian skipper, got one back, but that was all.

The Rumanians were another European side to win their first game—if such a word can properly be applied to their battle with Peru. The Chilean referee, Warken, held little more than a watching brief, giving free-kicks at random. Rumania's right-back, Steiner, had his leg broken in a clash, and

Above: *Vittorio Pozzo (left) and his relieved team at the end of normal time in the 1934 World Cup final; Orsi had equalised with a freak goal just eight minutes from time. Schiavio scored in extra-time to give Italy the last home success in a World Cup tournament for 32 years.*

Warken sent off De Las Casas, Peru's captain, whose tackling and gestures had grown increasingly violent, but who was guiltless in this particular unhappy incident. And so Rumania won, eventually, 3–1.

Uruguay then opened their programme against Peru, after day and night labour had at last readied the Centenary Stadium. A very tough game it was for them too, a laborious Uruguayan side prevailing by one meagre goal, scored in the second half by their centre-forward Castro, who had lost the lower part of one arm. Petrone now dropped out, Castro too, for the moment, and Rumania were swamped 4–0, Uruguay thus going on to the semi-finals.

The United States did splendidly in their group, despatching both the Belgians and the Paraguayans by the identical score of 3–0. Some excuse, perhaps, for their team manager, Wilfred R Cummings, loftily remarking before the ensuing semi-final with Argentina that they were 'only interested in the final'. With half-a-dozen British ex-professionals in the side, the 'Americans' played in highly modern fashion, three up and the rest back, the emphasis on power

and speed. In training, they amused the French by their compulsive lapping; but they played very well.

The semi-final draw pitted Argentina against the United States in the one match, and Uruguay against Yugoslavia in the other. The first semi-final turned out to be a 6–1 massacre, the unhappy 'shotputters' —though they had begun as favourites— simply not having the mobility to withstand the quick and clever Argentinians.

At half-time Argentina led by a solitary goal, scored by the rugged Monti, but in the second half, the floodgates opened and Argentina added five more. They scored their last three goals in a hectic nine-minute period, and then Brown, the United States outside-right, got his team's consolation goal a mere five minutes from the end of the game.

Yet the most celebrated moment of the game had nothing to do with the play. When Langenus blew for a foul against an American, the team's medical attendant rushed on the field to protest, threw down his box of medicaments, inadvertently smashing a bottle of chloroform, and was

Top: *Confusion in the Austrian net after Guaita's semi-final goal.*
Centre: *Internazionale's Giuseppe Meazza (right) one of two players to gain winner's medals in both 1934 and 1938.*
Bottom: *The Italian team at the end of the 1934 final.*

overcome by the fumes. He had to be helped from the field!

In the other semi-final the next day, the Uruguayans beat Yugoslavia by the same score, though the game was actually a good deal closer than 6–1 suggests. 80,000 spectators saw Yugoslavia astonish Uruguay by taking a fourth-minute lead through Seculic, a fine goal, but Cea and Anselmo soon wiped that out. Yugoslavia had an equaliser somewhat controversially disallowed just before half-time, then went to pieces in the second half, when Uruguay added three more to their 3–1 lead. The first goal of the half was scored by Iriarte, the left-winger, after clever play by Fernandez had caught Yugoslavia's defence unawares. Then Cea completed his hat-trick.

So the stage was set for a replay of the 1928 Olympic final, with Uruguay now enjoying the advantage of playing at home against their closest—in several senses—rivals.

The night before the game, boats set out in large numbers to cross the River Plate from Buenos Aires packed with fervent Argentinian fans, sent off from the quay by still more frenzied followers chanting, 'Victory or death!' On arrival, both at Montevideo and in the stadium, they were all searched for pistols. The players' residence was under a day and night guard, and the crowd in the new stadium was limited to 90,000, though capacity was 10,000 more. Not until just a few hours before the final was Langenus given the green light to referee by his fellow officials, greatly concerned for his safety. But in the event the only major disagreement was over the ball; each side wanted its own. In the end Langenus tossed up, Argentina won, and by half-time had a 2–1 lead.

Shortly before the match, the Uruguayan fans were distressed by the news that Anselmo was unfit, his place going to Castro. However, things looked better when Pablo Dorado, their right-winger, gave them a twelfth-minute lead. But ten minutes from half-time his counterpart, Carlos Peucelle, had equalised, and Stabile, despite offside appeals by Nasazzi, scored a second for Argentina. The crowd reacted with stricken silence.

Ten minutes after the break, Pedro Cea dribbled through brilliantly to equalise and Uruguay, a compound of skill and physical fire, were on top. Another ten minutes, and Santos Iriarte had put them ahead. In the last seconds, the 'despised' Castro vindicated himself by smashing the ball into the roof of Botasso's goal to make it a good-looking 4–2 win. The game had been surprisingly calm, and Uruguay were

2nd WORLD CUP Italy, 1934

First round

Italy	(3)7	USA	(0)1
Schiavio 3, Orsi 2,		Donelli	
Meazza, Ferrari			
Czechoslovakia	(0)2	Romania	(1)1
Puc, Nejedly		Dobai	
Germany	(1)5	Belgium	(2)2
Conen 3, Kobierski 2		Voorhoof 2	
Austria	(1)(1)3	France	(1)(1)2
Sindelar, Schall,		Nicolas, Verriest	
Bican		(pen)	
Spain	(3)3	Brazil	(1)1
Iraragorri (pen),		Silva	
Langara 2			
Switzerland	(2)3	Netherlands	(1)2
Kielholz 2, Abegglen		Smit, Vente	
Sweden	(1)3	Argentina	(1)2
Jonasson 2, Kroon		Belis, Galateo	
Hungary	(2)4	Egypt	(1)2
Teleky, Toldi 2,		Fawzi 2	
Vincze			

Second round

Germany	(1)2	Sweden	(0)1
Hohmann 2		Dunker	
Austria	(1)2	Hungary	(0)1
Horwath, Zischek		Sarosi (pen)	
Italy	(0)(1)1	Spain	(1)(1)1
Ferrari		Regueiro	
Italy	(1)1	Spain	(0)0
Meazza			
Czechoslovakia	(1)3	Switzerland	(1)2
Svoboda, Sobotka,		Kielholz, Abegglen	
Nejedly			

Semi-finals

Czechoslovakia	(1)3	Germany	(0)1
Nejedly 2, Krcil		Noack	
Italy	(1)1	Austria	(0)0
Guaita			

Third place match: Naples

Germany	(3)3	Austria	(1)2
Lehner 2, Conen		Horwath, Seszta	

Final: Rome 10.6.34   Attendance 55,000

Italy (0)(1)2   **Czechoslovakia** (0)(1)1
Orsi, Schiavio   Puc

Italy: Combi (capt); Monzeglio, Allemandi;
Ferraris, Monti, Bertolini; Guaita, Meazza,
Schiavio, Ferrari, Orsi
Czechoslovakia: Planicka (capt);
Zenisek, Ctyroky; Kostalek, Cambal, Krcil;
Junek, Svoboda, Sobotka, Nejedly, Puc
Referee: Eklind (Sweden)
Leading scorers: 4—Conen (Germany),
Nejedly (Czechoslovakia), Schiavio (Italy)

worthy victors of the first World Cup.

They would not compete in another World Cup for twenty years, and then they would win it again. As their coach for the 1966 World Cup, Ondino Viera, remarked, 'Other countries have their history; Uruguay has its football.'

The British associations watched the events of the summer of 1930 from a distance and with apparent distinterest. There was little thought of patching up the quarrel with FIFA—nor indeed much incentive, for the British nations had not been alone in sitting out the first World Cup.

That initial international defeat in Madrid had not shaken the apparently total belief in the supremacy of England, though there had been other warning signs. Shortly before the events in Uruguay, England had been held to a 3–3 draw by Germany in Berlin, all three of Germany's goals falling to Richard Hoffman, a protegé of Jimmy Hogan. Four days later, in Vienna, Austria took the credit from a 0–0 draw.

Worse followed a year later in Paris when France stormed to a 5–2 victory, but public opinion payed little attention to results in games which they saw as unimportant summer fixtures. Nor, sadly for the long-term prospects of English football, could any visiting international side conquer their nerves at facing their masters on their own terrain. Typical was the case of Spain who came to Highbury in October 1931 supposedly fortified by their achievement in Madrid. But England won 7–1 against opponents who paled in such surroundings, none more than goalkeeper Zamora, the hero of the match two years earlier.

Fourteen months later Hogan and Meisl brought their ever-improving Austria side to play England at Stamford Bridge. Christened the Wunderteam, they lived up to their title, particularly in the second half. But by then they were trailing—the Aus-

trian players too had shown signs of nerves—and England won by a short head —4–3 and most home supporters were desperate to hear the final whistle so in command were Hogan's team at the end.

But the England of the thirties were no world beaters, though had they entered the 1934 World Cup who knows what they might have achieved on reputation alone. A gauge of their form can be found in the fact that the winners of the Home International Championships of both 1933 and 1934 were Wales! Moreover when Hungary and Czechoslovakia both used visits by England as warm-up games for the Italian World Cup, both were successful, 2–1. For all the pompous self-belief of the English game, form would hardly have made them favourites as other teams collected in Italy to contest World Cup number two.

Perhaps the most pertinent summing up of the 1934 World Cup was made by Belgian referee, Jean Langenus, 'Italy wanted to win,' he wrote, 'it was natural, but they made it far too obvious.'

Win they did in the end, but they made hard work of it, very nearly going down to a brave Spanish side at Florence in the quarter-finals, and only scraping through in the Rome final against the Czechs after extra time, and that with the help of one of the flukiest goals ever scored.

The 1934 World Cup, if ignored by the British, was a much more representative competition than the first and depleted 1930 edition; even though the Uruguayans, the holders, refused to participate. They explained this on the grounds of pique: the Europeans had snubbed them, they said, when they staged the tournament, so they were doing the same thing. More to the point was the fact that there had been a strike among the Uruguayan players.

Argentina, beaten by Uruguay in the 1930 final, did send a team, but kept several

Above left: *The Italian side which delighted Mussolini by winning the second World Cup.*
Below: *A gold medal specially struck by the Italian FA to celebrate their victory.*

of their leading players at home, afraid they would be poached by the Italians as Luisito Monti, their attacking centre-half had been after the 1930 World Cup. Now Monti was fulfilling the same role in an Italian team which pivoted around him and which danced to the tune its manager, Vittorio Pozzo, had conceived when, as a poor student in England, he had watched the fine 1908 Manchester United team.

The 'natural' final, which in fact came to pass in the semi-final, was between Italy and Austria, which in turn meant the conflict of the two great managers and father-figures of European football at that time, Vittorio Pozzo and Hugo Meisl.

These two men could scarcely have been more different, though each had huge respect for the other. Pozzo was a Piedmontese who had been Commissario Tecnico of the Italian side for the first time at the 1912 Olympic Games, when Meisl had been managing Austria, then a much superior team altogether. Pozzo was a blatant egotist who inspired his players, drawing on the inflated patriotism and vulgar chauvinism of Fascist Italy for his own purposes. He was called by a French journalist 'the poor captain of a company of millionaires', and used every possible ruse to get his temperamental, selfish players to work to-

gether. 'Kind, but with a strong hand', was his motto.

If, during a training game, a player refused to do something Pozzo wanted him to do, Pozzo would return to him a few minutes later and remark guilelessly, 'You know, what you said was right. You should do so-and-so.' The player, flattered, would proceed to do it, quite forgetting that it was what Pozzo had wanted, not he.

If Pozzo knew that two players had quarrelled in a League match, he would put them in the same room, overruling their protests, insisting that 'we have to build a team.' Next morning he would look round the door: 'Well, cannibals, have you eaten each other yet?' Rueful protests would follow and later each player in turn would take Pozzo aside to say, 'He's not such a bad fellow, really. The public set me against him.'

Italy had besides Monti two other Argentinians, both wingers—Guaita and the brilliant Orsi. They had double nationality as *oriundi*, the sons of Italians, and Pozzo rationalised their choice on the grounds that 'if they could die for Italy'—that is be called up for the Army—'they could play for Italy.'

The Italians practised robust, sweeping football, though they had such artists as the splendid Giuseppe Meazza at inside-right, and Orsi, too. The Austrian 'Wunderteam' was more delicate. It had given England that terrible shock at Stamford Bridge in 1932 and had marvellous ball players such as Matthias Sindelar, a centre-forward nicknamed 'The Man of Paper', and a fine attacking centre-half in Smistik.

Hugo Meisl's right-hand man was still the little Lancastrian coach Jimmy Hogan, whose classical Scottish methods, keeping the ball along the ground and emphasising close control, had also been imparted to the Hungarians. They had been one of the earliest European countries to master the game and their clever side, with an outstanding centre-forward in the lawyer, George Sarosi, was also expected to do well.

This time a qualifying competition had produced a full house of sixteen teams, which were divided not into four qualifying groups, as in Uruguay, but into a straightforward knock-out competition. Italy had spent huge sums of money on organising the tournament, not least as a shop window for their Fascist regime.

Italy played the curtain raiser in Rome, where Mussolini looked on from under a yachting cap. They made the merest mouthful of the United States, whose team was by no means as strong as in 1930. Italy won 7–1, Schiavio, the centre-forward whose goal would eventually win the World Cup final, getting three of the goals, Orsi a couple. The American goal, ironically, was scored by a Neapolitan centre-forward called Donelli, who stayed on to play in Italy.

Then the other seven first-round matches took place. The Czechs squeezed through against Rumania in Trieste by the odd goal of three, after being behind at half-time.

The Rumanians, who included only two of their 1930 World Cup side, played extremely well, were unlucky to lose and were thwarted only by two marvellous saves by Planicka, the sturdy, acrobatic Czech goalkeeper and chief star of the side. The winning goal was especially fortuitous. In a bounce-up, Sobotka, the Czech centre-forward, won the ball and slipped it to the gifted inside-forward, Nejedly, who got the winner.

Both South American teams, Brazil and Argentina, went out at once; poor reward for travelling halfway across the world for three weeks. Brazil were beaten quite easily by Spain at Genoa. Spain, with the famous Zamora in goal, held a 3–1 lead by half-time and thereafter were content to save their energies for the next round. Brazil lacked a plan to fuse their unquestioned talents; De Brito, a manifest prey to nerves, even badly missed a penalty-kick.

Argentina went out 3–2 to Sweden at Bologna. The Swedes had none of Argentina's technique, but they were a better team, and they did not despair when Argentina went ahead with a thunderous twenty-five-yard free-kick taken by their left-back, Belis.

In Turin, France ran Austria surprisingly close. Hugo Meisl had been pessimistic about his country's chances. The team was tired, he said; yet he also claimed that one English player, Cliff Bastin, would enable them to win the title if they could have him! All the luck went against the French, whose centre-forward, Jean Nicolas, had a nasty head injury, though it did not prevent him from scoring. Finally, Schall scored a blatantly offside goal for Austria, who squeezed through 3–2 in extra time.

In Florence, the only side playing a third back game in the tournament, Germany,

The Tommy Walker penalty which defeated goalkeeper Ted Sagar and equalised for Scotland at Wembley in 1936. The day was a windy one and the ball kept blowing off the spot but Walker, in his first game at Wembley, was not perturbed.

overwhelmed Belgium 5–2 after a poor start to the first half. Conen scored three from centre-forward for the Germans. In Naples, Hungary's 4–2 win against Egypt brought solace for their amazing defeat by the Egyptians in the 1924 Olympiad, while Switzerland beat Holland 3–2 in Milan, Kielholz scoring twice.

The quarter-finals pitted Italy against Spain and the name of 'Zamora' was on every Italian fan's lips. In the past he had been a frustration to the Italians with his brave goalkeeping. This time was to prove no different. There were passages when Zamora, now a veteran, seemed to be playing Italy on his own. And though the game was weakly refereed, and Zamora given wickedly rough usage, Spain forced a draw. Indeed, they held a half-time lead, Regueiro's miskicked shot wrong-footing another illustrious goalkeeper in Combi. When Italy equalised just after half-time, it was largely because Schiavio impeded Zamora.

Zamora was unfit for the return, played the very next day between two subdued sides, both much changed. Meazza headed the only goal of the game for Italy, despite Noguet, standing in for Zamora, giving almost as impressive a display as Zamora had in previous matches.

In Bologna, those two old enemies Austria and Hungary clashed in what Hugo Meisl described as 'a brawl, not a football match.' Meisl brought in the dashing little Horwarth, a player scarcely cast in the mould of the elaborate Vienna School, but highly effective on the day. In the seventh minute he dashed in to end a fine movement with a scoring shot and Hungary, with Sarosi off form, were in trouble. Six minutes after the break, the famous right-winger, Zischek, moved into the middle to make it 2–0. Sarosi scored from a penalty, Markos, the Hungarian right-winger, was sent off, and the Austrians deservedly stayed ahead.

In Milan, under heavy rain, Germany just got the better of Sweden, who threw away a chance to lead which fell to Kroon. Hohmann, the German inside-right, proceeded to score twice, the second a fine solo goal. Though Sweden lost their left-half, they got a late goal back in the end through Dunker.

The best match of the round was staged in Turin and brought a Czech victory over the lively Swiss. Kielholz gave Switzerland a breakaway lead after eighteen minutes, but Svoboda equalised. In the second half, Sobotka made it 2–1. Switzerland reacted fiercely, and Trello Abegglen at length equalised; only for Nejedly to get the Czech winner seven minutes from time.

There was more heavy rain in Milan where Italy and Austria met in the semi-

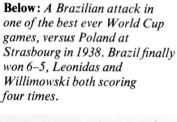

Below: *A Brazilian attack in one of the best ever World Cup games, versus Poland at Strasbourg in 1938. Brazil finally won 6–5, Leonidas and Willimowski both scoring four times.*

final. The clinging ground was just what the Austrians with their short, delicate game least wanted, and it bogged them down. Guaita, Italy's right-winger, got the game's only goal in the first-half, though in the last minute Zischek raced through alone, only in the event to shoot wide. And so Austria left the tournament.

In the other semi-final in Rome, the Czechs were far too quick and subtle for the plodding Germans, who badly missed the injured Hohmann. After twenty-one minutes, Nejedly gave the Czechs the lead after Junak's shot was parried, but after sixty-three minutes Planicka inexplicably allowed Noack's lob to sail over his head; a precursor of the final. Germany rallied, but after a mighty free-kick from the Czech left-winger, Puc, had hit the bar and been put in by Kreil, it was all Czechoslovakia, and Nejedly dribbled through for a third.

So the final would be between Italy and the Czechs—Germany meanwhile beating Austria comfortably at Naples for third place. Using the short pass admirably, the Czechs played with more consistency and determination in the final than in any previous round. Cambal, the attacking centre-half, was more than the equal of Monti, Puc a dangerous outside-left, while Svoboda at inside-right was deadly and Planicka supreme in goal. But the Italians were faster and harder, with Ferrari and Meazza keeping the attack on the move. Monti tackled bitterly, Monzeglio played well at right-back and Orsi and Guaita were lively on the wings.

For seventy minutes there were no goals. Then Puc, who had gone off with cramp, came back to take a corner. The ball ran back to him out of the goalmouth and he

drove it past Combi. 1–0 to Czechoslovakia. In despair some Italian fans seized a Czech's hair through the wire netting, and soldiers had to set him free.

Eight minutes from time Italy scored an extraordinary equaliser. Taking a pass from Guaita, Orsi ran through, feinted to shoot with his left, shot instead with his right, and saw the ball curl and dip diabolically over Planicka and into the net for a fluke goal. Next day he tried it twenty times with an empty goal and could not achieve it. Manager Pozzo danced behind the goal.

So the game went into extra time, which even though Meazza was limping, favoured the immensely fit Italian team. Indeed Meazza's handicap led indirectly to the goal, for the Czechs were not marking Meazza tightly when, seven minutes into extra time, he received the ball and served Guaita. On it went to Schiavio, who found new strength to beat a defender and then Planicka, and so give Italy the World Cup.

So Italy had achieved their ambition, and a beaming Duce presented the Jules Rimet trophy to Combi, the Italian captain. The general belief, however, was that Italy owed their triumph to their home advantage, and to the fact that the referees were intimidated by the fanatical nationalism of their crowds. Jean Langenus called it 'a sporting fiasco', and there is no doubt that a bitter taste was left behind everywhere but in Italy itself.

The following November the Italian team came to London to put their claim to the title of world champions at stake against England, whom everyone in the British Isles still believed to be the strongest footballing nation. The scene, Highbury, seemed set for a contest of gargantuan dimension. But few of the crowd, and indeed, the players, expected it to manifest itself in such a violent form.

A late reshuffle because of injury caused the home side to field seven Arsenal players—Moss, Male, Hapgood, Copping, Bowden, Drake and Bastin—in front of their own Highbury crowd. That may have been responsible for some of the marvellous team-work shown by England particularly during the early part of the game, but in no way does it explain the brutality.

That began when the titanic Monti had to be helped from the pitch after just two minutes with a broken toe. Monti imparted to the rest of his team before he left the arena his feelings that his injury had stemmed from a deliberate kick. That seemed improbable as play had not yet reached such cynical dimensions but nevertheless the World Cup winners felt they had a wrong to put right; they crudely set out to

Left: *The first round match at Toulouse where Cuba (in the dark shirts) held Rumania to a 3–3 draw. Appearing in their only World Cup finals so far, the Cubans then went on to win the replay 2–1 before going down 8–0 to semi-finalists Sweden.*

assault the English.

It was a foolish move. Not only did it destroy the pattern of their play, but they found themselves up against one or two opponents who knew a thing or two about the physical side of the game, notably Wilf Copping who tackled so forcefully that he pulled the ball away from others like a dentist pulling a tooth and with results just as painful. Though Hapgood suffered a broken nose from a shrewdly aimed elbow, England not only mastered this premeditated assault but struck back in the most effective way—with three goals. Eric Brook missed a penalty but compensated with two goals and Drake shot a third; only when Italy's steam evaporated did they produce their true form, and then their ten men scored twice, both goals from Meazza, and nearly equalised.

For England, then, prestige, but as Italy began their preparations for the defence of their title there seemed little indication that they had anything to fear from England even if the FA patched up their difference with FIFA. Still they psyched all foreign opposition in England, notably beating Germany 3–0 at Tottenham in 1935, Hungary 6–2 at Highbury in 1936, and Czechoslovakia 5–4 at Tottenham in 1937—in the latter case only with the help of a rare hattrick, all with his left foot, from Stanley Matthews. But, against this invincibility at

home, could be counted defeats in Vienna in 1936 and in Brussels three days later, then in Switzerland a few days before the 1938 World Cup, though the last defeat came just after the meritorious 6–3 win over Germany in Berlin where the players met Hitler and gave the Nazi salute. Nevertheless, England's status could still not be put to the test because of the disaffiliation from FIFA and the 1938 World Cup in France took place again without any of the four home countries.

The Italian team which won the 1938 World Cup in France was in every way a more attractive champion than its predecessor in 1934. Vittorio Pozzo's 1934 side made shameless use of its home advantage and the support of hysterical, Fascist-orientated crowds to win a tournament they would probably not have won outside Italy. But the 1938 side played purer football and prevailed on skill and merit alone. It had only two survivors from the 1934 team, its inside-forwards, Peppino Meazza and Giovanni Ferrari.

Though the shadows of war loomed over the tournament, its standard was high. The Nazi occupation had deprived it of the Austrians, several of whose players were co-opted by the German team, already under managership of the indestructible Sepp Herberger. Spain was locked in civil war. England, though still outside FIFA, were offered Austria's place but predictably declined, even though they now had a much more internationally-minded secretary of the FA in Stanley Rous.

Once again, after a qualifying competition, the tournament took the form of 'sudden death', with the Swedes drawing a bye in the first round.

The South American entry was limited to the talented Brazilians. Uruguay, still in the throes of developing professionalism, and still piqued by the way their own World Cup was snubbed by Europe in 1930, again decided not to come. The Argentinians too, who had sent a depleted side to Italy four years earlier and had been candidates to stage the 1938 World Cup, shillied, shallied, made demands, sulked, and finally stayed at home.

It was destined to be a tournament of great centre-forwards. Italy had the tall, powerful Silvio Piola, who vied for years with Meazza for the honour of being the most prolific scorer in Italian football. He did not play his last international until 1952.

Norway had the powerful, blond Viking, Brunyldsen, whom Pozzo, the resourceful Italian manager, was later to call 'a cruel thorn in my crown of roses.' In the Hungarian team, there was George Sarosi again, holder of a university doctorate, and his country's highest paid player.

The Czechs, runners-up in 1934, had the Nazis looming on their doorstep, but their football was still excellent, and the previous year they had been to Tottenham and frightened England.

France, the hosts, with a useful rather than a brilliant team, had just gone down 4–2 at home to England. Germany had been beaten by England too. Little Switzerland, however, had beaten the touring England side 2–1, and were to spring some surprises. Their star inside-forward, Trello Abegglen, a 1934 World Cup player, was with a French league side, as were Jaroslav Boucek, the Czech centre-half, and Willy Kohut, Hungary's left-winger.

Hungary, in the previous nine months, had scored a crop of goals, including no fewer than eight against the Czechs and their fine goalkeeper Planicka. Sarosi, having been switched to centre-half, was now back again at centre-forward, in splendid form, with a fine new lieutenant in the competent young inside-forward Szengeller.

As in 1934, the attacking centre-half still held sway. Pozzo had replaced the rugged Argentinian, Monti, in the Italian team with another ruthless South American in Andreolo, from Uruguay. The team of alleged 'amateurs' who had won the 1936 Olympic tournament had provided him with a new pair of full-backs in Foni and Rava, from Juventus.

Yet in Marseilles, the little-rated Norwegians gave Italy the shock of their lives. Certainly the Italians had been warned two years before when their Olympic team had only squeezed through by 2–1 against Norway in the semi-finals. Six of those Norwegians were there again at Marseilles.

Yet Italy had the immense incentive, Norway the sickening reverse, of a silly goal after only 105 seconds. Ferrari shot, Johansen, the Norwegian goalkeeper, dropped the ball, and Ferrari, following up, put it in. Norway took instant counter-measures. Eriksen, the centre-half, attached himself to Piola as a third back for the rest of the game, and largely subdued him, while Henriksen, the little right-half, took his place in midfield.

Just after half-time, Brunyldsen found Brustad, who cut inside Monzeglio, the right-back, and equalised. Brustad got the ball in the net again too, but this time he was offside, and Italy survived to extra time.

Within five minutes, Italy had retrieved the game. Again the goalkeeper could only block a shot, this time Paserati's, and Piola was at hand to score. It was a gloomy Italian team which took the train from Marseilles.

One of the great surprises of the round was the defeat of Germany by the lively Swiss. Herberger, taking over a German team low in morale after its thrashing by England, picked four Austrians in his so-called 'Greater Germany' side.

It was a tough game, Abegglen, injured in a collision with Kitzinger, had to leave the field. Soon after he came back, Gauchel

Left: *One of Italy's four goals in the 1938 final at Colombes, Paris, where they defeated Hungary 4–2.*

scored for Germany from a cross by the Austrian left-winger, Hans Pewser. But Abegglen himself equalised, heading in a cross by Wallaschek after Schnauss misjudged his back pass.

The game rolled on into extra time, and Pesser was sent off for kicking Minelli on the knee. Still there was no further score, and five days later the game was replayed; again in Paris, at the Parc des Princes. By half-time, Germany were two ahead and seemed to have the match in their pockets.

But, rather surprisingly, Switzerland's ten men were running the game by the time Aebi rejoined the game midway through he second half. A goal by Wallaschek, early in that period, had reduced the German lead, and Bickel equalised soon after Aebi's return. Then, to the delight of the crowd which loved him and knew him from his exploits with France's Sochaux, Trello Abegglen scored twice more to give the Swiss a fine 4–2 victory. So much for the Master Race.

Another, almost equally great, surprise was sprung in Toulouse, where the unknown, inventive Cubans held Rumania to a draw. Rumania had experience and tactical skill, the Cubans speed and control. Carvajeles, who had conceded only nine goals in the Cuban championship, was a superb keeper, and the score fluctuated until the end. Cuba, a goal behind early on to the veteran Covaci, went ahead in extra time, before Dobai equalised for Rumania. Cuba promptly dropped Carvajeles, picked a still more brilliant Ayra, and won the replay 2–1, even though the Rumanians again scored first. Although Cuba's winner

looked offside, and was in fact given offside by the over-ruled linesman, their victory was nonetheless a mighty feat by a team which had qualified only because Mexico withdrew.

At Le Havre, the Dutch took the Czechs to extra time, but then the loss of their inside-right Van der Veen in the second half, and the absence of their leading scorer, Bakhuijs, proved too much.

At Strasbourg, a Brazilian team including six new caps, met Poland, making their first appearance in the World Cup finals. Brazil had Leonidas and a brilliant inside-forward in Tim. Ernest Willimowski was an excellent inside-forward for the Poles. Indeed, he had helped Poland eliminate Yugoslavia to reach the last stages.

It was a fascinating, high-scoring game. Brazil led 3–1 at half-time thanks to a hat-trick by the black, dazzling Leonidas, small but infinitely gymnastic and elusive. Twenty-four years old, he could not have formed a greater contrast physically, with the tall, blond, strong Willimowski. Willimowski was the star of the second half when Poland fought back and conquered the midfield. Willimowski completed his own hat-trick, taking the final score to 4–4, which meant extra time. Willimowski got yet another goal for Poland, but only after Leonidas and the clever inside-right, Romeau, had scored for Brazil, and so the final score was a breathless 6–5. The sporting Poles sent Brazil a good luck telegram before their next game.

At Colombes, in Paris, the French hosts defeated their traditional rivals, the Belgians and at Reims, Hungary had no trouble in convincingly beating the Dutch East Indies 6–0, Sarosi and Szengeller getting a couple each.

In the second round, the Swedes, still fresh, thrashed the exhausted Cubans 8–0. Carvajeles, who had given a private press conference to forecast the 2–1 victory over Rumania, was back in goal, but was helpless to prevent the avalanche. 'Up to five goals,' said a French journalist, closing his typewriter in the press box at Antibes, 'is journalism. After that, it becomes statistics!' The Cubans returned home sadly via New York, where they watched Joe Louis knock out Max Schmeling.

58,000 spectators crowded into Colombes to see France play Italy, the nervous holders. The Italians played in Fascist black against a French team which only the previous December had held them 0–0 at the Parc des Princes, but now played like men without hope. They had no answer to a rampant Piola.

Colaussi, Italy's swift left-winger, gave Italy a freak lead after six minutes with what looked intended as a centre; Di Lorto, in the French goal, misjudged it. Within a minute, a clever French attack culminated in a goal when Aston dummied to Veinante's centre, and Heisserer beat Olivieri.

Half-time came at 1–1, but now Piola erupted. France unwisely committed themselves to all-out attack and Gusti Jordan, their Austrian-born centre-half, was stranded as Italy broke away. Piola took Biavati's long pass on to score, and then, to cap a brilliant performance, added the third by heading in Biavati's flick.

At Lille, the Swiss, without a key defender in Minelli, clearly felt the strain of their replay with Germany, and lost to the Hungarians. This was a relief to Hungary's sole selector, Dr Diest, who had promised to walk to Budapest if Hungary lost.

Bordeaux, where the new municipal stadium was inaugurated, produced a savage match between the Czechs and the Brazilians, one of the worst the World Cup has ever seen. Two Brazilians and a Czech were sent off and Planicka, the Czech goalkeeper, broke his arm. Nejedly—'pure as Bohemian crystal', according to a French journalist—broke his leg.

Brazil's Zeze began it all, early in the game, when he inexplicably kicked Nejedly, and got himself expelled. But on the half-hour, Leonidas gave Brazil the lead. Fourteen minutes later, Riha, the Czech, and the Brazilian, Machado, were sent off for fighting. A quarter of an hour after the interval, the gifted Brazilian back, Domingos Da Guia, probably the best in the competition, handled. Nejedly's penalty

equalised the score, and so it stayed after extra time.

All passion spent, the replay was surprisingly well-ordered, though admittedly Brazil made nine changes, the Czechs half-a-dozen. The Czechs took the lead through the busy Kopecky, moved up from wing-half to inside-left, but lost him with an injury after twenty-five minutes. Inevitably, Brazil dominated the second half. Leonidas equalised before Roberto volleyed the winner; yet there were those who believed that Senecky's shot had crossed the line when the Brazilian goalkeeper, Walter, retrieved it, just before Roberto's goal. So the depleted Czechs went narrowly out.

It was astonishing that Brazil should decide to confront Italy without Leonidas and Tim, their chief stars in attack. It seemed their team manager, Pimenta, had not been joking when he said: 'We are keeping them for the final.'

Yet perhaps they would still have won had the polished Domingos not allowed a vendetta with Piola to develop. Italy were leading 1–0 from Colaussi's goal when Domingos chopped Piola down. The centre-

First round

Switzerland	(1)(1)1	Germany	(0)(1)1	
Abegglen		Gauchel		
Switzerland	(0)4	Germany	(2)2	
Wallaschek, Bickel,		Hahnemann,		
Abegglen 2		Loertscher (og)		
Cuba	(0)(2)3	Romania	(1)(2)3	
Tunas, Maquina,		Covaci, Baratki,		
Sosa		Dobai		
Cuba	(0)2	Romania	(1)1	
Socorro, Maquina		Dobai		
Hungary	(4)6	Dutch East	(0)0	
Kohut, Toldi, Sarosi 2,		Indies		
Szengeller 2				
France	(2)3	Belgium	(1)1	
Veinante, Nicolas 2		Isemborghs		
Czecho-	(0)(0)3	Nether-	(0)(0)0	
slovakia		lands		
Kostalek, Boucek,				
Nejedly				
Brazil	(3)(4)6	Poland	(1)(4)5	
Leonidas 4, Peracio,		Willimowski 4,		
Romeu		Piontek		
Italy	(1)(1)2	Norway	(0)(1)1	
Ferrari, Piola		Brustad		

Second round

Sweden	(4)8	Cuba	(0)0	
Andersson, Jonasson,				
Wetterstroem 4,				
Nyberg, Keller				
Hungary	(1)2	Switzerland	(0)0	
Szengeller 2				
Italy	(1)3	France	(1)1	
Colaussi, Piola 2		Heisserer		
Brazil	(1)(1)1	Czechoslovakia		
			(0)(1)1	
Leonidas		Nejedly (pen)		
Brazil	(0)2	Czechoslovakia		
Leonidas, Roberto		Kopecky	(1)1	

Semi-finals

Italy	(2)2	Brazil	(0)1	
Colaussi, Meazza (pen)		Romeu		
Hungary	(3)5	Sweden	(1)1	
Szengeller 3, Titkos,		Nyberg		
Sarosi				

Third place match: Bordeaux

Brazil	(1)4	Sweden	(2)2	
Romeu, Leonidas 2		Jonasson, Nyberg		
Peracio				

Final: Paris 19.6.38 Attendance 65,000

Italy	(3)4	Hungary	(1)2	
Colaussi 2, Piola 2		Titkos, Sarosi		

Italy: Olivieri; Foni, Rava; Serantoni,
Andreolo, Locatelli; Biavati, Meazza (capt),
Piola, Ferrari, Colaussi.
Hungary: Szabo; Polgar, Biro; Szalay,
Szucs, Lazar; Sas, Vincze, Sarosi (capt),
Szengeller, Titkos.
Referee: Capdeville (France)
Leading scorers: 8—Leonidas (Brazil)
 7—Szengeller (Hungary)
 5—Piola (Italy/

Above right: *The winning
Italian team of 1938, a far
more attractive combination
than their predecessors of four
years earlier.*

forward rolled over histrionically, and Meazza scored from the penalty. Two–nil, and though Romeu got a goal in the second half, Brazil had shot their bolt.

In the other semi-final, Hungary had a surprisingly easy 5–1 win over Sweden at the Stade Colombes. Rudi Hiden, the famous Austrian goal-keeper now playing in Paris, dismissed it as a mere training game for the Hungarians against good amateurs. This despite the fact that Sweden took the lead through Nyberg, their left-winger, in a mere thirty-five seconds. A large blackbird roosted undisturbed in Hungary's half for much of the second period.

Brazil, at Bordeaux again, won the third place match 4–2 against Sweden, Leonidas returning, though it did not matter, to score twice.

The final, between Italy and Hungary, at Columbes, drew only 45,000. Some thought the Hungarians, despite their five against Sweden, would be too slow to hold the bustling Italians; though things might be different if the purist Sarosi could discover the form which had so far just eluded him.

In the sixth minute, after a Hungarian corner, Biavati ran almost the length of the field before finding Meazza, who sent Colaussi through to score. Undaunted, Hungary equalised within a minute, Sas crossing, and Sarosi finding an unmarked Titkos. But Hungary's own marking, especially of the Italian inside-forwards, was slack, and Meazza calmly put Piola

through to score. Ten minutes from half-time, Meazza put Colaussi through for the third. Sarosi reopened the game twenty minutes after half-time with an unexpected goal, but Italy were the masters.

Ferrari and Colaussi were too good and quick for the slow Hungarian right flank and, with ten minutes left, a fourth goal came. Biavati and Piola combined perfectly for Piola to finish it off with a crashing shot from Biavati's back-heel.

With Vittorio Pozzo again creating iron discipline and high morale, Italy's muscular, intelligent, flexible football had fully deserved its triumph. 'We played for the Cup', said Pozzo, 'leaving aside all flourishes.' But they played football, too, attractive football of a high standard unlike so many later Italian sides.

In October 1938 England met a FIFA representative team at Highbury, and, though they had lost 4–2 to Wales in Cardiff four days earlier, they beat a strong European team 3–0. In the following May they met Italy again, this time in Milan and drew 2–2, but later that week virtually the same side lost 2–1 to Yugoslavia in Belgrade. It was a fact not lost on Jimmy Hogan or a few other coaches with foresight, but as war began to beat its drum again England still remained unbeaten on her own soil at the game the British had given the world. It was an achievement worthy of praise, but no longer because it proved England was invincible. The fall, though, was still fourteen years away.

THE CHAPMAN ERA
England 1919-1939

The story of English football for twenty years can almost be told in just one game. That was the 1930 Cup final, the game which provided Arsenal with their first major honour. To achieve it they beat Huddersfield Town 2–0, Alex James controversially scoring the first after taking a quick free-kick and a return from Cliff Bastin while the Huddersfield defence protested their unreadiness. Centre-forward Jack Lambert scored the second.

Such are the facts about a game that summed up a soccer generation in a way that no game has ever done before or is ever likely to do again. As a microcosm of football in the inter-war era it is also easily remembered as the Graf Zeppelin final, Germany's giant airship dipping low over

Below: *One of the most famous of all Wembley goals, Alex James' for Arsenal in the 1930 Cup final. The referee nodded for James to take a quick free-kick, he took a return from Bastin and scored while the Huddersfield Town players protested their total unreadiness.*

Below: *1930 was also the Graf Zeppelin final, when the pride of a soon to be resurgent Germany dipped low over Wembley in salute.*

Top right: *The Huddersfield–Arsenal Cup final was the first for which the players took the field side by side, a tradition which has been observed ever since.*

Bottom right: *Happier days for Huddersfield, who lost the 1930 Cup final 2–0. In 1924–25 they established a record by not conceding more than two goals in any League match. That included this game at Highbury. At the end of the season Huddersfield manager Herbert Chapman was to leave the League champions and move to Arsenal.*

Wembley, a portent of things to come midway between two World Wars. Similarly memorable was the close relationship between the teams—they took the field together (the first time this had happened) and shared a banquet in the evening.

Such significance was given to the occasion by a man named Herbert Chapman, whose ideas were totally to dominate English football for nearly two decades. In that period he managed just two clubs—Huddersfield and Arsenal—and with both he built sides good enough to win a hat-trick of Championships. They remain the only clubs ever to have achieved this feat, and Arsenal, in particular, owe most of their history and their current standing in the game to this man. It is indicative of Chapman's reputation that, whenever Arsenal appoint a new manager, the nation's press invariably prints the same picture. It comprises the aspirant standing before the statue of the great man in the main hall at Highbury. And the captions always ask the same question: 'Have the Gunners found an equal?' The answer, one supposes, must always be no. For no man-

ager will ever again have the scope that Chapman had, nor conditions so conducive to his kind of autocratic control, nor, perhaps, his insight into the way to win football matches.

On the field of play the system that Chapman had devised became the norm for thirty years. But it was not only on the park that Chapman showed football the way of the future. In Tom Whittaker, appointed in February 1927, he found and encouraged the first of the genuine physiotherapists. In Highbury he built the best club ground in Britain. In advocating floodlights, numbered shirts, white balls, goal judges, independent time-keepers (he installed a 45-minute clock at Highbury only to have it banned by the FA), savings schemes for the players and even supporters trains he was way ahead of his time.

His influence extended everywhere. He changed the old style of strip acquired from Nottingham Forest to give the Arsenal players a distinctive look and introduced blue and white socks so that players could distinguish each other in a melée (not, as he kidded, because red runs in the wash). But Chapman was not in any way regarded as a godsend by the ultra-conservative administrators of the day. The Football League thought white balls a ridiculous idea and condemned his idea for numbering players' shirts as 'a stunt'. He tried to get the League to limit transfer fees (many

were convinced the game was facing ruin even then) and when it refused went out and paid a record for David Jack. He tore like a typhoon into a cosy world of semi-amateurs.

These were days when major clubs were happy to meander along, appointing an old player as Secretary-Manager, reaching the odd semi-final here, the top five of the League there, letting the senior players run the team. That was success, that was football.

Chapman came from another world, in fact another generation. He was the first true professional in a world of amateurs. The remarkable thing about Chapman,

even in comparison with managers like Busby and Revie, whose achievements are not totally out of proportion with his own, is that his influence extended far beyond the game itself. What is probably his greatest achievement off the field is still visible to the millions who travel on London's Piccadilly Line. There, sandwiched between Finsbury Park and Holloway Road, is Arsenal underground station. Not Gillespie Road, as the London Transport Passenger Board had originally called the stop, nor Highbury Hill, a compromise suggestion later put forward but plain, unadorned Arsenal. Chelsea are on the doorstep of Fulham Broadway station, West Ham next door to Upton Park—what more needs to be said about the powers of persuasion of this remarkable man?

In fact Chapman's success was all the more spectacular following, as it did, a relatively undistinguished playing career with Grimsby, Swindon, Northampton, Sheffield United (where he was a first team regular), Notts County and Tottenham. In 1907 Chapman stumbled into management back with Northampton Town—applying after the Spurs centre-half Walter Bull had turned the job down. Within two years

Above: *The bust of Herbert Chapman that stands in the entrance hall of Highbury's main stand.*
Above right: *A debonair Chapman with his trainer Tom Whittaker.*

Northampton were Southern League champions, but in 1912 Chapman was to return to his native West Riding (he was born at Kiveton Park in 1875) as the manager of the Second Division club Leeds City.

They had a successful spell through the First World War, winning the Wartime Championship play-off in 1918. But Chapman suffered with the club when they were unceremoniously thrown out of the League in 1919 for refusing to open their books when accused of making illegal payments to their players.

Leeds' place was taken by Port Vale, who were to suffer a similar fate half a century later. Vale, however, were re-elected; Leeds were not and their players were ignominiously auctioned to the highest bidders. Chapman was suspended for a while after a timely burning of the club's books, and took a partnership in an engineering firm. His suspension was lifted a year later and, predictably, he joined Huddersfield Town, first as assistant manager, becoming manager in September 1920.

Huddersfield themselves had very nearly left the League in November 1919. The directors, tired of small gates and a town obsessed with rugby league, (Huddersfield's 'Team of all the Talents' of the previous decade is still regarded as the greatest of all rugby league club sides) had recommended moving the club, lock, stock and barrel to Leeds. This could conveniently kill several birds by taking advantage of City's troubles (Huddersfield actually proposed to rename themselves Leeds United), maintaining a senior league club and increasing the potential audience. A group of supporters had, however, come up with enough cash to keep the club functioning in Huddersfield. The revitalised side was good enough to reach the 1920 Cup final (losing to Aston Villa) and Chapman found himself in the fortunate position of inheriting an already proven team.

In two years Huddersfield were back at Stamford Bridge, beating Preston in a dreadfully rough final with a Billy Smith penalty. The FA actually reprimanded both clubs afterwards, but Preston had to wait sixteen years for their revenge—reversing the tables in the 1938 final in identical fashion with a George Mutch penalty. In 1924 Huddersfield won their first Championship—albeit on goal average from Cardiff. In the Welsh club's last match of the season, against Birmingham, Cardiff got a penalty. Several players declined to take it but finally Len Davies agreed. If he had scored Cardiff would have been League champions for the only time in their history. He missed and the game ended in a goalless draw. Huddersfield were champions. The next year Huddersfield won it again with a new defensive record for a 42-match season (only 28 goals conceded) and went on to a hat-trick in 1926.

By then, however, Chapman had gone. He had achieved all that he could in that relatively small Yorkshire woollen town. It was a move that made sense to those who knew the man; Huddersfield could never, no matter how successful they were, become a club of lasting greatness. The town was too remote, too small, too devoted to the rival rugby league, thus, inevitably, too poor. Arsenal, twenty minutes away from Piccadilly Circus, offered not just the bright lights but the biggest city in the world, an enormous hinterland which had yet to acclaim a League Championship. To take Arsenal to greatness would be to tap the potential support of millions. And, perhaps, the fact that they were the arch rivals of the club with which he had ended his playing career might have been an influence.

No club, including Arsenal, could have failed to be impressed by his remarkable record at Huddersfield in the face of small crowds, little money and the rival code. He had few outstanding players—Alex Jackson of the 1928 Wembley Wizards was the key and played all over the park and ex-Aston Villa captain, Clem Stephenson (who had won Cup winner's medals with Villa in 1913 and 1920) provided the experience. The full-backs, Barkas and Wadsworth, were excellent and largely responsible for Huddersfield's magnificent defensive records. In the three seasons between the Cup win in 1922 and Chapman's departure in 1925 the Huddersfield defence conceded precisely 101 goals in 137 Cup and League matches. They were also the first side to go through a whole forty-two match First Division season without having more than two goals scored against them, and set up a remarkable and still standing record in avoiding defeat in eighteen consecutive away games.

The Arsenal of 1925 was by no means the Arsenal of 1976. At the same time that the Huddersfield directors were advocating a move to Leeds, Arsenal were creeping into the First Division in the most unsavoury circumstances. In the last pre-War season they had finished sixth in the Second Division. In 1919 the First was to be extended from twenty to twenty-two clubs, and the obvious thing to do seemed to be to leave the bottom clubs of 1914–15 (Chelsea and Spurs) where they were and promote the top two from the Second. Somehow or

Left: *Chapman and Whittaker with the 1929 Arsenal side. Chapman's two League clubs, Huddersfield and Arsenal, are the only two ever to have won a hat-trick of League championships.*

Charlie Buchan, the man the selectors said was 'too clever to play for England'.
Above: *Climbing above Villa keeper Jackson to head down.*
Right: *Last days with Arsenal and a well balanced shot against neighbours Tottenham.*

other, Arsenal chairman Henry Norris (who had been chairman of Fulham until 1910) got his club voted up, and at the expense of Tottenham Hotspur. This, coupled with Arsenal's unheralded arrival in north London in September 1913, when Norris had uprooted them from Plumstead (south of the river) to the grounds of a theological college, are the root of the understandable north London rivalry.

Nonetheless Arsenal proved no great revolutionary force in the premier division and were no better than adequate before Chapman's arrival. Fortunately, however, this date coincided with the most important change the game has seen this century.

The immediate cause of this revolution was the change in the offside law on 12 June 1925, when the 'fewer than three players between the attacker and the ball' clause was changed to 'fewer than two'. The results were startling. In the 1924–25 season, the final one prior to the change in law, 1192 goals were scored in the First Division. In the next season that figure rose to 1703 —an increase of nearly fifty per cent, or, more graphically, an extra goal for every match played.

But while the immediate result was to move the advantage from defence to attack, the long term effect was probably negative, for the tactical result was, at its simplest, that one attacker became a defender. Credit for devising the 'third back game', as it became known, has never been adequately apportioned. Bob Gillespie, of Queen's Park, quickly made it his job to blot out the opposing centre-forward but folklore has it—with some concrete support—that the man behind the innovation was Herbert Chapman.

Almost Chapman's first action on joining Arsenal had been to acquire a scheming inside-forward. His choice was Charlie Buchan, then aged thirty-four, from Sunderland, the man selectors said was 'too clever to play for England'. The fee was an imaginative £2,000 down and £100 for every goal he scored in the subsequent season. Buchan scored nineteen in the League and two in the Cup. But it was a transfer significant beyond its immediate impact and strange terms.

In 1929 Henry Norris, Arsenal's chairman, sued the FA for libel after he had been suspended for making illegal payments. The Buchan case was particularly mentioned and it was shown that Buchan had been offered other inducements to join the club. Norris lost his case and far more, for, when he died in 1934, he was an exile from football and the club that he had dragged from obscurity.

Charlie Buchan's return to Arsenal, the club he had actually walked out on before the War over 11 shillings (55p) expenses, was not a very happy one. One of his, and Chapman's, earliest matches for the club was a humiliating 7–0 defeat at Newcastle on 3 October 1925. Buchan was so upset at such a return to the North East that he and Chapman organised an immediate tactical discussion. One or the other (accounts vary as to which it was) proposed that Arsenal's centre-half, Jack Butler, should adopt a purely defensive role and that one of the inside-forwards should drop back to supply the creative link between defence and attack that the centre-half could no longer provide.

Oddly enough Newcastle's centre-half, Charlie Spencer, claimed he had played just such a defensive role in that vital match, and Arsenal's plan may have come from observing Newcastle's success. Before 1925 the centre-half performed exactly the functions his title implied—playing in the middle of the field, helping in defence and instigating attacks.

Buchan expected to be given the creative inside-forward's job himself, but Chapman valued his goalscoring abilities too highly and detailed a reserve inside-forward, Andy Neil, to perform the midfield role at Upton Park the following week on Monday 5 October. Arsenal won 4–0, with Buchan scoring twice. Chapman gradually revised his team by pushing the full-backs out to mark the wingers and using both his wing halves (now free from their close marking duties) to perform midfield roles along with the withdrawn inside-forward. The scheme worked well enough, but was not perfected until Chapman purchased the vital creative link, Alex James, from Preston in 1929. Thus the team played in a formation which could be loosely described as 3–4–3 or 3–3–4, rather than the 2–3–5 of earlier times and later programme design.

Chapman, needless to say, had to find the right players to fit his tactics. His ability was in choosing and moulding those players as parts of a whole. At Huddersfield he inherited a good side, having to buy only Clem Stephenson to make it really effective. At Arsenal he found a frankly mediocre team (their League positions since reaching the First Division had been tenth, ninth, seventeenth, eleventh, nineteenth and twentieth) and it took several years to create the blend that is remembered today.

The vital stopper centre-half was quickly found—'Policeman' Herbie Roberts arriving from Oswestry for £200. Right-back Tom Parker was signed from Southampton to act as Chapman's captain, and his successor, Eddie Hapgood, came from Kettering for £750 where he had spent his time outside football working in a dairy. And his full-back and England partner, George Male, was converted from an undistinguished half-back already on Arsenal's books.

Chapman's approach was again a subtle combination of buying, finding and bringing through the ranks. When he thought he had the right man he was unstoppable. David Jack replaced Buchan in 1928 having commanded the first five-figure fee (actually £10,370) and the last, most vital link, Alex James, arrived in 1929 from Preston. This was a remarkable acquisition in that Preston had previously turned down a reputed bid of £15,000 from Manchester City for James—arguably the best player of the day. Chapman acquired him for £9,000 (helped by the promise of a job as football demonstrator in Selfridge's) and set him to work as the vital midfield link. It took some time to persuade James to play the role required; at Preston he had been a real forward, scoring 53 goals in 147 games.

Life at Highbury was rather more serious (James openly confessed to regarding Second Division football as fun) and he eventually learned to conform—bringing the ball out of defence and spreading those long passes inside the full-backs for wingers Hulme and Bastin. Bastin was another even more celebrated example of Chapman's acumen. He had played only seventeen

Below: *A meeting of authoritarians, albeit of a different kind. Arsenal liked to undertake a continental summer tour and this one took them to Rome, where they posed with Mussolini. The Italian dictator signed a copy of the photograph for Chapman (bottom right).*

games for Third Division Exeter when Chapman bought him for £2000 as a true goalscoring winger. His total of thirty-three goals in the 1932–33 season still stands as a First Division record for any conventional winger.

It is worth remembering that Norris, like most football club chairmen, had his prejudices. He disliked small players intensely, loathed paying large transfer fees and had long imposed a maximum of £1000. His advertisement for a new manager in the *Athletic News* (to which it is assumed that Chapman responded although Norris was visionary enough to have approached him) read '. . . anyone whose sole ability to build up a good side depends on the payment of heavy and exorbitant transfer fees should not bother to apply.'

In Chapman, however, Norris had more than met his match and the manager simply ignored his chairman's instructions. Success came quickly. At the end of his first season, 1925–26, Arsenal were League runners-up to Huddersfield. It was as high as a London club had ever finished; the great days had begun.

The following year Arsenal were at Wembley, there to lose the only final won by a non-English club. Cardiff City's Hugh Ferguson scored with a long, speculative shot that keeper Dan Lewis fumbled, and then seemed to throw over his own goal line. Sheen on a new jersey was blamed— and the club have made a point of washing new goalkeepers' jerseys before use ever

since. 1928 and 1929 saw them tenth and ninth in the League and then came that definitive game at Wembley in 1930. It was Arsenal's first major trophy—they were on the verge of greatness. For Huddersfield it was the final gesture of a glorious decade— they would never win anything again. The following year Arsenal won their first Championship—with a record of sixty-six points that stood until Leeds bettered it by one in 1969.

The next year, 1932, saw the 'over the line' final, and one of Wembley's most disputed goals. Richardson, the Newcastle inside-right, had chased a long pass which seemed to have crossed the goalline when he reached it. He centred nonetheless and centre-forward Allen flicked it home. Hapgood, who had been marking Allen, had run across the line when he saw the ball go out. What pictorial evidence there is, and the views of those in line, seems to support Arsenal but the game had swung at that point and the Gunners were not to recover. Less than a year later they lost yet another Cup game, at Walsall, which was to become even more famous and is still revered as the greatest giant-killing act of all time.

Outside its context this assessment seems a little extreme. Arsenal, though leading the First Division, had won the League and Cup only once each. This was to be the first season of their hat-trick. Walsall, for their part, were a steady Third Division side—certainly not comparable with Yeovil when they defeated Sunderland, Hereford when they beat Newcastle or, far more praiseworthy, Wimbledon when they won away at Burnley in 1975, the only non-League club to win on a First Division ground since the formation of the Third Division.

But the Arsenal–Walsall game needs placing in historical context. The 1930s were, for most of provincial Britain, the worst decade for almost a century. Unemployment touched three million, and in some textile, mining and shipbuilding towns half of the workforce was on the dole for literally years on end. To these towns, with their fierce emotional commitment to football as one of the few sources of local pride still available, Arsenal came to represent the wealth, affluence and unfair advantage that London, still relatively unaffected by unemployment, seemed to have stolen from the rest of the country. Arsenal was the symbol of the south—rich, mean and successful. And in those days there was no television to say that it was not all true— just word of mouth and a once a year visit from this tactical monster 'Lucky Arsenal'.

That was the cry that flitted across a decade. Time after time, Arsenal seemed

Below: *Cliff Bastin attacks the Portsmouth defence. Chapman bought Bastin after he had played only seventeen first team games for Exeter City. Running on to the famous long through passes of Alex James, Bastin established a record for a conventional winger in 1932–33; thirty-three goals in the season.*

Above: *Tom Whittaker, first of the real trainers and Chapman's right-hand man from 1927.*

happy to absorb the pressure of less talented sides and win games by the simple expedient of a breakaway goal. It was difficult to convince the unsophisticated terraces or the ageing boardrooms of the 1930s that 80 minutes of unrewarded pressure was less valuable than one goal from a few sudden breaks by Hulme and Bastin. Arsenal played a smash and grab game on the field —fully confirming their similar reputation off it; a quick ball inside the full-back from Alex James to Cliff Bastin and back to London with the points—leaving the local team's supporters with the illogical conviction that the best side had lost. It was to be thirty years before British fans fully appreciated that the better of two teams is, by definition, the one that scores more goals.

But Arsenal were not really negative. In 1930–31, for instance, they scored 127 League goals. However, when Arsenal arrived at Walsall on 14 January 1933 Chapman was certainly not without his problems. Left-back Hapgood, left-half Bob John and the two centre-forwards Jack Lambert and Tim Coleman were all down

with flu, while Hulme had been off form and had not been considered. As a result Chapman played four total unknowns— left-back Tommy Black, outside-right Billy Warnes, centre-forward Charlie Walsh and half-back Norman Sidey—the only one with any first team experience and that limited to one game. Nonetheless, the other seven members of the team were all internationals and included the likes of David Jack, Alex James and Cliff Bastin.

It is unlikely that Chapman underestimated the opposition—even if the press took great delight in pointing out that Arsenal had paid out more for their boots that season than the whole Walsall side had cost in transfer and signing on fees. Walsall had drawn three of their previous four games, and lost the other 5–0. Arsenal, for their part, were probably at the peak of their abilities—just three weeks before (on 24 December 1932) they had produced what was probably their best performance of the whole decade in defeating Sheffield United 9–2 at Highbury. Lambert scored five and Arsenal had gone six points clear at the top of the division.

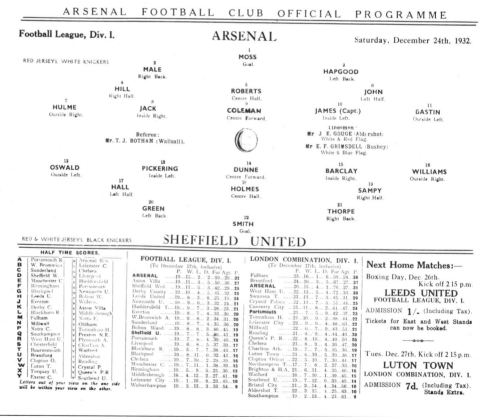

Football League, Div. I.

ARSENAL

Saturday, December 24th, 1932.

RED JERSEYS, WHITE KNICKERS.

1
MOSS
Goal.

2
MALE
Right Back.

3
HAPGOOD
Left Back.

4
HILL
Right Half.

5
ROBERTS
Centre Half.

6
JOHN
Left Half.

7
HULME
Outside Right.

8
JACK
Inside Right.

9
COLEMAN
Centre Forward.

10
JAMES (Capt.)
Inside Left.

11
BASTIN
Outside Left.

Referee:
Mr. T. J. BOTHAM (Walsall).

Linesmen
Mr J. E. GOUGE (Aldershot)
White & Red Flag.
Mr E. F. GRIMSDELL (Bushey)
White & Blue Flag.

12
OSWALD
Outside Left.

13
PICKERING
Inside Left.

14
DUNNE
Centre Forward.

15
BARCLAY
Inside Right.

16
WILLIAMS
Outside Right.

17
HALL
Left Half.

18
HOLMES
Centre Half.

19
SAMPY
Right Half.

20
GREEN
Left Back.

21
THORPE
Right Back.

22
SMITH
Goal.

RED & WHITE JERSEYS, BLACK KNICKERS.

SHEFFIELD UNITED

HALF TIME SCORES.

A	Portsmouth R.	v	Arsenal Res.
B	W. Bromwich	v	Leicester C.
C	Sunderland	v	Chelsea
D	Sheffield W.	v	Liverpool
E	Manchester C.	v	Huddersfield
F	Birmingham	v	Portsmouth
G	Blackpool	v	Newcastle U.
H	Everton	v	Wolves.
J	Leeds U.	v	Bolton W.
K	Derby C.	v	Aston Villa
L	Blackburn R.	v	Middlesbrough
M	Fulham	v	Notts F.
N	Millwall	v	Oldham
O	Notts C.	v	Tottenham H.
P	Southampton	v	Preston N.E.
Q	West Ham U.	v	Plymouth A.
R	Brentford	v	Charlton A.
S	Bournemouth	v	Watford
T	Brentford	v	Aldershot
U	Clapton O.	v	Reading
V	Luton T.	v	Crystal P.
W	Torquay U.	v	Queen's P.R
Y	Exeter C.	v	Southend U.

Letters out of your view on the one side will be within your view on the other.

FOOTBALL LEAGUE, DIV. I.
(To December 17th, inclusive)

	P.	W.	L.	D.	For	Agt.	P.
ARSENAL	19	15	2	2	59	29	32
Aston Villa	19	14	3	5	67	27	37
Sheffield Wed.	19	11	4	4	52	29	25
Derby County	19	10	4	5	45	32	25
Leeds United	19	8	3	8	25	19	24
Newcastle U.	18	9	6	3	32	21	21
Huddersfield T.	19	9	7	3	28	23	21
Everton	19	8	7	4	33	30	20
W.Bromwich A.	19	9	8	2	34	31	20
Sunderland	19	8	7	4	35	36	20
Bolton Wand.	19	8	8	3	40	45	19
Sheffield U.	19	7	7	5	46	41	19
Portsmouth	19	7	8	4	37	34	18
Liverpool	19	6	8	5	37	30	17
Blackburn R.	19	5	7	7	38	43	17
Blackpool	19	8	11	0	32	41	16
Chelsea	19	7	10	2	29	39	16
Manchester C.	19	7	11	1	39	39	15
Birmingham	19	5	9	5	25	30	15
Middlesbrough	18	4	12	2	27	41	10
Leicester City	19	4	11	4	33	49	12
Wolverhampton	19	3	13	3	33	54	9

LONDON COMBINATION, DIV. I.
(To December 17th, inclusive)

	P.	W.	L.	D.	For	Agt.	P.
Fulham	23	16	1	6	59	24	38
Brentford	24	16	3	5	67	27	37
ARSENAL	20	15	4	1	76	27	31
West Ham U.	22	13	5	4	72	33	30
Swansea T.	23	13	7	3	45	31	29
Crystal Palace	22	13	7	2	51	44	25
Coventry City	21	11	8	2	61	47	24
Portsmouth	21	7	5	9	42	37	23
Tottenham H.	21	10	9	2	48	44	22
Leicester City	22	9	9	4	48	63	22
Millwall	22	6	7	9	43	51	21
Reading	21	8	9	4	44	49	20
Queen's P. R.	22	8	10	4	40	50	20
Chelsea	21	8	9	4	30	47	20
Charlton Ath.	19	7	7	5	35	36	19
Luton Town	21	6	10	5	39	38	17
Clapton Orient	22	6	10	7	30	44	17
Northampton T.	17	7	8	2	27	33	16
Brighton & H.A.	21	6	11	4	35	46	16
Watford	18	7	10	1	39	45	15
Southend U.	19	7	12	0	33	49	14
Bristol City	23	3	14	4	34	56	10
Aldershot T.	22	3	15	4	25	63	10
Southampton	19	2	13	4	23	61	8

Next Home Matches:—

Boxing Day, Dec. 26th.
Kick off 2.15 p.m.

LEEDS UNITED
FOOTBALL LEAGUE, DIV. I.

ADMISSION **1/-** (Including Tax).

Tickets for East and West Stands can now be booked.

Tues. Dec. 27th, Kick off 2.15 p.m.

LUTON TOWN
LONDON COMBINATION, DIV. I.

ADMISSION **7d.** (Including Tax).
Stands Extra.

90

Nevertheless, Chapman understandably felt that his reserves, with a first team place to play for, would fight as hard as Walsall in what was, inevitably, going to be a tough game. It did not work out that way. Walsh, recruited from amateur soccer, was so nervous before the game that he put his boots on before his stockings, missed several easy chances (including the best of the game when he hit a centre with his shoulder

Opposite top: *Fred Keenor leads the Cardiff players down the Wembley steps at the end of the 1927 Cup final. The Welshmen had defeated Arsenal to take the Cup out of England for the first and only time.*
Inset: *Hugh Ferguson's goal, the only one of the 1927 final. Arsenal keeper Dan Lewis appeared to have gathered the ball and then seemed to throw it back into his net. Grease on a new jersey was the explanation.*
Opposite bottom: *The height of Arsenal's powers— Christmas Eve 1932 when they defeated Sheffield United 9–2. Lambert replaced the programmed Coleman as centre-forward and scored five of the goals.*
This page: *The most contentious goal ever scored in an FA Cup final—Newcastle's first in the 1932 Cup final. Richardson, the Geordies' inside-right, chased a long pass down the right but it seemed to have crossed the goal-line when he reached it. He centred nonetheless and Allen flicked the ball home—though at least one Arsenal defender who could have intercepted (bottom right) had run out of play assuming a goal-kick would be given.*

91

The 1923 Cup final, the first played at Wembley and attended (they could not possibly all have watched) by the largest crowd ever recorded at any sort of football match in Britain. Though the official attendance was only 126,047, with all turnstiles broken down and the pitch swamped it is unlikely that less than 200,000 were present.

rather than his head) and had a wretched match. Warnes did not enjoy the hard tackling and Black was responsible for sealing Arsenal's fate by giving away a penalty in the second half. But for an hour the Londoners survived and, despite the pressure, they were beginning to breath a little more easily; no score and seemingly, at worst, the prospect of a Highbury replay. Then it happened. Walsall won a corner, Lee centred and Alsop headed home. Then came Sheppard's penalty after Black's foul on Alsop and Arsenal were out.

Chapman reacted, probably over-reacted, violently to the defeat by blaming his reserves. Poor Walsh was transferred to Brentford within a fortnight—and had to carry the ghost of this game throughout his career. Warnes soon went to Norwich and

Black seems to have been banned from ever visiting Highbury again. He was sent straight home from Euston and transferred to Plymouth a week later. It was an unfortunate name to carry that black day in the Black Country.

The Walsall game is instructive of a lesser known side of Chapman—his rigid authoritarianism. He was allowed to rule the club with a rod of iron, on one celebrated occasion sacking his trainer (and replacing him with Tom Whittaker) for supposedly coaching from the touch-line, a duty which Chapman reserved totally for himself. Walsall, needless to say, were knocked out in the next round 2–0 by Manchester City and the freak result had no lasting effect on Arsenal—who went on to win the first of their League hat-trick. Chapman was not to see

the morning of Arsenal's next game—against Sheffield Wednesday on the Saturday. The game, according to a report of the time, was 'played by weeping players before a weeping crowd'. In 1936 Arsenal unveiled the majestic bust of Chapman in the main hall of the lush new Highbury stand, commemorating the anniversary of his death with two minutes silence and the laying of a wreath and flowers. The silence was carried on for over two decades; the flowers remain today.

After Chapman's death radio commentator George Allison took over, sensibly leaning heavily on the real team manager, trainer Tom Whittaker, and his own assistant, Joe Shaw. New players were in the tough, Chapman mould—the likes of half-back Crayston and centre-forward Drake,

Top: *A panoramic view of the game in progress.*
Left opposite: *The famous white horse in effective action.*
Centre: *The walls were reputed to be as high as Jericho's, but more than a few scaled them.*
Above: *The scene at official kick-off time, 3pm.*

all those successes; by a sad irony he was with neither Huddersfield nor Arsenal when they won their third successive trophy. Within a year of that traumatic day at Walsall Chapman was suddenly, unbelievably, dead.

It was January 1934 and Arsenal were typically top of the First Division. Herbert Chapman caught a cold, went to watch a third team game at Guildford one Wednesday, retired to bed that night and died on

Above: *The Bolton and West Ham players wait for the game to begin. They did not go off at half-time, simply changing ends.*
Opposite top: *A Bolton shot flies just over the West Ham bar. Note the spectators on the stand roof and the strategically placed feet.*
Opposite centre: *John Smith, scorer of Bolton's second goal, shoots just wide.*
Bottom: *The aftermath.*

and they built a reputation that perhaps only Real Madrid have ever rivalled—not to mention a superb club stadium that has remained unchanged for forty years and was not to be bettered for facilities in Britain for nearly thirty.

In the end Arsenal must be Chapman's epitaph. Mention of the word in any soccer conscious country does not instantly mean a place where ammunition is kept. It means a football club so strong that seven of its players were chosen to represent England and defeat new world champions Italy in 1934—at Highbury of course!

It would, nonetheless, be churlish to decry the other teams and events of the era— and there was one particularly significant development soon after the First World War which has come to be central to the English game, the building of Wembley Stadium (or, more accurately, The Empire Stadium, Wembley). After the end of the First World War the Football League had extended the First and Second Divisions to twenty-two clubs each, soon added the Third Division by absorbing the First Division of the Southern League, and later a fourth, designating the latter two 'Third Divisions North and South'.

But the FA Cup was still the major attraction, particularly for the south (which lacked any serious competitor in the League) and here the Football Association found itself with something of a problem. Crystal Palace, the pre-War venue, was still in use by the Army and would not be available for several years. It was, anyway, a poor stadium with no cover and no real terracing. As a stopgap Chelsea's Stamford Bridge was chosen to house three dreadful finals (1920, 1921 and 1922) all of which ended 1–0 and seemed thoroughly suited to that dreary setting.

At the time plans were being aired for a British Empire Exhibition to be held at Wembley, then on the outskirts of urban London surrounded by fields and farms. Part of the planning included an enormous stadium in which major events—such as circuses, rodeos and the Empire Pageant— could be held. The Football Association, showing unusual foresight, took an interest as early as 1921 and promised its support (the stadium has always been a private company). As a result the stadium was begun in January 1922. It took a mere 300 working days to complete, costing only £800,000, using 25,000 tons of concrete and 1,400 tons of steel to replace the 250,000 tons of earth that had to be removed from the slightly elevated site. It was 890 feet long, and the terracing rose 76 feet from ground level. The walls, said the press, were as high as the walls of Jericho, and yet

who remains the holder of a First Division record with his seven goals from eight shots in a League game against Aston Villa. Even as they declined, unconvincingly winning the Cup with another Drake goal in 1936 and the Championship with only 52 points in 1938, Raich Carter could say of them: 'They were not merely a great side; they towered so much above every other club. We were in total awe of them.' By that time only Hapgood, Male and Bastin survived from Chapman's great team. Even James retired that year, later to die at the early age of fifty-one. When Arsenal strove to rebuild their fortunes after the War they were to find that their reputation was as big a handicap to them as it had been to their rivals before 1939. The War had left them effectively without a side. Ten of the team that had played their last League game in 1939 were unavailable when normal peace-time football resumed in 1946.

Forty years after Chapman's death it is almost impossible to imagine just how totally his influence pervaded the game in the inter-war period. Combine the Leeds of the late sixties and the Manchester United of 1957 and you have the sort of awe in which Arsenal were held during the 1930s. He led his men, and the game, by what would today be called charisma. Nevertheless Chapman's sides were never great entertainers, not to be compared with the Manchester United of 1948 or the Tottenham of 1961, but they won football matches hundreds were to scale them at the very first Cup final.

As an aside, the exhibition itself cost £12,000,000 and came and went, losing a fortune and leaving just a sad series of pavilions down Olympic Way, now used as warehouses or simply derelict. 'A vast white elephant, a rotting sepulchre of hopes and the grave of fortunes', one contemporary newspaper report commented. It is probable that only the stadium saved it—certainly that was the only part to survive. After army regiments had walked round and round the concrete terracing to ensure its solidity, the stadium was opened in 1923 —a year before the rest of the exhibition.

As only 53,000 had turned up to see Chapman's first major honour with Huddersfield's Cup win in 1922, the Football Association was quite confident that Wembley's 125,000 capacity would be sufficient for everyone who wanted to see the first game to be played there, the 1923 Cup final. This view was not altered by the unexpected and rare appearance of a London club—Second Division West Ham United—to contest the game with the usual Lancastrians, this time Bolton Wanderers.

In normal circumstances, the Football Association would undoubtedly have been correct in its assumptions. Unfortunately the appeal of this magnificent new monument to the age of ferro-concrete had rendered the occasion rather abnormal and, by midday on 28 April 1923, something like half a million fans were probably on their way to north west London. By 2 pm the situation at the stadium had deteriorated into complete chaos. Standing accommodation was full but there were probably still one hundred thousand outside. They simply stormed the barriers and walls of the stadium—partly through disbelief that the stadium could be full, partly because the pressure of the crowds made it impossible to go backwards.

After a while barriers and turnstiles had simply disappeared—the day abounds with stories of old men hacking down fences or scaling the walls up drainpipes. At 3 pm, when the game should have begun, not a blade of grass could be seen, and the bands of the Irish and Grenadier guards, like bad children, could be heard but not seen.

It was around this time that PC George Scorey and his white horse Billy made their immortal appearance and began clearing crowds from one goal-line. Scorey was not the only mounted policeman there—he drew attention because of the white horse—and, interestingly, no newspaper other than the *Athletic News* mentioned his contribution the following day. The directors of the stadium were in no doubt, however, and

BAILY (A)

BAILY (B)

later expressed the view that it was largely through Scorey that the game was played at all. Scorey, incidentally, was not a football fan and later confessed to never having gone to another football match. The official attendance was later given as 126,047, but it was certainly at least 150,000, probably 200,000 and possibly 250,000—which would have made it the biggest attendance ever at a football match.

The game was finally started at 3.44 pm with the crowd literally standing on the touch line. By 3.46 pm David Jack had become the first man to score a goal at Wembley. The half lasted over an hour, having to be stopped once to clear the pitch of spectators. The players turned straight round and Bolton scored again in the second half, Ted Vizard apocryphally re-

ceiving a pass from a spectator (who put his foot over the line to stop the ball going out) before chasing down the wing and centering for John Smith to volley home and bring spectators behind the goal down like bowling pins. Vizard later said that this did happen at some point during the game, but not on that particular run. Like most good football stories, however, it persists.

West Ham found some consolation two days later when they won 2–0 at Hillsborough and had their promotion to the First Division for the first time confirmed by Leicester's defeat the following Saturday. Bolton needed no such consolation—they were to return to Wembley twice more in the decade and to win on both occasions —1–0 against Manchester City in 1926 and 2–0 against Portsmouth in 1929. Five

DUQUEMIN

Left: *Corner-kick controversies at White Hart Lane.*
Top: *In 1924 the Scottish FA had proposed that it should be possible to score direct from a corner-kick. This was accepted by the International Board, but they failed to study the wording of their new law very carefully. The Everton right-winger, Sam Chedgzoy, was not so lax. Early in the following season Everton visited White Hart Lane and Chedgzoy took a corner. Rather than cross the ball, he simply dribbled it into the net while the Spurs players stood around perplexed at this strange behaviour. At first the referee refused to allow the goal, but a heated argument ensued and the goal was eventually recorded. The law was quickly changed to 'the kicker shall not play the ball a second time until it has been touched by another player'.*
Bottom: *Nearly thirty years later, in 1952, a comparable incident was also to occur at White Hart Lane. Spurs were playing a Huddersfield team fallen on hard times and facing relegation. Eddie Baily shaped to take a corner with his left foot but was stopped by the referee, who indicated that the ball was not within the quadrant. Baily then took the corner with his right foot and it struck the referee in the back as he sprinted towards the middle, knocking him flat and suggesting that Baily had playfully avenged the rebuke. As the ball rebounded, Baily chipped it in to Len Duquemin who nodded the game's only goal. Huddersfield rightly protested that Baily had played the ball twice and that this was against the rules. But the referee had been unsighted, gave the goal and, despite Huddersfield's further protests (the point from a draw was vital to them), the League let the goal stand.*

players—Pym, Howarth, Seddon, Nuttall and Butler—played in all three games, and all except Howarth played for England.

Bolton were always a Cup rather than League side—during the twenties they never came closer to the Championship than third and in 1929 had lapsed as far as fourteenth. Their third Cup win was something of a final fling for their great side. They struggled for four seasons and were finally relegated in 1933. That was the year Lancashire neighbours (and the most prominent side of the inter-war era after Arsenal and Huddersfield) Everton won the Cup for the second time. The Merseysiders had a remarkable record between 1927 and 1933, a time when they were noted for the presence of one Bill Dean (he always disliked the name Dixie, which stemmed

from his crinkly black hair).

Dean had been signed from Tranmere, been seriously injured in a motor accident in 1926, and had consequently made little impact until the 1927–28 season. The previous year (when Everton had finished twentieth in the First Division) Second Division Middlesbrough's George Camsell scored fifty-nine goals in thirty-seven games, including nine hat-tricks, the latter a record which still stands. This was the time of centre-forwards unashamedly revenging themselves on defences after the alteration of the offside law—an era of flying wingers and crosses back from the bye-line for the iron foreheads of thundering strikers. Camsell, incidentally, had been on offer for £50 at the end of the previous season.

Anyway, Dean, after scoring only

an away match against Charlton at The Valley, on 7 February 1931, all five forwards—Stein, Dean, Dunn, Critchley and Johnson—scored in the space of eighteen minutes. They immediately won the Championship again in 1932 and the Cup in 1933 —easily beating Manchester City 3–0 in the first final in which players were numbered, from 1–22. Joe Mercer, who had just joined Everton, says of Dean: 'He wasn't a clever player, but he had the ability to stand still until they went for him—and then he wasn't there. He had no time for team talks and tactics. After one particular defeat Dean walked in, put his feet up on the table and said "It's this lot, they can't bloody play" and then he dozed off.'

Towards the end of the thirties another club, Wolves, began to test Arsenal's power. They were managed by a man who, being another authoritarian, is often compared with Chapman. But Chapman's parallels with that man, Major Frank Buckley, really end there. Throughout his managerial career at Wolves, Buckley had always to find young players, develop their abilities, and then balance the books by selling them. This reached its peak (as did the fury of Wolves' supporters) in 1938 with the sale of the superb Welsh scheming inside-forward Bryn Jones to Arsenal for a record £14,000. There were near riots in the Black Country (this was not uncommon when Buckley sold players—on one occasion fans invaded the pitch and made off with the goal posts by way of protest) after Jones' sale but, in the end, Wolves got a marvellous bargain —£14,000 for a player who, because of the War, was only to play 74 more First Division games and never did become the new Alex James that Arsenal had wanted.

It took Buckley a decade from his arrival in 1927 to develop a young side based on the principles of youth, hard work and discipline—a decade in which he pulled Wolves round from near bankruptcy to being a very rich club. He relied on uncompromising defence, fast running wingers and fearless centre-forwards, and during the thirties acquired a reputation for innovation and public relations surpassed only by Chapman at his best. He did not have a station to re-name Wolves, but even his arrival in 1927 caused something of a sensation. There was a new gymnasium, strict regulations for the players, and virtually a new team. The old faces went, usually for cash, and in came young hopefuls, discards and anyone the Major could buy for next to nothing. The policy produced financial profits for a decade, and in 1937 began to show profits on the field. In 1937 they came fifth, in 1938 second just a point behind Arsenal, and in 1939 second again and

Above: *Newcastle United captain Frank Hudspeth and friend with the FA Cup at the end of the 1924 final, in which Newcastle defeated Aston Villa 2–0. Hudspeth and his full-back partner Bill McCracken (inset) were largely responsible for the change in the offside law a season later.*
Opposite top: *George Mutch scores the only goal of the 1938 final against Huddersfield. It was from a penalty awarded in the last minute of extra-time and went in off the crossbar. For Preston it was appropriate revenge for their 1922 final defeat—when they had lost 1–0 to the same opponents.*
Opposite bottom: *William Dean's goal in Everton's 3–0 defeat of Manchester City in the 1933 final. This was the first game in which players had been numbered—from 1 to 22.*

twenty-one goals in 1926–27, suddenly found unstoppable form and Everton rose from twentieth to first in Division One. On the very last day of the season Everton played Arsenal at Goodison and Dean stood on fifty-seven, two below Camsell. Arsenal scored, Dean equalised, Dean scored from a penalty, Arsenal equalised but, finally, with just twelve minutes left, Dean leaped to a high centre, met it superbly and the record was broken. The game finished 3–3. During that season he scored eighty-two goals in first class matches—League, Cup, Internationals, International trials and Inter-League games. That has never been beaten and he and Camsell remain the only players to score more than fifty goals in a season in either of the top two divisions.

Everton's perverse behaviour continued. The next year they dropped to eighteenth and Dean scored only twenty-six. Things got rapidly worse; the following year they were relegated, only to bounce straight back in 1931. That was a good year for Everton—they scored 121 goals and during

reached Wembley for their first final since 1921.

There have probably never been hotter favourites. All the Major's efforts for over a decade, both on and off the field, reached their culmination that spring day, 29 April 1939. His side had been the talk of the season. The League had been forced to regulate the watering of pitches after Buckley consistently kept Molineux soft to help his young side and hinder the opposition, and he had intrigued the sporting press with talk of the 'monkey gland' treatment of his players.

Buckley had always been obsessed with physical fitness, rightly deducing that a fully fit team invariably went on the pitch with the game half won. In 1935 he had become interested in the effects on human glands of animal secretions from oxen or monkeys. The result was an FA inquiry which decided to leave the whole thing to the players, and at least one refused any treatment. But it was a ready-made press sensation and the Wolves team were obviously expected to produce a freakish brilliant display at Wembley in the last of the pre-War Cup finals. Freakish it was, brilliant it was not.

Goalkeeper Scott had a particularly bad game, and Portsmouth made up for their disappointments of 1929 and 1934 with nothing more than manager Jack Tinn's 'lucky' spats. The only survivor from the 1934 team was right-winger Fred Worrall, who had an excellent game and made two of the goals for outside-left Cliff Parker. Portsmouth played far above anything that had been expected of them and Wolves, after scoring 19 goals and conceding only three in the earlier rounds, lost 4–1, and thus ended in the unenviable position of runners-up in both competitions. At least

they were in good company—the only two clubs to have previously ended the season similarly were Huddersfield in 1928 and Arsenal in 1932.

Portsmouth, for their part, held the Cup for longer than any other club had before or have done since—though only because of the intervention of the Second World War which closed down first class football for seven years. The League did manage three fixtures of the 1939–40 season and then expunged the results from the record books. For the record, Blackpool were top of the First Division, the only club with a maximum 6 points from their three games.

Seven years later the 1946–47 season was opened with exactly the same fixture list. The War was exceptionally unkind to Buckley. His side would have reached its peak in the early 1940s and could arguably have been as good as Arsenal. But they weathered the War wonderfully well; the players were young and healthy, partially because of Buckley's fitness fetish, partially because he had sold anyone with experience. It reassembled under the pre-War captain, Stan Cullis, but by then Buckley had gone—his great ally, chairman Ben Matthews, had retired, and the manager, resenting interference, resigned in February 1944. He later drifted from club to club, ending up at Walsall and achieving little, while just five miles away Cullis had developed Buckley's team and tactical ideas into the great Wolves side which won two FA Cups and three Championships in twelve seasons. It is a remarkable tribute to Buckley that his name is so well remembered *despite* the fact

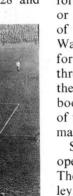

that he never won a major honour.

Buckley bought many of his players—like Bryn Jones—from South Wales, an area for which the depression years were disastrous in footballing as well as human terms. An area of exceptionally high unemployment, South Wales lost Aberdare Athletic in 1927 tying on the vote with Torquay, and losing on a second ballot) and Merthyr Town in 1930. Merthyr conceded 135 goals that season (only Nelson, with one more, have a worse record in a 42-game season) and Coventry City still have the cheque they received as their share of the receipts from a midweek fixture in April that year at Merthyr's Penydarren Park. It is for 18s 4d (92p). Newport left the League in 1931—though they came back a year later in place of Thames of east London. Even Cardiff had to apply for re-election in 1934—just seven years after winning the FA Cup. Gates at Ninian Park then were down below 5000.

The North East suffered similarly—losing Durham City in 1928 and Ashington, birthplace of the Charlton brothers, a year later. In 1930 South Shields became another slump victim and moved to Gateshead, changing their name along the way. Gateshead were to survive until 1960, when they were unceremoniously thrown out to make room for Peterborough, despite finishing only third from bottom and having applied for re-election just once before.

The North West was the other unfortunate area; Stalybridge Celtic left in 1923, and the minor clubs had a terrible time at the beginning of the 1930s. Nelson disappeared at the end of the 1930–31 season, and then, on 26 October that year, Wigan

Borough became the first club to resign from the League during a season. Accrington, of course, did the same some thirty years later but Borough's action has been a major factor in preventing their successors, Athletic, from achieving a Football League place ever since. At the end of that same season Rochdale may well have wished they had also resigned. They had set a League record by losing seventeen games in succession: on 7 November 1931 they beat New Brighton 3–2, but then failed to gain another point until their 1–1 draw with the same team on 9 March 1932. New Brighton, incidentally, finished next to bottom. Rochdale also lost a record thirty-three out of their forty matches and their eleven points is the lowest recorded in any division since the First World War. Another of Rochdale's claims to fame in this period is their failure to win an FA Cup match for seventeen years between 1928 and 1945.

During a period when the most notable footballing event was the swing in the balance of power from the North to London, in the shape of Arsenal, it is worth remembering that this was an accurate reflection of the economics of depression. The terrible times of the 1930s are illustrated in the plight of many football clubs in the depressed areas, not all of them, like Cardiff, by any means small clubs either. While Arsenal strutted on a national and international stage, and are rightly remembered for it, we should not forget the two decades of struggle that faced the majority of League clubs—struggles that were not overcome until the euphoria and enormous attendances of the late 1940s.

Opposite top and centre: Jimmy Dimmock, the white shirted player on the right hand side of the penalty area, scores the solitary goal that beat Wolves in the 1921 Cup final (one of three played at Stamford Bridge) and enabled Spurs to drive back to north London in fine style.

Opposite bottom: Spot the ball, Stamford Bridge style, in 1924. Chelsea's Hughie Gallacher (near right) argues vehemently that a West Bromwich defender played him onside before a goal which referee Denton clearly disallows. The West Brom defenders appear to disagree.

Above left: The biggest Cup final upset of the inter-War period— the 1939 defeat of Wolves by Portsmouth. Anderson has just evaded Stan Cullis's (centre) tackle to put Pompey 1–0 up. They went on to win 4–1.

Above: While the team that he had built are winning the first of their three Championships of the decade, just five miles away in Wolverhampton, Major Frank Buckley (with spectacles) sits in the dug-out at Walsall's Fellows Park.

THE DEVELOPMENT OF TACTICS
The Game 1863-1976

There was much to admire in the play of Holland in the 1974 World Cup finals. In Johan Neeskens they possessed a complete footballer whose intuitive skills were toughened by a keen if sometimes overenthusiastic sense of competition; Ruud Krol similarly moved as nimbly as an inside-forward without relinquishing any defensive resilience; Johnny Rep raided with brave gusto; Wim Van Hanegem clipped left-footed passes with the precision of a golfer going round in ten under par; and Johan Cruyff lived up to the boasts of those who de-

scribed him as the best individual player in the world.

But it was the deployment of these talents by team manager Rinus Michels which caught the eye of the professional observer. For the Dutch team eased its way over a series of hurdles of ever-increasing heights with a style of play of flowing, liquid elegance. That they fell at that last fence—in the final to West Germany—told more about a weakness in character than in any failing in their system. The admirers reached for a label and found one which had been

Opposite: Joe Mercer (left) who took over the England team for a brief spell between the reigns of Ramsey and Revie. On the right is Les Cocker, the England trainer. **Below:** *The original English 'dribbling' game, in which the man with the ball ran until dispossessed. This was the result of the common school offside law under which anyone in front of the ball was offside.*

CENTRE-HALF

Above: *By the 1880s, England had adopted the Scottish offside law and Preston North End had won the first Football League Championship and Double with a pyramid w-formation defence. The key figure in this style was the centre-half, who helped in defence and initiated attacks. The last club to succeed in English football using the style was Huddersfield's Championship hat-trick side of 1924–26, with the capped Wilson (a celebrated Huddersfield name) at centre-half in the blue and white stripes.*

used more in hope than expectation earlier in the decade about the style of one or two Football League clubs—'total football'.

The totality came from a lack of limitation placed on individuals, particularly defenders. Holland's flank defenders Suurbier and Krol owned sufficient initiative and skill to participate in the heart of attacking movements; Haan and Rijsbergen, neither central defenders by upbringing, added further dimensions to their makeshift roles by being allowed to stride forward into offensive positions. The midfield men would be the most advanced attacker one moment and in the heart of the defence the next. Cruyff, nominally a central attacker, pulled markers wide and deep, and Holland became known as the team without a centre-forward.

Helmut Schoen, the man who finally drilled a hole in the Dutch dyke in Munich, had been among those who recognised the need for change some ten years earlier. Speaking as a guest lecturer at an FA coaching course in 1964 he said: 'Something must be done to open the game up again. It would be better if football could find the answer within its coaching and among its players. But if that isn't possible we may have to alter the laws.'

Holland's performance, and that of West Germany (whose own attacks lacked the Dutch fluidity largely because of the absence of outstanding individuals rather than ambition) impressed a school of English coaches who travelled to the World Cup finals. None watched with greater concentration than Dave Sexton, a manager of slavish dedication to the game who had already tasted European success when in charge of the Chelsea side which lifted the European Cup Winners Cup in 1971. Sexton was to move a few miles across London to Queen's Park Rangers before the events of Munich had faded from the immediate memory, and he took with him what he had learned from the World Cup.

While the Football League prepared for the 1975–76 season under storm clouds of gloomy forebodings, Sexton took his team to Germany and Portugal on an arduous pre-season tour. While the Queen's Park Rangers players, somewhat to their own surprise, were training three times a day, football's future within the confines of the Football League seemed bleak; the goals in the 1974–75 season had dropped to barely 5,000; Derby County had averaged marginally over a goal and a half a game to win the Championship.

CENTRE-HALF

British football seemed once again to have reached stagnation point. But Sexton's squad provided a glimmer of encouragement. Queen's Park Rangers achieved a memorable 4–1 win in Germany over Borussia Monchengladbach, the new Bundesliga champions. Shortly afterwards they defeated Benfica, champions of Portugal, 4–2 in Lisbon. And with the British season only a week old, they completed an astonishing treble by beating Derby County, England's champions 5–1. Three away wins, thirteen goals scored, three champions defeated. There was hope that the tactical wheel had begun, thoughbeit slowly, to turn again. And yet from the game's very beginnings it was British thinking and tuition which had fostered worldwide interest in the most unified of all team sports. What began as an exercise in individuality quickly became a classic of teamwork and concerted effort as players realised the need to husband their stamina.

Attack separated from defence. The need to prevent goals was clearly important if the contest was to assume any validity. And it was this which provided the framework of team play.

The steady development of individual technique, especially by attackers, led to the need for more organised systems of play and a numerical balance between attack and defence.

By the turn of the twentieth century football had taken hold throughout the world and it was the missionary influence of British tourists which helped to establish the early fundamentals of team play. At the outset, the game was steeped in individualism. Eight attackers made solo sorties on a goal covered by the keeper who was aided by at best two defensive henchmen. The bulk of the attacking force supported the individual in possession, moving in when his run faltered. It was only when Scottish football realised the potential of passing and use of the whole playing area, that team play finally did creep into the game.

Scotland had one considerable advantage. Their football was played to a consistent pattern of rules. In England, each public school, the breeding ground of the game, played to its own set. And one common feature was the use of what is still the rugby offside law—a player could only be onside behind the ball. This virtually condemned the prevailing style of play to be based on dribbling as the ball could only be passed backwards. Even when the 'three-

Above: *Huddersfield's manager, Herbert Chapman, moved on to Arsenal and devised a new defensive formation there to cope with the change (in 1925) to a new offside law (two defenders rather than three between forward and goal). The centre-half (in Arsenal's team, 'Policeman' Herbie Roberts) fell back to mark the opposing centre-forward and reduce his new-found freedom. This formed a back line of three defenders. The inside-forwards (one or both) also fell back to fill the centre-half's midfield role and leave a formation roughly classifiable as 3–4–3 or 3–3–4. Arsenal were to win the only other hat-trick (1933–35) of English Championships with this system, which became the norm for thirty years.*

BOZSIK

HIDEGKUTI
9

5

JOHNSTON

KOCSIS

PUSKAS

RAMSEY

Above: *How Hungary pulled England apart at Wembley in 1953. With ostensible centre-forward Hidegkuti playing deep, centre-half Harry Johnston was pulled out of position. Because the England system had the full-backs wheeling up behind the centre-half to provide cover and search out the wingers, Hungary's strikers Kocsis and Puskas could run through behind Johnston with little fear of being caught offside. It should be said, however, that Hungary were a great side essentially because they had three or four great players—not because of their tactics, which were the result, not the cause, of their talented team. The withdrawn centre-forward tactic was not copied often, perhaps because it took a particularly perceptive player to perform the role. Don Revie, however, did so with similar success for Manchester City in beating Birmingham in the 1956 Cup final.*

man' offside rule was accepted, English players found it difficult to re-learn the game and adopt new patterns.

Only after Scotland had achieved a total dominance over England in the late 1870s and the following decade was the 'passing' tactic finally accepted south of the border and further counter-measures were taken.

Instead of the eight attackers there were now only five with three players operating in the middle of the field as half-backs and two behind them as full-backs. This 'Pyramid' system was the basis of modern strategy. Preston North End in 1888–89 sailed proudly to the League and Cup Double using this system of play.

The full-backs stationed themselves within the penalty area to deal with attacks which had pierced the first defensive screen, and they marked the opposing inside-forwards.

In time the two flanking half-backs would play critical roles as linking attackers, but in the beginning they were almost exclusively defenders and it was the centre-half who was allowed the freedom to circulate.

Modification was inevitable and what began as a line of five attackers became a split formation with the inside forwards dropping back to act as links. Football had quickly confirmed that it was a thinking game and the more perceptive players were to have a great effect on development.

Several of them—the most famous, Billy McCracken of Newcastle United—perfected a trap to catch forwards within the law dictating when a player was offside. The law as it stood decreed that a player was offside unless there were three players including the goalkeeper between him and his opponents' goal when the ball was last played.

The astute saw this as a means of killing off attacks at the halfway line. The full-backs simply moved forward and the practice threatened to kill football's appeal. The monotony of offside decisions forced a change in the Laws.

It was the Scots, speaking with powerful authority in the councils of the game, who proposed the change at a meeting of the International Football Federation in 1925. Following that proposal, the Law was altered so that a player could not be offside if two instead of three opponents were nearer to their own goal-line when the ball was last played.

As a result the game was handed back to attackers. In the season immediately preceding the change a total of 4700 goals were scored throughout the Football League. In the season which followed it the total rose spectacularly by almost a third to 6373.

The centre-half was still an attacker, and with the change in law defences were im-

BOZSIK

HIDEGKUTI

KOCSIS

PUSKAS

mediately vulnerable to assaults through the middle. If the full-backs continued to push up on the halfway line, an attacker could lie between them leaving himself with only one man to beat. If they played wide on the touchlines they left an inviting gap in the middle of the defence. If they moved in tighter the opposing wingers had too much freedom.

The middle had to be closed and the man given credit for doing this was Herbert Chapman, the farseeing manager whose fame was to outlast even his enormous influence on strategy. Chapman had already established himself with two successive Championship triumphs at Huddersfield (and a third followed the year he left) when he joined Arsenal, who had just sacked Leslie Knighton. As we have seen, he proved to be a man of tremendous vision. But it was his tactical appreciation which was particularly to help build Arsenal into a dominating power.

Chapman began badly and on 3 October 1925 he had to suffer the humiliation of a 7–0 defeat at Newcastle. That disaster finally convinced him that it was now necessary to block the middle of a defence which could not cope with the licence forwards were allowed by the new offside law.

The following Monday at West Ham, he re-arranged his team with Jack Butler operating deep between his full-backs.

Arsenal won 4–0. It was perhaps the most significant result in the history of the game. Butler was only a stop-gap until Chapman could find the right type of player to function as his 'third back' or 'stopper'.

That man was Herbie Roberts, a tall redhead who was to personify Chapman's theories about the role of the centre-half. Roberts was no stylist, but he won the ball consistently in the air and effectively closed up the middle of the defence.

Around him, Chapman built a highly functional system of play. Systems can only be successful if players have the willingness and imagination to fill them out. Arsenal obtained these players. Full-backs whose sound sense helped them to swing or pivot on Roberts provided the defence with balance and cover.

While Roberts policed the middle, refusing to be drawn to the touchlines to hunt attackers, full-backs Male and Hapgood responded to the immediate point of attack. If an attack was being built up on Hapgood's flank, he closed down in the area of the ball while Male swung round and infield to provide cover for his centre-half. When play switched to Male's flank, the roles were reversed.

The two later wing half-backs, Jack Crayston and Wilf Copping, helped to fill out the middle of the formation forming a linking parallelogram with Alex James and

Above: *How Brazil's 4–2–4 system, devised before the 1958 World Cup finals, would have coped with the Hungarian attack. Because it was zonal rather than man-for-man, the number 5 would not have been drawn to Hidegkuti but would have left him for a midfield player to pick-up. The four defenders would thus have been left across the back of the defence and, by moving upfield together, could have created an offside problem for Kocsis and Puskas.*

LEADBETTER

2

4

PHILLIPS

CRAWFORD

3

Above: *The Ipswich tactics in their Championship winning season 1961–62 involved a withdrawn left-winger, Jimmy Leadbetter, who would draw the right-back towards him and create space in the defence. The long, diagonal ball was then met by Ray Crawford and Ted Phillips.*

David Jack. As the back line swung to meet an attack Crayston and Copping adjusted their angle accordingly.

With wingers Cliff Bastin and Joe Hulme operating wide on the flanks and a centre-forward—first Lambert and later Drake—playing up as a powerful strike force through the middle, the team shaped itself into what was called a W–M formation.

It was an outstanding success. Although

Chapman died before he saw the full fruits of his planning, Arsenal dominated the game. James could initiate counter-attacks with the devastating accuracy of his long-range passing and the forwards were ideally equipped to press them home with speed and power. The system, widely adopted, proved so successful that it lasted as the basis of play for over twenty years.

Had Chapman lived he might well have

changed it. But there were few with his foresight and in time English football was to pay the penalty for turning a deaf ear to the rumbling of new ideas which began to come from other corners of the world. English football sat back, blind to its deficiencies and unwilling to learn, cockily convinced that no one could teach it anything. The price was a heavy one.

Arthur Rowe, Spurs centre-half and an England international, figured prominently among the British players and coaches who travelled to spread football's gospel in the thirties. Rowe was a thinker, a man with the unyielding conviction that the game was all about simplicity and movement. In time he was to build a magnificent Spurs team around the fundamental principle of 'Keep it simple. Make it quick.'

But as the threat of War increased almost

Above: *In the 1962 Charity Shield Cup winners Spurs found the answer. By refusing to allow right-back Baker to be drawn, centre-half Norman was able to 'tidy-up' while full-backs Baker and Henry marked Crawford and Phillips. That problem solved, Spurs then attacked and won 5–1.*

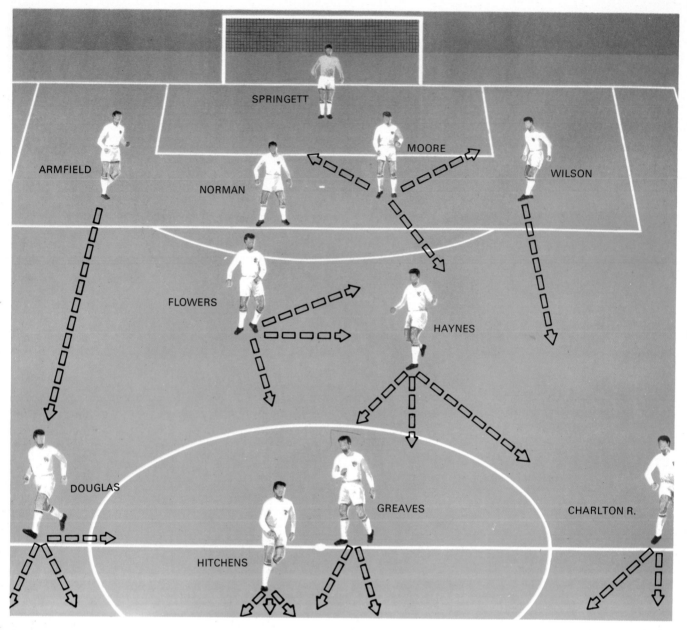

SPRINGETT

ARMFIELD

NORMAN

MOORE

WILSON

FLOWERS

HAYNES

DOUGLAS

GREAVES

CHARLTON R.

HITCHENS

Above: *The basic pattern used by England in the 1962 World Cup. Moore was the covering centre-back, Haynes the creative midfield player, and the scheme was essentially 4–2–4.*

daily in the decade's latter years, Rowe was in Hungary, dispensing ideas which were to be incorporated into the ultimate destruction of the complacency that had resulted from Herbert Chapman's successful revolution in the late twenties.

Rowe was an uncommonly sophisticated centre-half at a time when the position had been taken over by burly, uncompromising stoppers who stood at the heart of defensive play. He recalled: 'There was no hint of what the Hungarians would later achieve. They were little more than apprentices at that time. And yet in 1953 they had the finest team in the world. They didn't have any secret. They were a great team because they had something like six world-class players. It was as simple as that.

'When they murdered England at Wembley in 1953 there were still people who looked at the wrong things. Skill, thought

and mobility didn't take much recognising.'

England's hooded attitude to world football enabled the Hungarians to sneak into London with their brilliant talent concealed. Olympic champions the previous year, they were virtually unknown in a country which had chosen to isolate itself from the rest of the game. Ninety minutes at Wembley changed all that.

It was clear that the Hungarians, while remaining true to the basic principles of defensive play as laid down by Chapman, had modified attacking strategy. Hidegkuti, a great centre-forward, dropped off into the middle of the field leaving Puskas and Kocsis to pursue through passes cut through the heart of England's defence. The wingers, too, came deep adding to the confusion of players who had become chained to complacent thinking.

Centre-half Harry Johnston of Blackpool

Players labeled on the field: BANKS, COHEN, CHARLTON J., MOORE, WILSON, STILES, PETERS, CHARLTON R., BALL, HUNT, HURST

was never sure whether he should follow Hidegkuti or stay in the heart of the defence, while the covering full-backs, swinging round to give the defence depth, merely created space into which the Hungarians could hunt passes without fear of being caught offside.

But, however salutory the lesson, English football simply would not learn or see the true reason for a shattering defeat. It was blamed on poor selection. The critics, at least, were true to form.

One man who did see, who could recognise, was Walter Winterbottom. As England team manager he had to bear the brunt of the attacks which were aimed at those responsible for the international side.

A studious, approachable man, Winterbottom had a background in physical education and had played immediately prior to the War for Manchester United. He be-

came the first manager of the England team, although his influence was consistently diluted by a selection committee system which survived until Alf Ramsey appeared on the scene.

Winterbottom was at his happiest in his other role as Director of Coaching. He was to inspire a host of young managers who would eventually help to restore Britain to a prominent position in world football. But when attempting to build a successful national team he was stuck with prevailing attitudes and the strategy which dominated League football.

With little time for preparation it was impossible for him to try to create the new strategy which he knew was essential. When he took the Hungarians on for the second time the following year, he fared even worse as England were crushed 7–1 in Budapest.

Another World Cup came and went in

Above: *By 1966, Ramsey had adapted the England system to 4–4–2 or 4–3–3, depending on where Ball played. Moore was still the covering central defender, but Stiles played an auxiliary sweeping role in front of the line of four defenders and Bobby Charlton shared the creative role with Martin Peters. The most contentious feature was the lack of wingers, Ball and Peters patrolling the touchlines as part of a wider brief. Hurst and Hunt covered most of the field upfront with Charlton coming from behind to score vital goals against Mexico and Portugal.*

Switzerland in 1954 with no sign that England were willing to look ahead. It was won, surprisingly, by the West Germans when Hungary were firm favourites and yet again the wrong things were seen to be important.

That World Cup simply revolutionised fashion in England without refashioning football. Lighter boots, more streamlined kit. It was as though looking like Continental players was a guarantee that the British would play like them. A system of play, invalidated by consistent failure, remained largely unaltered; again it offered opportunities to the thinkers.

When Manchester City used Don Revie as a withdrawn centre-forward, dropping him back to link with Ken Barnes as Hidegkuti had done with Bozsik in the Hungarian team, they were an immediate force.

It was an indictment of the British game that Revie was able to capitalise on something as simple as the number on his back.

Numbers merely identified the players. But they had come to assume ridiculous importance.

Revie threw confusion into defences partly because he wore a number nine on his back while playing in the middle of the field.

He recalled: 'If they had bothered to think about it, there was no great problem. But players and managers were chained to straight up and down attitudes. As the centre-forward I was the responsibility of the centre-half. And when he attempted to follow me a great hole was left in the middle of the defence. All they had to do was detail someone to pick me up, leaving the centre-half where he was, ready to take over when I appeared in an advanced position.'

The deployment of a deep lying centre-forward was probably the first definite attempt to counter Chapman's principle of play which had lasted for over twenty-five years. But more revolutionary things were happening elsewhere, and for Brazil they reached fulfilment in Sweden in 1958.

Brazil won that World Cup handsomely, introducing Pele's prodigious talent to a marvelling congregation. More important for the rival managers and coaches was the way in which the Brazilians had chosen to arrange their team.

Blessed with superb individuality, they ordered it within a framework which was to take football by storm. It was based on the simple principle of maximum security in defence and maximum support in attack. A name was quickly found for it: 4-2-4.

The back line of four rarely ventured over the halfway line. The two middle men had the responsibility for building attacks. Wingers played wide and two strikers shared a thrusting role through the middle. The full-backs no longer swung around to cover the centre-half. They played wide and tight on the opposing wingers and the two central defenders pivoted on each other when danger threatened through the middle. The defence still had depth, and extra cover was provided by the full-backs who drifted in tighter when play was on the opposite flank.

Opponents found that through passes were being stifled by offside decisions and the overall effect of the system was to force the opposition into adopting the same pattern. Four men were needed to deal with four attackers, two to deal with the men in the middle.

Brazil had actually modified the system even before it took hold. Their left-winger in Sweden was Mario Zagalo, who was to manage the team in Mexico twelve years later. When Brazil found themselves under pressure in the final against Sweden, who

had been splendidly coached by an Englishman George Raynor, they instructed Zagalo to drop back and make a third man in the middle of the field.

It was the beginning of the 4-3-3 system which was to be the platform for England's later World Cup success. In 1959 4-2-4 swept through British football, but it was not established without anguish for many managers. West Ham, under manager Ted Fenton, flirted with 4-2-4, but dropped the pattern after losing 3–1 at Wolves in the first game. Swansea and Coventry were among the other clubs who gave 4-2-4 brief and inconclusive trials.

Many of them ignored the fact that systems were only as good as the players who filled them out. Brazil's full-backs were quick, mobile and skilful. By tradition their British counterparts relied on strength and aggression. Few of them were equipped to cope with the subtleties demanded by the change and it took time before clubs were able to dovetail the thinking of the two central defenders. Some teams suffered shattering defeats as they were caught square and without cover either by piercing through passes or swift running forwards.

It meant that 4-2-4 never completely took on. A well-balanced system, it was only truly effective (like all systems) when outstanding players were involved in it, but it eventually led to a variety of changes. The principle of tight marking full-backs and cover through the middle was freely adopted although many British clubs remained true to a man-to-man marking technique.

But while football moved nearer to completely organised and eventually negative play, two British teams, Manchester United and Spurs, refused to abandon their adventurous policies.

Real Madrid, when dominating the early years of the European Cup, showed that the initiative of truly great players was all important. But there were never enough of them to go round and it was perhaps inevitable that a more thoughtful approach should lead to less appealing football. It was not possible to outskill the great teams. But they could be outrun and outfought.

Perhaps the most important factor in English League football was the removal of the insidious maximum wage in 1961. With no ceiling on salaries some players trebled their money overnight. In return they were expected to attain new levels of fitness and understanding.

The game would become more difficult to play and in Ipswich a former England full-back, Alf Ramsey, was about to fashion a system which would bring success to his country and controversy to his profession.

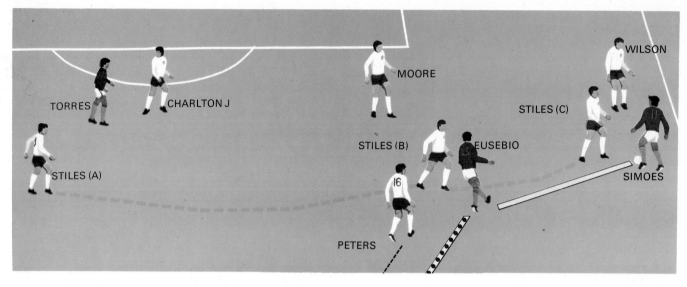

The players labelled in the diagram: TORRES, CHARLTON J, MOORE, WILSON, STILES (A), STILES (B), STILES (C), EUSEBIO, SIMOES, PETERS, 16

Above: *The role performed by Nobby Stiles in the England World Cup semi-final team against Portugal in 1966. Stiles played as a sweeper in front rather than behind the defence. He would shuttle across the pitch picking up any opponent who had broken free before one of the back four became committed. In this diagram, Stiles forces Eusebio to pass to Simoes and then moves across to challenge Simoes in turn. He has succeeded in giving Peters time to get back and mark Eusebio and another potential crisis has passed.*

Whilst Herbert Chapman in the thirties and the Hungarians and the Brazilians in the fifties had made differing overall changes that had a deep influence in the game, they had one concept in common. Particularly in the W-M system but also to a large extent in 4-2-4, players had defined roles which limited the areas of the pitch that they covered.

But eight years after Brazil had triumphed in Stockholm, England won the World Cup with a system of play that had its very essence in the complete mobility of the players. Alf Ramsey had not become England's manager until 1963, but he had been formulating his ideas since 1955, the year he was appointed manager at Ipswich.

It was a humble beginning in a part of the country that at best could be described as unfashionable, and at a club only seventy miles, but a far cry, from Ramsey's illustrious playing career at Tottenham. Apart from a co-operative board of directors and one of the best playing surfaces in the Football League, the new boss had very little going for him. Ipswich had no history. Ramsey was about to put that right.

In his first full season he won the championship of the Third Division and settled down to consolidate. Only four years later Ipswich arrived in the First Division and a new era was dawning in the game.

Far from struggling in the top class, Ipswich, their players revealing the total respect for their manager which was later to be matched by the national team, went out and won the Championship.

It was argued that the failings of more accomplished teams at a critical stage of the season contributed to Ipswich's success. And yet there was a firm professional opinion that Ramsey, with an astute appreciation of tactics and the ability to get the best out of his men, had worked a miracle.

Ramsey himself was more inclined to argue that he had simply given opponents the sort of tactical problems they were not conditioned to cope with. For instance, he took Jimmy Leadbetter, a spindle-legged, average half-back, gave him the eleven shirt, stationed him deep on the left touchline and watched him destroy some of the best defences in the business.

The strongest feature of Leadbetter's game was the accuracy of his passing. In the hurly-burly of midfield play he had spent much of his time trying to win the ball. Out on the left flank he merely had to receive it and use it.

Yet he was no orthodox left-winger. Coming deep to collect passes out of defence he would turn and float the ball forward where it was fought for by eager, powerful attackers.

There was no restriction on Leadbetter's passing angles. The opposing full-back, drawn forward, found that the ball was being dropped over him. Long passes were used to find Ted Phillips, Ray Crawford and Roy Stephenson, the opposite wingman who delayed penetrating forward runs.

The perfection of the Ipswich pitch had not been overlooked by Ramsey. The big men, Phillips and Crawford, suffered from deficiencies in their technique but at home, with the ball running true, they were a frightening proposition.

Ramsey was too shrewd to believe that it could go on for ever. Thinkers would counter his strategy and Ipswich's talent was thin on the floor beneath the concealing pattern of their tactics.

In the Charity Shield game at the start of the 1962–63 season they were destroyed by Spurs at Portman Road. After losing three points to Ipswich the previous season, Bill Nicholson, a former team-mate of Ramsey's, had worked it out. He told his right-back Peter Baker not to be drawn to

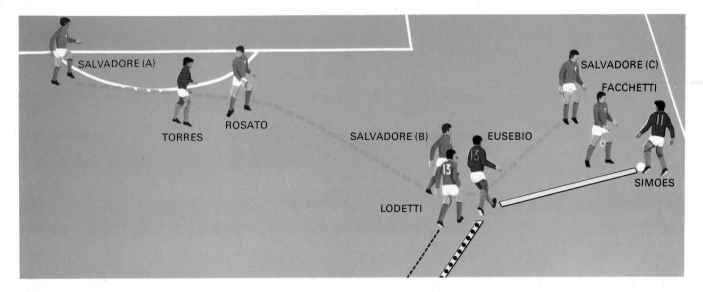

SALVADORE (A)

TORRES

ROSATO

SALVADORE (B)

EUSEBIO

SALVADORE (C)

FACCHETTI

SIMOES

LODETTI

Leadbetter. The job of closing him down went to one of the midfield men and Baker was left free to pick off the front runners. As the game progressed, Baker and Ron Henry, the left-back, picked up Phillips and Crawford. If the ball fell loose, centre-half Maurice Norman could tidy up.

With their defence intact, Spurs could concentrate on exposing ordinary players in vital positions. They won 5–1. The following October Ramsey was asked to become England team manager. One romance was over. Another was about to begin.

Malcolm Allison, whose personal extravagances could not alter the fact that he was one of the finest tutors in world football, was to say many years later that three men had influenced modern football, Herbert Chapman, Nereo Rocco and Alf Ramsey. Allison, probably deliberately, did not say whether any of these men had improved the game.

Chapman by his withdrawal of the centre-half, Rocco by his studied development of man-to-man marking backed by a sweeper, the infamous *catenaccio* of the Italian game and Ramsey's re-organisation of the balance between defence and attack and his search for an all-purpose team, all had led to a rechannelling of football thinking.

Ramsey's career as England's team manager ran into an immediate disaster, losing heavily to the French in Paris. For a while he flirted with the basic principles of 4-2-4 without ever being convinced that they were entirely workable. But all the time he was searching for players who could provide him with the midfield mobility which would be the basis of his team's play in 1966.

The first obvious clue came during a summer tour in 1965. It was in every way successful. A draw in Yugoslavia, victories in Germany and Sweden. The victories were significant. England were seen to have numerical strength in the middle of the field and to be sending these players forward to support the furthermost attackers.

The following December in Madrid, just twenty-four hours after Scotland had gone out of the World Cup qualifying competition in Italy, the next move was made. Roger Hunt, a powerful, muscular Liverpool forward, was used as a twin striker with Joe Baker. Alan Ball pushed forward along the touchlines. Bobby Charlton, George Eastham, and Nobby Stiles played in echelon behind them, covering the full width of the field.

The strategy was publicly labelled 4-3-3 but the absence of wingers hogging the touchlines meant that so much more was asked of each player.

With the framework established, Ramsey now sought to fill it out with as many complete players as possible. He left it late, as late as England's last warm-up game before they opened the 1966 competition against Uruguay at Wembley.

For the final game of the pre-World Cup tour he brought in Martin Peters of West Ham to play on the left side in midfield. Nobby Stiles, whose enthusiasm had been immediately infectious, was stationed across the back line of four defenders, sweeping in front and not behind the defence. The marking system was zonal with attackers being passed across from one defender to another so that width was always maintained.

Peters and Bobby Charlton filled out the midfield with Stiles. Ball, always willing to fill in there when required, pushed forward to support the front men, Hunt and Greaves.

Ramsey was to make one more change, electing to play without Jimmy Greaves in the latter stages of the competition and replacing him with Geoff Hurst. Hurst was an international apprentice when the competition began. A hat-trick in the final altered that overnight.

Above: *The way Italy, with their orthodox sweeper system, would have met the same threat. With the back four marking man-for-man, sweeper Salvadore would have run out from behind the line to hold up Eusebio. Then, when Eusebio's marker Lodetti had regained his position, Salvadore would have resumed his covering role in readiness to meet any threat from Simoes.*

JENKINS

FISHER

DAVIES

O'NEIL

CHANNON

PAINE

Above: *The influence in the 1960s of home-and-away ties in European football led to tactical changes in domestic football and a greater concentration on defence away from home. Southampton are a particular example of a team which changed its tactics during a spell in the First Division around the turn of the 1970s. Home at The Dell (above) they would play two central forwards, initially Davies and Chivers, later Davies and Channon, and two reasonably conventional wingers, Jenkins and Paine.*

England's strategy that afternoon was in marked contrast to that employed by the West Germans, who used Willi Schulz as an orthodox sweeper behind tight man-to-man marking.

This system, largely perfected in Italy from Rocco's influence, called for the markers to cling tight to opponents, sure in the knowledge that there was insurance should early tackles fail. On the other hand if they won the ball they could use speed to counter attack quickly.

It was inevitable that Ramsey's system would encourage the imitators in the game. The most ordinary League clubs could arrange themselves as England had done and work for a greater level of fitness and combative attitude.

But there was a backlash. When employed by ordinary players, the system became dull and negative. It did not require genius to make life difficult in the middle of the field. It did require genius to overcome the difficulties of playing in a confined space.

England were to discover in Mexico in 1970 that altitude and heat were so weakening that the essential mobility of the system could not be sustained. Their two strikers,

Hurst and Francis Lee, were invariably left to battle alone.

Yet there was considerable irony in the defeat by West Germany which ended England's interest. England, playing their best football in four years, were almost comically unlucky losers in the quarter-final played in Leon. But Hurst's superb play as a target for passes out of defence was instrumental in giving England overall superiority in a contest lost during the drama of the final twenty minutes.

The Germans went on to lose in the semi-finals to Italy but within two years they had threatened to dominate the world game. They remained true to their man-to-man system but by the time they beat Russia in the European Championship in 1972 they had made subtle alterations to their mood.

Schulz as their sweeper had influenced a defensive attitude. With his retirement, the German manager Helmut Schoen conceded to Beckenbauer's eagerness to take over the role. Beckenbauer was an attacker by instinct and the Germans began to attack.

Like the Dutch and European Champions Ajax, the Germans made decisive use of the space which defenders could find

HOLLYWOOD

FISHER

GABRIEL

O'NEIL

10

8

7

PAINE

CHANNON

2

KIRKUP

3

when coming from the back. Schoen said: 'We use footballers who can defend rather than defenders who might be able to play a bit of football.'

In some ways it was a defence of Ramsey's principles. Schoen with his victory over England simply had better players. And his keen tactical awareness and appreciation was to keep Germany ahead of the world two years later. Holland may have had the technically better and more attractive team, but Germany certainly won the 1974 World Cup final through their superior tactics.

But for all the efforts of the Dutch and West Germans in the first half of the seventies, others found it an example that was hard to follow. The essence of successful team tactics will always be the fitting of the strengths of the available players into a system which suits those strengths, and a lack of outstanding players began to limit the ambitions of many clubs. As had happened some fifty years earlier defending had become very much easier than attacking.

It was a point not lost on one of Britain and Europe's most respected football intellectuals, Bill Nicholson. Speaking at the

outset of the 1975–76 season, he foresaw a need once again for change: 'We have got to play more attractive football to attract the crowds. You have one fellow perhaps two stuck upfield against four defenders. Even I get bloody bored sometimes. It's not like my day as a player. Then you went out to win. Now you go out not to lose. You're afraid to give a goal away.

'All this talk is not enough. You have got to act. The ground prices have gone up and the Football League have given the public nothing in return. Something must be done to encourage more goals.'

The 1974–75 Football League season had produced just over 5000 goals, many of them from free-kicks, corners and long throws, set-pieces which had increased in importance as routes to goals as scoring from free play had become increasingly harder. In 1925 a total of barely three hundred less had stimulated change; even in the reactionary world of football an alteration did not seem many years away.

Whatever form it might take, it would be another challenge for tacticians of the future, and the new generations of Chapmans, Roccos, Schoens and Ramseys would probably relish that.

Above: *When Southampton played away from home, Paine would be withdrawn to midfield to provide extra marking and cover. Occasionally manager Ted Bates would withdraw one of his three remaining forwards (usually Jenkins) and include an extra defender, sweeping up in front or behind the defence. Thus the system would change from approximately 4–2–4 to 4–4–2 and is illustrative of an attitude that came under increasing fire as 'negative' or 'stifling' as the 1970s wore on.*

THE TWO CLUB SYSTEM
Scotland 1893-1976

It has been said of Scottish football that its history consists of three great clubs, a century of battles with England and very little else. A little brutal, perhaps, but a statement with rather more than a grain of truth.

The first of those great clubs was Queen's Park—undefeated for nine years, founder of the Scottish Football Association and the Scottish Cup, the last amateur club to reach both the English and Scottish Cup finals, and the arbiter of the laws in Scotland for the first decade of organised football.

It is significant that as many as five of the team which played against England as late as 1893 were Queen's Park men, though there were also four from Celtic and the latter represented the future—a future that was to be confirmed just a month after that game. 1893 was one of the most significant years in the history of Scottish football, for it was then that the game finally succumbed to the 'evil' of professionalism.

The Scottish League had been in existence for three seasons when Celtic's J H McLaughlin made his emotional plea at the 1893 AGM of the Scottish FA: 'You might as well attempt to stop the flow of Niagara with a kitchen chair as to endeavour to

Opposite: *The face of Scottish football; Rangers McCloy saves from the Kilmarnock attack in the days before the three division system.*
Below: *More safe Scottish goalkeeping during the 1905 international against England. Held on 1 April at Crystal Palace, England won 1–0. The international against England has long been the highlight of the Scottish season.*

Right: *Glasgow belongs to Celtic.*
Far right: *The Heart of Midlothian side which won Edinburgh's first championship in 1895. In the background is the League flag which they also acquired. Hearts went on to win the Scottish Cup the following year before taking the Championship again in 1897.*

stem the tide of professionalism.' So, after three impassioned debates within a year, the motion was carried and club football in Scotland became the story of Celtic and Rangers. Between the first professional season of 1893–94 and the final one under the old two division system (1974–75) there were seventy-five League Championships. Of these Rangers (thirty-four) and Celtic (twenty-eight) won sixty-two—leaving just thirteen for the rest of Scotland's clubs.

For decades at a time, the Championship acquired the elements of farce rather than competition. Between 1904 and 1948, not exactly a short or insignificant period, only once (Motherwell in 1932) did the Championship not go to the Glasgow duo. The best the provincial clubs have ever been

able to offer is a string of near misses. Airdrieonians, for instance, were runners-up in four consecutive seasons (1922–26) and have yet to win the trophy. Motherwell, despite being regarded as the best team of their day, were runners-up four times between 1927 and 1934 and won the trophy only once.

The Scottish Cup has not been such a two-horse race—the two Glasgow rivals winning forty-three of the sixty-nine Cup competitions in the same period and sharing another in 1909 when they refused to contest a second replay after riots at the first. But here, at least, there are some signs of mortality. Rangers did not win the Cup between 1903 and 1928 and as recently as the late 1950 s there was a five year period

120

without either succeeding. However, in only four seasons have both major competitions been won by clubs other than Rangers or Celtic—1895, 1952, 1955 and 1958. The second and third of these were particularly significant for the League Cup was also won by an 'outsider'.

But these, for all their significance, are just bald facts. The inevitable question is why? Or rather, why not the other clubs? After all, Rangers and Celtic have no apparent advantage in Glasgow over, say, Partick Thistle or Clyde. There were six First Division clubs (under the old system) in Glasgow at times—none theoretically enjoying more proportional support than any other. Why, then, have these clubs not all shared success over the years in the manner of the London or Lancashire clubs in England? And why have the provincial clubs never been able to compete? Hearts and Hibs can command enormous followings while Aberdeen have an isolated captive audience in the north-east. Just what has given Rangers and Celtic such fanatical support, solid financial backing and success over such a long period? Sadly, the answer must be religion, for no other could possibly fit the facts.

Rangers and Celtic had, even by the end of the nineteenth century, become far more than football clubs—they were causes to be fought for and, if need be, died for on the streets of Glasgow. And the basic cause of this rivalry was not even a direct product of Scottish political or economic circumstances. In fact it was imported from across the Irish Sea, from Ulster to be exact, and stemmed from the centuries old battle between the Protestants and Catholics of that unhappy province.

Exactly when the religious rivalry began

is, however, obscure. Celtic were founded in 1887 by a Brother Walfrid of the Catholic teaching order of Marist brothers, and their initial aim was that of providing food for needy children in the east end of the city. An early impetus came from another club with Catholic connections, Hibernian, when, in 1887, they won the only Scottish Cup final ever contested at Crosshills. Celtic, in similar Irish green, rapidly became the club of Glasgow's Catholic immigrant population—underprivileged, deprived and poor even by contemporary Glaswegian standards.

Rangers have no such deep rooted affinity with Protestantism—indeed their fanatical support seems to have grown only as a direct counterpart to that of Celtic. It has been suggested that such support could just as easily have gone to Clyde, Partick or elsewhere but just happened to settle on Rangers. Founded in 1873 by a group of oarsmen who rowed on the Clyde, their name was chosen at random from a list of English rugby clubs. For fifteen years they achieved very little and, for a time in the 1880s, seemed near to disintegration.

In 1889, nonetheless, they opened their new Ibrox Park and invited English double winners Preston as guests. Apparently the referee blew early to save Rangers further punishment when Preston went 8–1 up. Still, matters improved rapidly and a year later a new club committee had steered the team to the first Championship (jointly with Dumbarton) and Rangers were on their way to becoming a Protestant bastion.

Oddly, Rangers as a club have always been far more scrupulous in observing the unwritten religious war than Celtic. They are thought to have accidentally signed a Catholic (or 'left footer') in the 1920s but

Near right: *Alan Morton in familiar Queen's Park strip.*
Far and centre right: *Jimmy McGrory, the most prolific goalscorer in British football. In 408 League matches he scored 410 goals, to become the only man to maintain a goal-a-game record throughout a first-class career. As late as the 1935–36 season, his 14th in first class football, he recorded 50 goals in 32 League games though, oddly, he was capped on only seven occasions. The centre picture shows an incident from the 1933 Scottish Cup final with a Motherwell defender handling to stop McGrory scoring. The penalty was missed but McGrory did score with a header to take the Cup back to Parkhead.*
Bottom: *Willie Struth in the Ibrox Trophy Room in 1949, a few months after he had taken Rangers to the first ever treble in Scottish football.*

quickly disposed of him when the 'error' was discovered. Celtic, for their part, judge a man solely by his ability. In part this can be explained by sheer pressure of numbers (there are far fewer Catholics in Scotland) but it also reflects a greater tolerance. Many of the club's greatest names—Bobby Evans, Bobby Collins, John Thomson, Ronnie Simpson (son of a Rangers centre-half) and Jock Stein to name but five—are Protestants.

But for all that the support for the two clubs in Glasgow is quite rigid—the Catholics, many of whose ancestors came to Glasgow in search of work at the end of the last century, for the green of Celtic; the Protestants for the royal blue of Rangers. The songs and the attitudes remain those of Northern Ireland—heightened in recent years by the civil war in that sad province. And it is that fanatic allegiance plus the cash it provides from fans all over Scotland (three-quarters of the population lives within fifty miles of Glasgow) that keeps Celtic and Rangers where they are and where, it seems, they will certainly stay. For the other clubs the argument has become circular—little success, small gates, inadequate income, the automatic sale of any good player to Celtic, Rangers or England, thus little success. It is many years since a provincial club really fought to keep a star player; if the price is right the offer simply cannot be refused. So Ibrox and Parkhead get the stars, and thus the fans, and any good Scottish player must inevitably wish to play for one or the other. The circle gets tighter.

The Scottish League was set up in 1890 as a direct copy of the English version and it was inevitably just as successful. After only one season there were sixty-four clubs in various associated leagues. Queen's Park soon learned to regret staying out—their major fixtures simply disappeared—and had to wait for an opportunity presented by one of the regular disagreements between the First and Second Divisions, in 1900, to squeeze in. For the first three full seasons the clubs were technically amateur but, from 1893–94, the Glasgow pair began to take over. In 1898–99 Rangers recorded the only clean sheet ever in either the English or Scottish Leagues. But, after winning all eighteen of their League games, they surprisingly lost all three Cup finals (Scottish, Glasgow and Charity) and thus missed an opportunity to match Preston's unique totally undefeated season.

Unlike the English League, the Scots continued throughout the First World War. Much of the football was below par—Celtic were even able to play two games in a single day at the end of the 1915–16 season. In the afternoon they beat Raith Rovers 6–0, in the evening Motherwell 3–1, and they won the Championship easily.

After the War, the sad drowning of manager Willie Wilton, who had been with the club since 1888, caused Rangers to appoint an ex-professional runner William Struth as their new manager. In his first full season, 1920–21, Rangers established a British record with 76 points out of a possible 84—losing only one League game and the Cup final to Partick Thistle. That was the start of Rangers' golden era. In the two decades between the wars Rangers won the Championship fifteen times and Struth's teams are still regarded as the finest Rangers have ever fielded, with magical names like Morton, Meiklejohn and McPhail.

Left-winger Alan Morton is probably felt by the majority of Scots to be the greatest player of all time. Signed from amateur Queen's Park he won game after game with his unstoppable bursts down the touchline. During easy games in bad weather he is supposed to have occasionally carried an umbrella and, when the Scottish FA held its Diamond Jubilee dinner in 1933, he was the only player to be invited—as much a comment on the attitudes of the Association as the esteem in which Morton was rightly held.

Morton is perhaps still best remembered for his part in the Wembley Wizards international of 1928, an unusually significant year for Morton and his Rangers colleagues. Despite their dominance of the League, Rangers had not won the Cup since 1903. In 1928 they reached the final to meet Celtic. In the first half Willie McStay punched out a Jimmy Flemming shot; a penalty. Captain Meiklejohn took the kick with John Thomson, arguably Scotland's best-ever goalkeeper, in front of him and twenty-five years of Cup failure behind. The ball flew home, the bogey was laid and Rangers won 4–0. Three years later, in a game between the old rivals at Ibrox, Thomson was to die diving at the feet of a blameless Irishman named Sam English. The Celtic and Scotland keeper thus became a martyr to the Parkhead cause. The irony is that he was a Protestant and, for a time, it seemed that the death would cool religious fervour; 30,000 turned out for the funeral. But within a year things were as bad as ever and, if anything, with Celtic now having a ready-made martyr, even worse.

Ibrox has seen more than its fair share of tragedy. In 1902, during the last England-Scotland international to be held there (the new Hampden was opened in 1903), part of the wooden terracing collapsed and twenty-five spectators died as they plummeted down through the struts. The match

Right: *Photographs used in evidence to show that Rangers forward Sam English was completely blameless in the death of Celtic's goalkeeper John Thomson at Ibrox in 1931. The top picture clearly shows English striking the ball with his right foot, while Thomson's brave, if foolhardy, headlong dive ends in contact with the Irishman's left knee.*

Opposite page: *Genuinely aggressive forward play from a Cologne forward during the second leg of a Dundee–Cologne European Cup tie late in 1962. Dundee had won the first leg by a remarkable 8–1 margin, the best Scottish display ever in Europe excluding Celtic's winning run in 1967. Bert Slater, Dundee's keeper, had already been injured in the first half of the return leg, hence the bandage. Cologne won 4–0 and provoked a crowd invasion but Dundee went on to the semi-final when they were defeated by AC Milan, the eventual winners.*

continued, ending 1–1, but was deleted from official records and replayed at Birmingham.

Some seventy years later, on 2 January 1971, stairway thirteen was the scene of an even worse disaster at the end of yet another Rangers-Celtic game. Celtic were leading 1–0 when, with literally seconds left, Colin Stein scored for Rangers. Fans who were already leaving turned to get back and see what had happened, meeting those who had jubilantly left after the goal was scored. Somebody stumbled, others fell and sixty-six were crushed to death.

It was easily Britain's worst sporting disaster but, given the crowds that Glasgow attracts, it is no surprise that it should have happened there. Hampden, for instance, holds most European as well as British attendance records. The largest for any game in Europe is the 149,547 who attended the Scotland-England international in 1937. The largest European Cup atten-

dance was for the 1970 semi-final between Celtic and Leeds and the largest European Cup final attendance was the 127,621 for the 1960 classic between Real Madrid and Eintracht Frankfurt. Ibrox Park holds the record for a League match in Britain with an astonishing 118,567 for the Celtic game in 1939.

The only period in the whole history of Scottish football during which the provincial clubs competed on near equal terms with the Glasgow duo was the years after the Second World War. This was largely because of the exceptional interest the game generated in the British Isles during the late forties and fifties. As a result of the enormous crowds—30,000 at Firhill or Tynecastle was not abnormal—the provincial clubs could compete financially with Glasgow in a way they have never managed before or since. The good players stayed longer because wages were comparable, and a little success bred confidence in the

future. Hibernian won the League in 1948, 1951 and 1952, coming second in 1947, 1950 and 1953. Aberdeen won the League in 1955, Hearts in 1958 and 1960 (plus the Cup in 1956), Dundee in 1962 and little Kilmarnock in 1965. Clubs as humble as Motherwell, Clyde, Falkirk, St Mirren and Dunfermline were also able to have their names engraved on the Cup.

Hibernian's post-War side is best remembered for its 'Famous Five' forward line of Gordon Smith, Eddie Turnbull, Bobby Johnstone, Lawrie Reilly and a later Scottish manager Willie Ormond. Edinburgh rivals Hearts almost matched its goal-scoring abilities a decade later with their inside-forward trio of Alfie Conn, Willie Bauld and Jimmy Wardhaugh. Behind them was the near-legendary Dave Mackay and in 1957–58 Hearts won their first Championship of the century with a record 132 goals.

Dundee, champions in 1962, were the last of the major provincial clubs to benefit from the relative decline of the Glasgow partnership. Gordon Smith, Alan Gilzean, Andy Penman and Alan Cousin starred in a side that went on to crush Cologne 8–1 in a European Cup tie the following season and eventually, to the surprise of all Britain, reached the semi-final. Dundee's later experiences, however, are a commentary on the times. The game was undoubtedly becoming more egalitarian in Scotland when a happening in England pulled the carpet from underneath the provincial clubs.

This was the abolition of the maximum wage, at that point only £20 per week and not comparable with the sums top Scottish clubs, free from such emcumbrances, could pay. Soon, however, £100 per week was commonplace south of the border and only Rangers and Celtic north of Carlisle could match it. As a result, the exodus began in earnest. The Dundee side of 1962 rapidly disintegrated—Ian Ure went to Arsenal for

Above: *The payboxes burn at Hampden Park at the end of the replayed 1909 Scottish Cup final, between Rangers and Celtic. Fans had demanded extra-time at the end of the replay, but this was not allowed under the rules then prevailing. Goalposts and fences were torn down and burnt with the payboxes. As a result, Rangers and Celtic refused to play another game and the trophy was withheld.*

Above right: *Hampden Park on a more mundane Saturday—with Queen's Park (in the stripes) performing in front of around 1500 people in a stadium that has held a hundred times that number.*

£62,000, Alan Gilzean to Spurs for £72,000, Alan Cousin to Hibs and Gordon Smith into retirement. Because of recent success the effect was more noticeable at Dundee, but it was a story paralleled, to an extent, throughout Scotland—even in the halls of Ibrox and Parkhead.

In fact, a slightly more transient phenomenon was attracting more attention at the time. The real problems of Scottish football were obscured by the remarkable achievements of Jock Stein and Celtic. It is true to say that a whole generation of football fans grew up never having known any other side at the head of the Scottish League.

Between 1965 and 1974 Celtic won a record nine Scottish Championships—unparalleled in any league in Europe. More significantly for Britain, Celtic also became the first club from the homeland of football to win the European Cup in 1967, and should have done so again in 1970 when Feijenoord were fortunate to catch them in a strangely muted mood.

The Celtic story is also the Jock Stein story—a miner, he had played for Celtic after the Second World War, causing no great excitement and moving to a Welsh non-league club Llanelli after three seasons. Celtic were not notably successful at the time—in April 1948 they found themselves having to take two points from a game at Dundee to retain the First Division place they had never lost. They succeeded, but it was to be a dull half a dozen years later before Stein returned to the club after two burglaries at a home he kept on in Hamilton. He had decided to return north and go back to the pits when Llanelli were knocked out of the FA Cup in 1954.

Oddly, Celtic made an approach at the same time—to ask him to play in the re-serves and look after the youngsters that the club was bringing along. He agreed, preferring football to the mines, but never played in the reserve team as the two senior centre-halves were both quickly injured. In a fairytale return for Stein, Celtic won the double, but they were to win neither major trophy again until Stein's second coming, this time as manager in 1965.

He had started his managerial career with lowly Dunfermline in 1960—a poor side almost certain to be relegated after a dreadful season. They won their next five matches, were saved, and reached Hampden for their first ever Scottish Cup final the next year. Happily for Stein they met and defeated Celtic. For the next four years Dunfermline were among Scotland's best, even without Stein who enjoyed a short but equally successful spell at Hibernian before returning to Celtic in March 1965. By one of these remarkable coincidences his first major game was the Scottish Cup final—against Dunfermline. Stein again managed the winning side, Celtic emerging 3–2 victors. The next nine years Celtic were virtually untouchable in Scotland with Ronnie Simpson in goal, whose first class career had lasted twenty-five years from the age of fourteen when he first appeared for Queen's Park, Billy McNeil at the centre of the defence, Bertie Auld and Bobby Murdoch controlling the mid-field, and Bobby Lennox, Steve Chalmers, Willie Wallace and the inimitable Jimmy Johnstone, a winger in the true Scots mould, up front.

It was sad, perhaps, that they did not reach double figures with a tenth consecutive Championship in 1975, as this was the last of the Championships to be contested in the traditional way. Rangers had finally emerged from their decade-long doldrums, in which they had only won the Cup twice and done very little else, to take the 1974–75 title. Ex-Hearts coach Jock Wallace had, after five years, moulded a team to be reckoned with. For the following season a much debated alternative pattern was to be tried—three divisions of ten, fourteen and fourteen clubs. The top ten clubs were to play each other four times, thus providing the same number of games (thirty-six) but, hopefully, much larger gates. Some argued that this would lead to more sterility, but the major sides were clearly in favour—it meant two home games against Rangers and Celtic for a start. The 1974–75 season was largely spent jockeying for position, with the east coast coming out right on top with six of the top ten placings—the two Edinburgh and Dundee clubs, Aberdeen and Perth's St Johnstone. Apart from the inevitable Rangers and Celtic the massive Glasgow connurbation could offer only Motherwell. Part-time Ayr United were the jokers in the pack.

The principle was a new departure for the Scottish League, which had never coped adequately with the problem of having Brechin City and Stenhousemuir (averaging gates of well under 1000) in the same structure as the likes of Rangers and Hibernian. It was not certain that the problem had been solved with three divisions—the distinctions between second and third being somewhat blurred with the second a sorry sort of no-man's-land for clubs like Kilmarnock, Airdrieonians, Morton and Partick Thistle.

From its inception the Second Division had never been completely clear about its position in the order of things. From foundation in 1893 through to the acceptance of a formal promotion/relegation

system in 1922 the two divisions were regularly at odds. The First insisted on 'electing' clubs from the Second to its ranks—thus in 1905, for instance, Falkirk (who finished second) and Aberdeen (who finished seventh in the Second Division) were elected to the First while League champions Clyde had to remain where they were. Some clubs suffered continually from this discrimination. Little Cowdenbeath won the Championship in both 1914 and 1915 but were refused admission. To rub salt in their wounds, the next time they won, in 1939, they were not promoted because of the Second World War.

Before the First World War, on the other hand, some clubs, particularly Queen's Park and Port Glasgow, retained their premier status despite regularly finishing at or near the bottom of the table. The discontent grew, stayed only by the First World

Above: *An English Rangers defeats a Scottish Rangers. Berwick, the Northumberland club which plays in the Scottish League, defeated mighty Rangers 1–0 in the first round of the Cup in January 1967. The Rangers keeper appears less pleased than his opponents with Sammy Reid's goal.*
Below: *The attractive face of the Scottish lower divisions— Arbroath's loyal supporters shelter under the stand at windswept and seaswept Gayfield Park. Arbroath hold one British record—that of the biggest ever first class win. Back in 1885–86 they defeated Bon Accord 36–0 in a Scottish Cup tie.*

War, and after hostilities had ceased the Second Division had disappeared to be replaced by a rebel Central League. This was a real money spinner outside the jurisdiction of the Scottish League and was concentrated in the eastern counties of Fife and Angus; clubs like Dunfermline and Cowdenbeath were soon tempting players away from the likes of even Celtic and Rangers with, for the time, massive wages and incentives. Dunfermline even persuaded the Scottish international centre-forward, Andy Wilson, to play for them although he was technically registered with Middlesbrough. They paid no fee and he won three caps while unofficially with them.

The Central League won its point and the automatic promotion/relegation system was introduced in return for the Central League clubs returning to the fold as the new Second Division. There was a continual fluctuation of membership throughout the next fifty years, including a spell between 1946 and 1955 of a three-division system with eight ex-Second Division teams comprising division 'C'. As recently as the 1966–67 season East Stirlingshire Clydebank split into its constituent parts and Ferranti Thistle changed their name to Meadowbank Thistle and were a new name for the 1974–75 season—the last under the two division basis.

It is not likely that three divisions will solve the essential dilemma facing the lower grades of the Scottish League—that the likes of Forfar Athletic and Berwick Rangers simply cannot aspire to the Championship. They are, simply, in another league from the Celtics and Aberdeens. In England *relatively* small towns like Carlisle, Ipswich and Derby can and do aspire to a First Division club on equal or nearly equal terms with the Liverpools and Arsenals—in Scotland Brechin and Stanraer must always be second or third rate citizens. The relative differences are far greater. Surprisingly the people who seem to mind least are the clubs themselves.

'The only way Scottish Second Division clubs can survive,' says a Stranraer official, 'is by opting out of the rat-race. The less ambition you have, the more money you can tote up, or, at least, the smaller overdrafts you accumulate. If you have any sense you simply don't think about promotion or anything silly like that.' With that approach clubs like Stranraer are healthier than their supposed superiors. It is the clubs on the fringe of the élite that suffer most, like Dunfermline after their successes under Stein in the early 1960s. By 1972 the strains of having to maintain top flight status on small gates got too much and Dunfermline were appealing for £50,000 to

save the club from extinction. They then fell back to a more modest station in life.

For the Stranraers and Brechins life can be well ordered, pleasant and profitable. The players are all part-timers—most live around Glasgow anyway—and with all but eight of the Scottish League sides in a belt no more than fifty miles wide, travel is not usually a great expense. The clubs act as a social centre in their communities, often as the major focal point for local interests. Where else do you hear the names Arbroath, Cowdenbeath and Stenhousemuir except on a Saturday night? Their role, therefore, is not to win the Scottish League, and it is not to be decried for that. In fact, it is remarkable that the Scottish League has maintained clubs as disparate as Celtic and Cowdenbeath, Aberdeen and Albion for so long. But as a measure of the real strength of divisions, only one side from outside the First Division has ever won the Scottish Cup or the Scottish League Cup—and in both cases that club was East Fife.

Their 1938 victory in the Cup was the more remarkable of the two. They had five replays during their Cup run—and somehow or other East Fife avoided playing any of the League's top five clubs, a remarkable feat in itself.

Their opponents in the final were Kilmarnock, themselves only eighteenth in the First Division and one point away from relegation—and the first game ended in a 2–2 draw. The replay had a similar score at full-time but the Fifers scored twice in extra time. It is unlikely that any club will ever match their feat—nor will any player match that of John Harvey who was transferred from Hearts before the replay and won a Scottish Cup medal in his first game. When they won cups they won them in style did East Fife—their 1948 League Cup win over Falkirk had a 4–1 score line to emphasise their superiority, even if it was after a goalless draw.

East Fife's unexpected success—their home of Methil is barely the size of an

Opposite page top: *Jock Stein and his wife hold the Scottish Cup in 1954 after he had captained Celtic to their first double for 40 years.*
Opposite page bottom: *Billy McNeill, a later Celtic captain, celebrates one of his side's four goals against Rangers in the 1969 Scottish Cup final.*
Above: *The 1967 European Cup triumph in Lisbon; Facchetti deflects a shot by Lennox. Despite being a goal down in seven minutes (a penalty by Sandrino Mazzola whose father had played his last game in the same stadium before being killed in the Superga air crash), Celtic fought back magnificently to score twice.*

Right: *Newspapers which tell their own stories of the two tragic Ibrox crowd disasters.*
Opposite page left: *Stairway 13 down which fans tumbled at the end of that game on 2 January 1971.*
Opposite page right: *The goal that caused it all; Colin Stein scores for Rangers in the final minute to equalise Celtic's earlier goal. Almost certainly, fans who had been disappointedly leaving early turned back when they heard the crowd roar approval, only to meet others who were leaving as the final whistle blew. The result was chaos, someone presumably stumbled and sixty-six people died.*

English market town—does in some ways parallel Scotland's own position in the footballing world. A tiny country with a population of barely five million, she has long held her own on the football field with countries many times her own size. But the most significant statistic of all is the record against England—at the beginning of 1976 Scotland had won thirty-six times to England's thirty-five with twenty-two drawn in the world's oldest international. For one hundred years the main object of Scottish football has clearly been to defeat England.

The Observer's Hugh McIlvanney has pointed out that when Pope Pius II visited Scotland (before his elevation to the title) in the reign of James I, he wrote that 'the greatest conversational pleasure of the populous was the abuse of the English.' For over a hundred years the main object of Scottish football has not been dissimilar, and nowadays the Scottish hordes remain a remarkable exposition of nationalism—over 200,000 wrote for the 3800 tickets available to postal applications for the 1975 game. This annual event has long been a cult—the ultimate testing ground of the power of Scottish football—but it did not really become an obsession until the 'Wembley Wizards' of 1928. That game remains the ultimate proof—to a Scotsman—that those born north of the border play football better than those born south of it.

That would be a surprising assessment to anyone who had witnessed the reception that the 1928 Scottish team announcement received in Glasgow a week before the game those five long decades ago. The now immortal forward line of Jackson, Dunn, Gallacher, James and Morton had no player taller than five feet seven inches and seemed certain to be beaten by the English.

The night before the game Captain Jimmy McMullan, looking at his pessimistic team, could give only one sentence by way of tactical advice, which was, 'Go to bed and pray for rain.'

Perhaps they did. The downpour the following day gave the forwards an enormous advantage over a rather ponderous English defence. Alex James, perhaps the greatest of all Scottish inside-forwards, played brilliantly and scored twice. Even more memorably, Huddersfield's Alex Jackson scored an identical trio of goals—each being headed in from a precise Alan Morton cross. A mining engineer who would often work on the morning of internationals, Morton was known by the English as 'Wee Blue Devil', a nickname originating from the journalist Ivan Sharpe after hearing him so described by a Lancastrian.

In the end the game was won 5–1 and was the inspiration for what has now become a biennial trek to Wembley. But, having praised the Scots, it is worth remembering this was the only season in the whole history of the Home International Championship that England lost all three of her games. Though the Scots clearly played well, an extremely poor England side greatly contributed to the result.

Though there has never been a performance approaching that of the 'Wizards' the most memorable Scottish displays certainly seemed reserved for Wembley rather than Hampden. Hearts' Tommy Walker who equalised with a penalty in 1936— an eerie goal this as the ball kept blowing off the spot in a gusty wind—won the game in 1938. In 1949 goalkeeper Jimmy Cowan had a great game and the Scots played superbly to win 3–1, a game captain George Young later called his most memorable

Above: *The game that started the real Wembley pilgrimage— the 1928 'Wizards' win by 5–1 over England. The picture shows one of Alex Jackson's three remarkable goals from Alan Morton crosses. As the Scots forward line was so small, the side's tactics had consisted of: 'Going to bed and praying for rain.' It poured and this became the only season that England has ever lost all three home internationals.*

Right: *A cartoon highlighting Jock Stein's problems before the vital 1965 World Cup qualifying match in Naples, when his team was decimated by injuries and the refusal of some English clubs to release their players. Scotland lost 3–0 and Italy qualified. Interviewed after the game Stein commented: 'Never again'.*

ever. Later keepers were not quite so happy —Martin of Aberdeen let in seven in 1955 (Denis Wilshaw of Wolves getting a record four of them), poor Frank 'Slap' Haffey saw nine go past in 1961 for a record defeat and Kennedy conceded another five in 1975. But in both 1963 and 1967 the great 'Slim Jim' Baxter (James' main rival for the mantle of Scotland's greatest) taunted and teased England to defeat. The 1967 loss was the first the World Champions had suffered at home since their success less than a year before—and that made it all the sweeter for the Scots, who had failed to qualify.

By that time the Scots were beginning to concede that defeating England was not everything, and that success on a wider stage had its attractions. For a long time however, the game's administrators seemed to do their best to actively discourage any involvement beyond the British Isles. Selection was by committee and often brought out the worst of petty rivalries. Tactics consisted of faith, hope and Alan Morton, George Young or Charlie Cooke —depending on the decade. Scotland has maintained her limited success on the international stage by continuing to produce the truly gifted exceptions—the Mortons, Cookes, Baxters, Laws and Bremners. But in 1950 it is unlikely that all of these in the same team together could have got Scotland to the World Cup finals. FIFA invited the top two clubs in the Home International Championship to take part in that year's contest in Brazil. Scotland finished second but refused to go—no one ever quite found out why but it was in keeping with an association that had taken fifty-six years to play a game outside Britain. 1950 was a bad year for the Scots, they lost their first home international against a foreign country, Austria, in December that year.

In 1954 Scotland did get further—even to the extent of appointing Andy Beattie as team manager (he was 'helped' in his selecting by the committee) but the results were even more disastrous. Captain George Young was left out, Beattie was allowed to take only eleven —nine outfield players and

JON'S SPORTING TYPES

" I recognise most of the Italian team, but who are those chaps in blue shirts ? "

Left: *Lou Macari and Denis Law confront Gordon Banks at Hampden Park.*
Bottom: *A chart showing the record of six major European nations in international matches against each other up to 1972. Considering Scotland's relative size and number of players, her percentage success rate is remarkably high.*

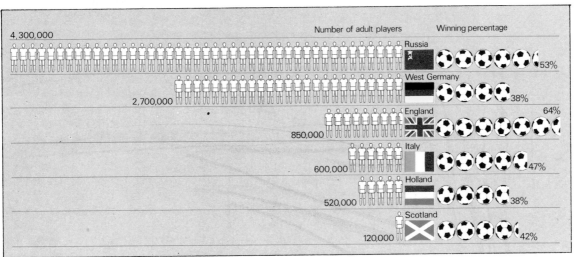

Number of adult players   Winning percentage

4,300,000   Russia   53%

2,700,000   West Germany   38%

850,000   England   64%

600,000   Italy   47%

520,000   Holland   38%

120,000   Scotland   42%

Classic Scots individualism: Jimmy Johnstone slips past Bobby Moore and Alan Ball.

and Shankly—had simply refused to release players from what they regarded as vital League matches. The Scots have had to live with this problem since, back in 1895, they finally decided to allow 'Anglos', to play for the national team, and so long as the great majority of talented players go south they will have to continue doing so. For that game in Naples, the country which had produced the likes of Hughie Gallacher, Jimmy McGrory and Denis Law played Liverpool centre-half Ron Yeats as a traditional number nine.

After losing it 3–0, Stein gave the job up, muttering 'never again . . .' and there followed the famous apotheosis of the Scottish game—an advertisement for the managership suggesting that: '. . . the job might suit a man with other business interests.' The best that could be said was that this at least marked the lowest point.

In 1970 the vital game was in Hamburg against West Germany. The Scots were more than a match for their hosts, who eventually reached the semi-finals in Mexico, but a strange tactical decision cost them a place. Tommy Gemmell, a fine overlapping full-back was on the left marking the conventional but fast Rheinhard Libuda. On the right was John Greig, a solid, competent but entirely defensive player without a winger to mark. Gemmell's attacking abilities were wasted as he held back to mark Libuda—indeed Gemmell's slowness on the turn was exposing the Scots. Though the obvious move seemed to be to swop Greig and Gemmell so that attacks could be initiated down the right, manager Bobby Brown did nothing —and paid the price. Towards the end of the game Libuda broke past Gemmell, scored and put his side on the plane to Mexico. Brown's reign lasted for another year, till a sorry 3–1 defeat at Wembley brought Tommy Docherty to the Scottish FA's headquarters at Park Gardens.

It was not until this point that a manager really took control of the team—and Docherty's successor, Willie Ormond, was able to emerge from the 1974 World Cup finals with the proud boast that Scotland had been the only team to go through the final stages undefeated. This was not quite so valuable in the light of the fact that a particularly weak performance against Zaire (Scotland scoring only twice when Yugoslavia managed nine) had let Brazil squeeze past them into the second round by just one on goal difference. Nonetheless, it was progress of sorts, even if by that stage Ormond was fighting to maintain control not with the selection committee but with the players. Scotland's international lot rarely seems to be a happy one.

two goalkeepers to Switzerland, and even that meagre number had to train in club jerseys as no national equipment had been provided. They got their just desserts— going down spectacularly 7–0 to Uruguay. Andy Beattie announced that he was resigning just before the match. Farcical would be too kind a word to describe the whole expedition. When the players returned one selector greeted them with the traditional exaltation: 'Never mind about Switzerland, just so long as we beat England.'

1958 in Sweden was better. Scotland got only a single point but had John Hewie's penalty kick not hit the post against France they might have gone further. Nevertheless it was to be another sixteen years before they qualified again.

In the interim committee selection ruled and it was this, more than any other factor, that created the sort of atmosphere in which there were ten managerial changes in the two decades after 1954. There were other factors; Jock Stein needed to win a game in Naples in 1965 to hope to qualify for the following year's finals, only to find himself left with half a team. The English clubs— most notably Scots managers like Busby

THE RISE OF SOUTH AMERICA
The World 1945-1962

Six years of war had intervened when England returned to action of a football kind on 28 September 1946 against Northern Ireland in Belfast. Of those who had played in the last pre-War international (in Rumania in 1939) only centre-forward Tommy Lawton remained. But though the faces had changed, the short-sighted pride in domestic football certainly had not. In England the belief still persisted that British football was best. But the events of the next fifteen years were to prove the fallibilities

of the game, notably in the British Isles, but also throughout Europe. The era was to belong to South America.

England won 7–2 in Belfast that day, with a young blond wing-half, Billy Wright, beginning an international career that was to endure thirteen years. Victories over the Netherlands, France, Portugal and Belgium, by large margins, soon brought back that aura of invincibility that had been so much a part of the pre-War era, even if a 1–0 defeat by Switzerland in Zurich was

Below: *Neil Franklin, the Stoke and England centre half (left) dispossesses Argentina's Afredo Rial during a game for Santa Fe of Bogota. Franklin left England in April 1950 for supposed riches which, as the thin crowd suggests, never materialised. For the national team the loss was enormous for Franklin was unavailable for the World Cup that year.*

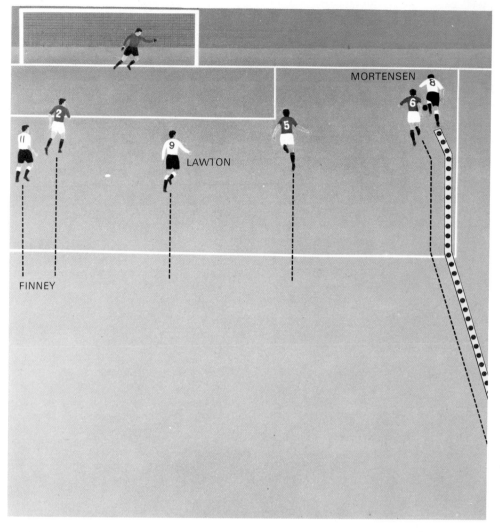

Right and opposite: *Stan Mortensen's astonishing early goal from the edge of the penalty area against Italy in Turin in 1948. A comparative newcomer, Mortensen had been playing for the national team for less than a year. In what promised to be England's most difficult post-War international thus far, Mortensen ran forty yards to the touch-line and decided on a totally unexpected shot rather than a centre to Tommy Lawton. 'It was as good a goal as I ever scored', said Mortensen. England went on to win 4–0 for one of their most memorable victories.*

conveniently pushed under the carpet. And when the mighty Italians were on the wrong end of a 4–0 scoreline in Turin in 1948, England's stock had never been higher.

Or so it seemed, particularly to the officials of the four British national associations. Those heads, buried deep in the sands, failed to notice any significant challenge from abroad—not just in playing standards but also in terms of preparation. The Football Association's only concession towards a more detailed approach to international matches came in the appointment of a team manager, though Walter Winterbottom only managed a list of players given to him by the FA selection committee and then under the awesome handicap of meetings so rare that team members often had their first conversations in the dressing-room prior to kick-off.

A second concession was a return to FIFA, which meant that the top two teams in the Home International Championship of 1950 would compete in that year's World Cup. England won and duly prepared for their journey to Brazil with the same attitude of a monarch touring to

show the flag in the colonies; Scotland, the runners-up, astoundingly declined the invitation, piqued because they had not been the British champions.

Undoubtedly England were expected to make a grand showing, but those whose expectations were high ignored results in 1949 like a 3–1 defeat in Stockholm and a 2–0 home defeat by the Republic of Ireland at Goodison Park, technically England's first at home by a foreign country. The monarch was about to be overthrown.

Late withdrawals, an ill-conceived pattern and inept organisation helped to rob the 1950 tournament of much of its significance. It was, of course, the first World Cup held since 1938, the 1942 and 1946 competitions having been rendered impossible by the War. Where the 1934 and 1938 World Cups had been run on a straight knock-out basis, meaning that some South American countries travelled thousands of miles to play but a single match, the 1950 competition—organised on a league system —was a throw-back to the initial World Cup of 1930, the only previous one to take place in South America.

There were, it is true, differences, and

MORTENSEN

not really for the better. In 1930, four qualifying groups produced four semi-finalists. This time, four groups would provide four contestants for the final pool, which would again be run on the basis of a miniature league, its winner taking the World Cup.

This was a well-meant attempt to make the tournament look more equitable and significant, but it foundered on the rock of a host of withdrawals, and the inflexibility of FIFA's World Cup committee. Moreover, the concept of playing each group in a single venue had inexplicably not yet been arrived at, so that the countries involved—Brazil excepted—had to travel huge and wearying distances between matches. This was what caused the French to withdraw.

The Czechs made a surly exit, the Scots their childish one. Billy Wright, now the England captain, pleaded with his Scottish counterpart, George Young, to persuade the officials to change their minds, stressing that the presence of Scotland would be a great help to England. But the Scottish FA remained adamant, even turning down a subsequent invitation to compete when several teams withdrew, and so England travelled alone.

Austria decided not to come on the weird grounds that their team was 'too young', although it had been quite good enough to beat Italy, the holders since 1938, on the eve of the tournament. Hungary was maintaining a splendid isolation from which she would not emerge until 1952. The Germans were still excluded from the competition, and the Russians had been holding aloof ever since the Moscow Dynamos returned to the Soviet Union in 1945, after their successful European tour.

Italy's team had been wrecked by the dreadful Superga air crash in May 1949, when seventeen Torino players, most of them Italian internationals, died on a hillside outside Turin. Stunned by Superga, the Italians travelled on a white ship called the *Sises*. By the time it docked in Sao Paulo, to be greeted by 200,000 Italo–Brazilians, the team manager Ferruccio Novo had quarrelled with his lieutenant, the Tuscan journalist Aldo Bardelli, and sacked him. Vittorio Pozzo, architect of the victories of 1934 and 1938, had been dethroned as *commissario tecnico* the previous year; the end of a mighty era.

England were suffering the loss of their brilliant centre-half, Neil Franklin of Stoke City, the incumbent for five years. Franklin had that summer been lured off to Bogota, the capital of Colombia, to join the Santa Fe club at a reputedly huge salary. Colombia, then outside FIFA's jurisdiction, had been luring Argentinians for years. Franklin, giving the Football Association the excuse that his wife was having a baby, withdrew from the World Cup party, then decamped to Bogota, where it all ended in tears and a sad return.

England still had plenty of talent, even though it was only a grudging last-minute decision which added the great Stanley Matthews to the squad, he having left to tour Canada with an FA party. There were Stanley Mortensen, a superb opportunist, and the brilliant Wilf Mannion at inside-forward, Preston's gifted Tom Finney on the wing, Bert Williams, the goalkeeper who had already saved England once against Italy, Billy Wright, an exuberant young wing-half, and the solid, thoughtful Alf Ramsey of Spurs, at right-back.

Brazil and England were the favourites. The Brazilians, talented failures in 1938, had by now made great strides. Their skilful, volatile players were virtually confined in a house just outside Rio, liberally accoutred free of charge by manufacturers. In charge was the serious, moustached Flavio Costa, at that time manager of the Vasco da Gama club of Rio, and said to be earning £1,000 a month. There were two

doctors, two masseurs and three chefs. England, amazingly, still travelled without a team doctor; a fact which said a good deal about the official attitude to the players.

Sweden, though their stars had been pillaged by Italian clubs, still brought a lively side under the bubbling little Yorkshireman, George Raynor, a fine tactician.

Uruguay had had yet another players' strike, which had forced them to send a team of youngsters to the 1949 South American championship. Absurdly, they had only to encounter feeble Bolivia in their group, the others having withdrawn; Italy's group had just three teams, England's and Brazil's four; an unbalanced arrangement indeed.

A massive new treble-decker stadium had been built beside the Maracana River, its seats painted blue on the advice of a psychologist; he considered it a peaceful colour. Shades of Uruguay's Centenary Stadium twenty years earlier, it was still not finished.

Still, Brazil were able to play Mexico there in the opening game; one which they won with little hardship. There were fireworks, 5000 pigeons fluttered aloft, a 21-gun salute was fired. Brazil had the lithe Ademir and Jair as inside-forwards, flanking Baltazar, a powerful black centre. Ademir scored two of the goals in a 4–0 win.

The first surprise took place at Sao Paulo where, despite the local support, a strangely selected Italian side went down 3–2 to Sweden. Palmer and Skoglund backed up forceful Hans Jeppson, the blond centre-forward. He was too much

even for Italy's elegant centre-half, Carlo Parola, and scored twice. The Swedes then drew with the Paraguayans and went through.

England won their first game, against Chile, 2–0, with goals from Mortensen and Mannion, but the muggy air of Rio did not agree with them. At Curitiba, in the group's other match, the Spanish team was given a surprisingly hard game by the United States, their attack generalled by John Souza, who scored America's goal in a 3–1 defeat. Eddie McIlvenny, a Scot given a free transfer by Wrexham of the Third Division North only 18 months earlier, captained the States, who also had a Belgian left-back and a Haitian centre-forward.

That was in Pool Two. In Brazil's pool, Yugoslavia beat the Swiss 3–0 at Belo Horizonte. Yugoslavia's excellent, well-balanced side included Mitic and Bobek, both fine inside-forwards, Vukas on the left wing, and the bustling Cjaicowski as their right-half and captain.

Now England travelled north to Belo Horizonte where the mountain air was invigorating. The players stayed at a British-owned gold mine, and even Bill Jeffrey, the Americans' dedicated coach, a Scot from Pennsylvania State University, gave his team no chance. Indeed, half of them stayed up into the small hours the night before.

And yet, sensationally, they won, fighting magnificently on what was then a rudimentary ground, hard and bumpy, without even decent dressing-rooms. England's defence, with young Laurie Hughes of Liverpool taking over coolly at centre-half,

ENGLAND FALL TO U.S. AMATEURS

From JOHN THOMPSON

BELO HORIZONTE (Brazil), Thursday.

ENGLISH Soccer was humbled as it never has been before in the little stadium here today, when America beat us 1—0 in the World Cup match. The Americans, who entered the competition on a "hiding-to-nothing" basis and completely unfancied, were the better team, and fully deserved their victory.

And win is a 'must'

England's defeat has led to a tense situation in Group "B" of the World Cup competition.

Spain now head the Group with two wins from two games, and they meet England on Sunday. Spain need only to avoid defeat in that game to shatter all hope of England going forward to the final pool. United States, by beating Chile could, in the event of an English win, force a triple tie in this pool.

Italy, holders of the Jules Rimet World Cup, have failed to survive for the final because of Sweden's draw yesterday with Paraguay. Sweden top Group C with one game to be played.

	England		USA	
			○	29 June 1950
	○○○○○○		○○○	8 June 1953
	○○○○○○		○	28 May 1959
	○○○○○○			27 May 1964
	○○○○○○ ○○○○○○ ○○○○○○		○○○○○	Aggregate
24				5

Larry Gaetjens, the Haitian centre forward who scored the only goal of the game.

Top: Newspaper reaction to what arguably remains the biggest international upset of all time. One newspaper assumed their teleprinter operator had made a mistake and printed the score as 10–1 to England.

Centre: The first 4 post-War games between England and the United States. Unfortunately the latter won the only one that mattered—a match that later came to be called the Great American Disaster.

Bottom: Larry Gaetjens, the Haitian centre forward who scored the only goal of the game.

139

Top: *After their sensational defeat by the United States, England had to defeat Spain in Rio de Janeiro to stay in the World Cup. But they lost 1–0, thwarted by Ramallets, the Spanish goalkeeper, with saves like this.*

Bottom: *Earlier, Sweden had created the first shock of the tournament when they defeated Italy, here shaping to defend, 3–2. A year earlier Italy had lost the whole of their great Torino team in the Superga air crash—an experience to be closely paralleled by England at Munich eight years later.*

looked solid and the forwards were expected to run up a cricket score.

What happened was more like a nightmare, with the English players making dozens of chances but missing them all, thanks to the splendid play of Borghi in goal and Colombo, a centre-half playing in gloves. Gradually the English attackers grew desperate; and then, after 37 minutes, the United States scored.

Behr, the left-half, crossed, Larry Gaetjens got his head to the ball, and it flew past Bert Williams into the net. England were one behind to a goal scored by a Haitian centre-forward, who would twenty years later disappear in mysterious circumstances in that troubled country.

So the score stood, despite a header by Jimmy Mullen from Alf Ramsey's free-kick which seemed to cross the goal-line. United States 1, England 0. Now England must beat Spain in their last game in Rio to survive.

Less surprising, but still a shock, was Switzerland's draw with Brazil in Sao Paulo. Many thought the Swiss deserved to win. Brazil picked a 'political' team based on Sao Paulo players and it creaked. It did hold a 2–1 lead, but two minutes from time, Tamini scored a breakaway goal to make it 2–2. Yugoslavia beat the Mexicans 4–1, which meant that all would depend on the meeting with Brazil at the Maracana.

Spain beat Chile 2–0, Basora and Zarra getting the goals; the Chilean attack was led throughout by George Robledo, Newcastle United's half-Chilean, half-Yorkshire centre-forward.

Uruguay's solitary game against Bolivia at Recife was an absurd 8–0 canter, with Juan Schiaffino scoring four of the goals. The Uruguayans were still stubbornly and successfully playing with an attacking centre-half, the massive captain Obdulio Varela. Brazil, still uneasy about the third-back game, played a so-called 'diagonal' system in which the left-half marked the opposing right-winger.

England brought in four new players against Spain in Rio, including Stanley Matthews, and two players—Eddie Baily and Bill Eckersley—won their first caps. But a goal headed by Zarra beat a demoralised England, even though Jackie Milburn had what looked a perfectly good goal ruled out, for alleged offside.

Brazil, however, managed to beat Yugoslavia 2–0, though the Yugoslavs were bitterly unlucky when Mitic, their inside-right, cut his head on a girder while leaving the dressing-room and eventually played with it bandaged. For the first time, Brazil fielded their now legendary inside-forward trio of the wiry Zizinho, Ademir and Jair, backed up by Bauer, a splendid attacking right-half. After only three minutes, with Mitic off the field, Bauer passed to Ademir, who scored. It was Bauer's pass, too, which sent Zizinho away on a typically sinuous run to make the game safe in the second half.

So Brazil, Spain, Sweden and Uruguay contested the final pool. In their first two matches, the Brazilians were irresistibly brilliant, putting seven past the Swedes and six past the Spaniards, who had replaced their fine reserve goalkeeper, Ramallets, a hero against England, with Eizaguirre.

Ademir scored four against Sweden, Jair and Zizinho three of the goals against Spain, who in their opening game at Sao Paulo, had held Uruguay 2–2 with another two goals from Basora. Uruguay stuck to it, however, with a rather lucky win against the Swedes; 3–2 at Sao Paulo. Sweden would do still better in their last game, beating Spain 3–1 to take third place, but meanwhile the stage was set for the great confrontation between Brazil and Uruguay.

Flavio Costa was far from over-confident. The Uruguayans, he pointed out, had always been the Brazilians' bogey team; and

so they proved yet again.

Wonderful embattled defence allowed Uruguay to survive the first half, Maspoli making save after save, Varela inspiring his men, the little, black Andrade, nephew of a 1930 World Cup medalist, doing splendid things out on the left flank.

Not until a few minutes after the interval did the Uruguayan goal fall at last to Friaca, the Brazilian right-winger, but already Uruguay had shown signs of attacking life, and the mighty Varela was beginning to come forward.

After 65 minutes, Varela trundled the ball upfield, sent Ghiggia flying down the wing, and the unmarked Schiaffino smashed home his centre for Uruguay's equaliser.

There was room to spare on the Brazilian left, where Bigode and the diagonal system were found wanting, and eleven minutes from the end, Ghiggia took a return pass from Perez, sped in on goal, and crashed a right-footed shot past Barbosa to make Uruguay World champions.

'Our team is a strange one,' said Andrade, afterwards, 'It is capable of anything.' Indeed it was.

One sad fact about England's humiliation by the United States was that it happened so far away. Press coverage of the tournament was sketchy and there was no television, so much of the impact was lost. The result was acclaimed as a freak, and the malignant symptoms of England's first sortie into international competition were ignored.

So it was, too, when in 1951 the Argentinians came to Wembley and led from the eighteenth to the seventy-ninth minute before England scored twice to snatch victory; again when Austria drew 2–2 in the same stadium later that year, and again when a last-minute penalty from Ramsey protected that much-vaunted undefeated home record in a match versus the Rest of Europe in October 1953.

It was to be but a short stay of execution. On 25 November of that year, England entertained Hungary in a match which captain Billy Wright later remembered as: 'One which we expected to win; we had been conditioned always to expect to win at Wembley.' But Hungary led after only sixty seconds. Before half an hour had been played they were 4–1 ahead, and the final victory margin of 6–3 flattered England.

The Hungarians revealed a style of play so far advanced of the cliche of the English game, that the very best of the home players were bewildered. Nor were the lessons heeded; in the return the following May Hungary produced a shattering 7–1 win. The 1953 game was to be Alf Ramsey's last international, the 1954 game England's last game before the World Cup, but if the players had learned anything from these fearsome beatings, the narrow-mindedness of the FA surely stopped them benefitting. Again Winterbottom was a manager who not only did not select his players, but rarely saw them—in stark contrast to the Hungarians who had spent years in intensive collective preparation. At least this time Winterbottom was to have some domestic company. Scotland qualified and deigned to participate, though the nation's predilection for footballing suicide was to ruin their chances of success.

Just as in 1950 when Brazil, the favourites, were caught at the post by Uruguay, so in 1954 the brilliant Hungarian side suffered the same fate. It was West Germany, re-admitted to the fold of international football after a long absence, who astonishingly won the World Cup—after losing 8–3 to Hungary only days earlier in an eliminating game, and after being two goals down to them in the final itself. And just as Brazil in 1950 were the 'moral' victors, having more than convincingly dealt with the opposition

they encountered before losing in the final to Uruguay late in the game, so in 1954 the Hungarians deserved a better result.

Hungary were the outstanding team of their era but West Germany arrived as really remote outsiders. It was only at the very last moment that Sepp Herberger, manager of the international team since 1938, decided to recall Helmut Rahn, a massive, raiding outside-right, from a successful tour he was making in Uruguay with his club; and it was Rahn who would prove the decisive figure of the World Cup.

The Germans scarcely looked the kind of team to trouble the dazzling Hungarians, and, in retrospect, many questions still hang over their victory. What, for example, would have happened had Werner Liebrich, the burly German centre-half, not severely kicked Ferenc Puskas in the course of Hungary's 8–3 victory? If Puskas had not talked his way back into the final before he was fully fit—and talked Budai out of the team into the bargain? If a more rational, less madly intricate, method of playing the competition had been chosen, avoiding the paradox of a well-beaten team reaching the final? If Puskas's late 'equaliser' in the final had not rather contentiously been given offside?

It was a highly dramatic and attacking World Cup. Uruguay scored seven against the discomfited Scots. Turkey got seven against Korea, Germany seven against Turkey, Hungary eight against West Germany and nine against the Koreans. England drew 4–4 with the Belgians, while Austria beat Switzerland 7–5 and then went down in the semi-final to West Germany by 6–1! What games! What floods of goals!

Hungary came to Switzerland full of goals. They had a marvellous attack; Nandor Hidegkuti played as a deep-lying centre-forward, behind Puskas—with his deadly left foot—and Kocsis, who headed the ball so well. On the left wing, Zoltan Czibor used his speed cleverly. The defence was strong enough too, with Zakarias, the left-half, playing as a second stopper, allowing the right-half, Josef Bozsik a member of the Hungarian parliament, to make repeated surges upfield. Gyula Grosics, in goal, was so adventurous as to be almost an extra back.

England's chances, after their thrashing in Budapest, looked thin. Under the continuing team management of Walter Winterbottom, they lacked both tactical cunning and drive, though with such splendid wingers as Matthews and Finney to call upon, and Nat Lofthouse to lead the attack powerfully, they were obviously to be respected.

Scotland arrived with a team manager—

4th WORLD CUP Brazil, 1950

Group 1

Brazil (1)4 **Mexico** (0)0
Ademir 2, Jair
Baltazar

Yugoslavia (3)3 **Switzerland** (0)0
Tomasevic 2, Ognanov

Yugoslavia (2)4 **Mexico** (0)1
Bobek, Cajkowski 2, Casarin
Tomasevic

Brazil (2)2 **Switzerland** (1)2
Alfredo, Baltazar Fatton, Tamini

Brazil (1)2 **Yugoslavia** (0)0
Ademir, Zizinho

Switzerland (2)2 **Mexico** (0)1
Bader, Fatton Velasquez

	P	W	D	L	F	A	Pts
Brazil	3	2	1	0	8	2	5
Yugoslavia	3	2	0	1	7	3	4
Switzerland	3	1	1	1	4	6	3
Mexico	3	0	0	3	2	10	0

Group 2

Spain (0)3 **USA** (1)1
Basora 2, Zarra Souza (J)

England (1)2 **Chile** (0)0
Mortensen, Mannion

USA (1)1 **England** (0)0
Gaetjens

Spain (2)2 **Chile** (0)0
Basora, Zarra

Spain (0)1 **England** (0)0
Zarra

Chile (2)5 **USA** (0)2
Robledo, Cremaschi 3, Pariani, Souza (J)
Prieto

	P	W	D	L	F	A	Pts
Spain	3	3	0	0	6	1	6
England	3	1	0	2	2	2	2
Chile	3	1	0	2	5	6	2
USA	3	1	0	2	4	8	2

Group 3

Sweden (2)3 **Italy** (1)2
Jeppson 2, Carapellese,
Andersson Muccinelli

Sweden (2)2 **Paraguay** (1)2
Sundqvist, Palmer Lopez (A), Lopez (F)

Italy (1)2 **Paraguay** (0)0
Carapellese, Pandolfini

	P	W	D	L	F	A	Pts
Sweden	2	1	1	0	5	4	3
Italy	2	1	0	1	4	3	2
Paraguay	2	0	1	1	2	4	1

Group 4

Uruguay (4)8 **Bolivia** (0)0
Schiaffino 4, Miguez 2,
Vidal, Ghiggia

	P	W	D	L	F	A	Pts
Uruguay	1	1	0	0	8	0	2
Bolivia	1	0	0	1	0	8	0

Final pool

Uruguay (1)2 **Spain** (2)2
Ghiggia, Varela Basora 2

Brazil (3)7 **Sweden** (0)1
Ademir 4, Chico 2, Andersson (pen)
Maneca

Uruguay (1)3 **Sweden** (2)2
Ghiggia, Miguez 2 Palmer, Sundqvist

Brazil (3)6 **Spain** (0)1
Jair 2, Chico 2, Igoa
Zizinho, Parra (og)

Sweden (2)3 **Spain** (0)1
Johnsson, Mellberg Zarra
Palmer

*****Uruguay** (0)2 **Brazil** (0)1
Schiaffino, Ghiggia Friaca

	P	W	D	L	F	A	Pts
Uruguay	3	2	1	0	7	5	5
Brazil	3	2	0	1	14	4	4
Sweden	3	1	0	2	6	11	2
Spain	3	0	1	2	4	11	1

Uruguay: Maspoli; Gonzales (M), Tejera; Gambetta, Varela (capt), Andrade; Ghiggia, Perez, Miguez, Schiaffino, Moran
Brazil: Barbosa; Augusto (capt), Juvenal; Bauer, Danilo, Bigode; Friaca, Zizinho, Ademir, Jair, Chico
Leading scorers: 7—Ademir (Brazil)
5—Basora (Spain),
Schiaffino (Uruguay)

*Deciding match of final pool. Played at Maracana Stadium, Rio de Janeiro, 16.7.50
Attendance: 199,854
Referee: Reader (England)

Left: *The final game of the final group at Maracana, unexpectedly won by Uruguay after Brazil had just missed this chance. This was the only World Cup in which there was a final group rather than a final tie. Fortunately, the last game was between the top two teams and thus doubled as the 'real' final. Had Brazil even drawn they would have won the Cup.*

their old left-back, Andy Beattie—though with manifest reluctance, for the officials were anxious to maintain their influence, and so, at the last, it ended in chaos and recrimination.

The formula of the competition was a kind of madman's flytrap. The sixteen teams were this time divided into four pools of four teams each. But instead of playing one another, to make three games, each team played only two matches. This was because two sides in each group were seeded, thus not meeting one another, but only playing the other two, non-seeded countries. In the event that two teams were to finish level on points for second place—which was highly probable—they would play off for the place in the quarter-finals, at which point the tournament would become a knock-out affair.

In the event, Brazil and Yugoslavia qualified without play-offs in Group One as did Uruguay and Austria in Group Three. But in Group Two West Germany had to play off against Turkey, while there was a play-off between the Italians and the Swiss in Group Four.

It was a violent World Cup, featuring above all the notorious Battle of Berne, in which the Hungarians and the Brazilians set about each other both on and off the field. There were high jinks, too, between Italy and Switzerland, not to forget the kick with which Liebrich lamed Puskas and possibly won West Germany the World Cup.

Group One was fairly straightforward. It produced an excellent match between two wonderfully talented sides, the Brazilians and the Yugoslavs, which ended in a 1-1 draw. Brazil had the two Santoses as overlapping full-backs, and Didi, playing in his first World Cup, as a scheming inside-forward. They also had a superb outside-right in the powerful, fast Julinho, a brooding, copper-coloured figure with a glorious technique and a powerful right foot.

For Yugoslavia, the agile Vladimir Beara played in goal and Cjaicowski and Boskov (later national team manager), were admirable wing-halves. The forward line, including Mitic and Bobek again at inside-forward, Zebec and Vukas as goalscorers, and the gifted young Milutinovic on the right wing, was brilliant.

It was Milutinovic whose goal beat a talented French team 1–0 in the opening match, a French side including Jonquet, Penverne, Kopa and Vincent, names to become more famous four years later. Brazil

Above: *Alf Ramsey preserves England's undefeated home record with a last minute penalty against Austria at Wembley in 1951. The game ended 2–2.*
Right: *Gyula Grosics pushes the ball behind for a corner during England's traumatic 6–3 defeat by the Hungarians in November 1953.*

accounted for Mexico 5–0, who then lost 3–2 to France, while at Lausanne Brazil and Yugoslavia were playing their fine draw.

England, fresh from the disaster of Budapest, began their programme in Group Four with a wasteful draw against Belgium in Basle. At half-time, England were 2–1 up, but were caught at 3–3 by the end of ordinary time, and ultimately drew 4–4. The score is sufficient commentary on a rocky defence that lacked a firm centre-half —until Billy Wright moved there in the next game—and a reliable goalkeeper. Gil Merrick, shaky and demoralised by the Hungarian fusillade at Wembley the previous November, was for some reason retained in goal. It would prove a disastrous and decisive error in the quarter-finals.

Using Wright as stopper, and with Mullen coming in for Matthews, who had pulled a muscle, England qualified by beating the Swiss 2–0 on a steaming hot day in Berne. The Wolves men, Mullen and Denis Wilshaw, scored the goals.

For Switzerland, this was a relatively calm oasis in two violent matches against Italy. The weakness of the Brazilian referee helped to ruin the first encounter. The Swiss defenders were allowed to handle the Italian forwards very roughly, so that at the outset the Italian defenders retaliated in kind. One Swiss forward was kicked in the back, another in the stomach. Surprisingly, the Swiss won 2–1, Joseph Hugi, switched to the wing, getting the winner in the second half.

So all was set for more carnage when the two countries had to meet again in the play-off. Perhaps it would not have been needed if Benito 'Poison' Lorenzi had not needled the referee by consistently disputing his decisions, so that when he scored, it was dubiously given offside. Italy now beat Belgium at Lugano, but in Basle the Swiss struck astonishing form, and thrashed

them 4–1. They were 2–0 up before Nesti, one of the Internazionale 'block' of defenders, scored for Italy, but Hugi got his second goal of the match, and little Jacky Fatton, the left-winger, hit the fourth just on full-time. Swiss dash had overwhelmed Italian technique.

Scotland, in Group Three, played moderately well losing against Austria. But a clash with the officials now moved an exasperated Andy Beattie to resign in midstream as team manager, and the sequel was disastrous. Uruguay, the holders, who had beaten the Czechs 2–0 without impressing, won 7–0 at Basle in dazzling sunshine, their wingers, Abbadie and Borges, ripping Scotland apart on the flanks, and the great Juan Schiaffino, a hero and scorer in the decisive 1950 World Cup match against Brazil, impressing Tommy Docherty of Scotland as the best inside-forward he had ever played against. It had been a humiliation and a rout.

Hungary amassed no fewer than 17 goals in their group, nine against the South Koreans and eight against a West German side far below full strength, Sepp Herberger, its wily manager, having decided that this was a good game to throw away. The Germans showed what they were truly made of by annihilating the Turks 7–2 in their Zurich play-off, Morlock, the powerful inside-right scoring three times.

The quarter-finals now produced the notorious game between Hungary and Brazil in Berne, when two gifted teams lost their heads.

Things first went wrong for Brazil when Nandor Hidegkuti belted a left-wing corner into the net—and had his shorts ripped off him in the process. There was rain and plenty of mud, too, which upset the Brazilians' game. Five minutes after Hidegkuti's goal, Brazil went two down when Kocsis, the 'Golden Head', nodded in Hidegkuti's centre. Brazil scored from a penalty by Djalma Santos after Indio was brought down, and by half-time the game was already slipping out of control. Hungary themselves scored a penalty, by Lantos, after Pinheiro had handled. There was no sign that they were missing the injured Puskas, for whom Czibor deputised brilliantly. Julinho, with a glorious run and shot, made it 2–3; then Nilton Santos and Bozsik came to blows and were sent off by Arthur Ellis, the referee. Djalma Santos at one point chased Czibor all over the field, and Humberto Tozzi, Brazil's inside-left, was expelled for kicking an opponent— though he fell to his knees and pleaded with Ellis to change his mind. A minute later, Kocsis headed the fourth goal for Hungary.

But all was not over. The enraged Brazi-

lians invaded Hungary's dressing-room to continue the brawl, having turned out the lights in the tunnel and laid in wait for the enemy. When the fists and the boots began to fly in the darkness, Hungary, of course, gave as good as they got. Altogether it was a shameful end to a shameful match—though curiously Brazil were later to benefit from it. When they got home, the authorities decided that the Battle of Berne had exposed a Brazilian weakness—their willingness to retaliate. From then on, Brazilian teams were more disciplined, and that discipline paid off in Brazil's later World Cup successes.

In Basle, England went down to Uruguay in a fine game they might have won with sounder goalkeeping. Billy Wright was dominant in the heat at centre-half, and Obdulio Varela was an equally splendid roving centre-half for Uruguay.

Borges put Uruguay ahead with a superb goal after five minutes, though Matthews sent Wilshaw quickly through to make an equaliser for Lofthouse, and England pressed. But, against the play, Varela beat Merrick with a long shot he might have saved; then went off with a pulled muscle.

Andrade and Abbadie were limping too; the dice seemed loaded in England's favour. Instead, Merrick was again slow to Schiaffino's shot after Varela had taken a free-kick by kicking the ball illegally as it dropped from his hands without let or hindrance. Finney made it 2–3, Matthews hit a post; then Uruguay got away for a counter-attack in which Ambrois made it 4-2.

In Geneva, against West Germany, despite dominating play for an hour, Yugoslavia could not score, and then fell behind when the giant Horvath's pass back sped into his own goal. Kohlmeyer saved three times on the German line and four minutes from time the hefty Rahn broke away to make it 2–0—a cruel result.

In Lausanne, Austria won an astonishing 12-goal game against the Swiss by 7–5, after being 5–4 up at half-time. Wagner, their skilled inside-right from Wacker, got three of the goals, Ballaman and Hugi a couple each for the Swiss.

The semi-finals produced what is still regarded as one of the most brilliant World Cup matches of all time: Hungary's 4–2 win over Uruguay, in extra time at Lausanne. The Hungarians led 1–0 at half-time

Right: *Gil Merrick, Birmingham and England goalkeeper, can do little to stop Hungary's fifth goal at Wembley. In the background, Alf Ramsey adopts a vain posture in what was to be his last international.*
Below right: *More problems for Merrick; he conceded 13 goals against Hungary in 6 months. This was one of seven scored by the Magyars in Budapest in 1954.*
Opposite page: *Puskas, number 10, shows his delight after scoring Hungary's third goal at Wembley in 1953.*

against a Uruguayan team without the injured Varela, Abbadie and Miguez; Czibor volleyed in Kocsis's header. It became 2–0 when Hidegkuti headed in Budai's cross and, with 15 minutes to go, that seemed to be that. Then Schiaffino took a hand, twice sending the naturalised Argentinian, Juan Hohberg, through to score. So extra time was needed.

Perhaps Uruguay would have done it had not injury struck again, this time to Schiaffino, who had played so well. As it was, Sandor Kocsis headed two late goals, and Hungary survived.

In Basle, Austria's famous goalkeeper, Walter Zeman, succeeding Schmied who

had played the quarter-final, had a dreadful day, and a muscular German side took full advantage, winning 6–1 with two goals from corners, two from penalties, each scored by a dazzling Fritz Walter, while his brother Otmar at centre-forward himself got two.

So, in the final, Germany would meet Hungary, the team which had trounced them 8–3. Meanwhile, a jaded Uruguayan side lost 3–1 to Austria and Ocwirk for third place.

The final, in Berne, saw Puskas resume his place; expensively for Hungary as it turned out. Yet how well they started! In heavy rain, they scored twice in the first

146

eight minutes. First, Bozsik sent Kocsis through, and when the shot was blocked, Puskas drove in. Two minutes more and Czibor slipped in from the right-wing to get another. The Germans, admirably fit and full of spirit, hit back three minutes later, when Morlock stretched out to Fritz Walter's swift centre. A still greater shock came soon after when Germany equalised, Rahn thumping the ball in after a corner.

Turek's fine saves prevented another Hungarian goal and, with Puskas clearly labouring and missing chances, Budai's absence was clearly felt. Hidegkuti and Kocsis went close, both hitting the wood-work, but it was not enough. Germany held out, and Eckel and Mai, the wing-halves, began to take command. Suddenly, Fritz Walter's centre was only half cleared, and Rahn smashed in a 15-yard shot. Germany were ahead.

There were five minutes left, and all at once Puskas, long invisible, raced on to Toth's fine diagonal pass to beat Turek. A goal? After all, he seemed to have spurted past Posipal. But the Welsh linesman, Mervyn Griffiths, had his flag up. The World Cup had been dashed from Hungary's grasp, and within a couple of years, their great team was no more than a memory.

England regained a measure of pride by beating the World Champions, 3–1, at Wembley the following December. And in the four years up to the 1958 World Cup they produced some praiseworthy per-formances, notably a 4–1 win over Spain in November 1955, a 4–2 success over Brazil in 1956, both games at Wembley, and a 3–1 beating of West Germany again

in Berlin the same year. In the latter matches, the Manchester United trio of Roger Byrne, Tommy Taylor and Duncan Edwards were outstanding; tragically all three had perished by the time the next World Cup came round, victims of the Munich air catastrophe, and with them died many of England's hopes.

That disaster also cost Scotland a mana-ger, for the extent of the injuries sustained by Matt Busby robbed him of that new position. But Scotland did qualify, at the expense of Spain. Also into the last sixteen went Northern Ireland who were enjoying the best series of results in their history. Astutely guided by the sensitive hands of Peter Doherty, as manager, and Danny Blanchflower and Jimmy McIlroy, on the field, they put out Portugal and Italy—finally beating the latter, who had never previously failed to reach the finals, in an emotive encounter in Belfast. Sandwiched amidst these fine results was their first Wembley triumph, a 3–2 win masterminded by Blanchflower's direction. And Wales made up a full complement for the Home Countries when they too qualified, though only after Uruguay had withdrawn and given them the opportunity to beat Israel in the play-off for the last place in Sweden.

Sweden were again under the manager-ship of little George Raynor, the York-shireman who had taken them to third place in the 1950 World Cup. Professional-ism now being recognised in Sweden, he was able to recall such players from Italy as Nils Liedholm, a member of the 1948 Olympic winning side, Kurt Hamrin, a tricky outside-right, Nacka Skoglund, the Inter winger, and Julli Gustavsson, centre-

This page: *A Pathe News still and diagram of that classic third goal at Wembley, one of the best ever scored there. Billy Wright, England's captain, was completely fooled by Puskas pulling the ball back with the sole of his left foot. With Wright gone galloping past, Puskas whipped the ball into the net before Merrick could intervene.*

Opposite page: *A moment of danger for West Germany as Hungary's Kocsis waits to pounce on the ball during a group game in the 1954 World Cup final. Hungary won 8–3, in what was to be the first game ever lost in the World Cup final stages by the eventual winners.*

JOHNSTON

MERRICK

WRIGHT (A)

WRIGHT (B)

10

PUSKAS (B)

PUSKAS (A)

half, while another 1948 star, Gunnar Gren, ex-Milan, was back in Gothenburg. Gothenburg was where England's group played. To Raynor's amazement—'Isn't it a sin and a shame?'—England installed themselves bang in the middle of town in the Park Avenue hotel, having failed to get quarters, like the Russians and Brazilians, in idyllically wooded Hindas. They did not bring either Nat Lofthouse or Stanley Matthews—in fact they did not use their full complement of 22 players. The team relied heavily on the strategy of the Fulham inside-left Johnny Haynes, but he, like the Blackburn men Douglas and Clayton, had had a wearying season in the battle to get out of the Second Division.

The holders, West Germany, playing in Ireland's group, were again under the shrewd command of Sepp Herberger, and the captaincy of Fritz Walter. Herberger had again resuscitated Helmut Rahn after he had run to fat and dissipation. Horst Szymaniak, a muscular left-half, was a new star.

Brazil began with a 3–0 win over Austria at Boras which did not satisfy their team manager, the plump, explosive Vicente Feola. Pele was unfit, and Feola was dissatisfied with his 19-year-old centre-forward, Jose 'Mazzola' Altafini, already

signed expensively by Milan. Nor did he much like the presence of an official psychologist, an amiable, unshaven man with glasses and jerseys who said that he liked to get players to draw pictures to see whether they were instinctive or intelligent players. He did not, he explained, believe in talking to players individually, since this could serve to magnify their problems. Nor, on the other hand, did he believe in haranguing them in groups. Feola shrugged. 'How,' he demanded, 'can he know all the circumstances?'

Feola's initial forward-line was based on the Flamengo (Rio) attack. Not till the third game, against Russia in Gothenburg, would the sensational Garrincha appear on the right wing; and then it required a special deputation by the players to achieve it.

Sweden played the opening game, in the afternoon of Sunday 8 June, in Stockholm, comfortably beating Mexico 3–0 in a Group Three match. Two of the goals went to a vigorous young centre-forward, Agne Simonsson. At Sandviken, in the same group, Wales bravely held Hungary to a 1–1 draw. The Hungarian Revolution had laid waste a once great team, though Grosics, Bozsik and Hidegkuti all played. John Charles, the mighty centre-forward

Above: *Bauer, Brazil's captain, tries to restore order during the infamous 'Battle of Berne' against Hungary in 1954.*
Above right: *Nat Lofthouse wins a corner for England during their quarter-final against Cup holders Uruguay. The British sides found little joy against the Uruguayans— Scotland collapsed 7–0, England 4–2.*

released by Juventus for the tournament, headed the Welsh goal from a corner. Fresh from easy victories against local sides, the Welsh had great confidence.

England's 2–2 draw against Russia in Gothenburg was a patchy affair. They had recently drawn with the Russians in Moscow and now Russia, in their first World Cup, had to play without their fine captain and left-half, the blond Netto.

England had been shattered by a 5–0 defeat in Yugoslavia on their way to the World Cup, a result which cost the young Bobby Charlton his place in Sweden, despite a spirited press campaign. They were only slightly reassured by their draw in Moscow and so when the match began, they had much the worst of the early play. The goalkeeping of Colin McDonald from Burnley and the courage of Billy Wright at centre-half, helped keep the score to 1–0 at half-time, but Ivanov added to Simonian's goal early in the second half. In the last half-hour, Tom Finney began to roast Kassarev. And it was he who got the equaliser from a penalty after Derek Kevan had jumped superbly to head a goal. ('England score goals with the outside of their heads, not the inside' commented Vittorio Pozzo.) But Finney was injured and took no further part in the tournament.

Northern Ireland, though the loss of their centre-half Jackie Blanchflower after the Munich crash had gravely affected their tactics, forcing Danny Blanchflower to play more cautiously, began splendidly with a 1–0 win over the Czechs at Halmstad. Wilbur Cush got the vital goal. Also

in Group One, at Malmo, the robust Germans, with two goals from Rahn, beat a labouring Argentinian team 3–1. In Group Two, a revitalised French side, inspired by its stay in the Swedish village of Kopparberg, under the management of Paul Nicolas, routed Paraguay 7–3. It was the unveiling of the marvellous partnership between the deep-lying little Raymond Kopa, back from Real Madrid and the shadow of di Stefano, and the sturdy Just Fontaine, who in fact scored three of France's goals. Scotland, in the same group, came out evens 1–1 with the Yugoslavs, finishing very strongly.

England had perhaps their most distinguished game against Brazil. Bill Nicholson, Spurs' coach, who was in Sweden as Winterbottom's assistant, had studied the Brazilian 4–2–4 tactics and worked out a plan to counter them. This involved playing Don Howe, a clever right-back, in the middle, leaving Bill Slater to mark Brazil's midfield schemer, the black Didi, with Clamp in the role of an attacking right-back.

With ineffective forwards, Haynes and Robson out of form, and Kevan a bull at a gate (though he might well have had a first-half penalty) England's defence took the laurels. Indeed, in the second half, England looked the better side, having come under heavy pressure in the first. A goalless draw, it would prove the only occasion on which Brazil did not score. But Pele, Zito and Garrincha were waiting in the wings.

At Halmstad, the Irish faltered against the Argentinians, who turned on their undoubted skills and won 3–1, while West

Germany were being held 2–2 by Czechoslovakia.

Group Two produced surprises. Paraguay beat Scotland 3–2, despite the fine centre-half play of Bobby Evans, and Yugoslavia beat France 3–2; a travesty of a result. In Group Three, Sweden disposed of Hungary 2–1 in a mediocre game in Stockholm, after which George Raynor announced, 'Sweden are the slowest team in the competition. If there was a relay race over a hundred yards between all the different countries, Sweden would finish last. But we'll still reach the final!' And so they did. Wales, meanwhile, were held to a disappointing 1–1 draw by Mexico, but were 'allowed' through when Sweden put out several reserves in the final match, and they drew 0–0.

Happier against power than artistry, Northern Ireland revived to force a 2–2 draw with West Germany at Malmo, Harry Gregg keeping a superb goal, and Peter McParland getting both Irish goals. The Czechs routed Argentina 6–1 in an astonishing game. The poor Argentinians, who, the previous year, had lost several of their most gifted young forwards to Italian clubs, were overwhelmed by—of all unexpected things—the Czechs speed. They were pelted with rubbish on their return to Buenos Aires.

France beat a brave Scottish team, which brought in Dave Mackay at left-half, 2–1, to win Group Two. Dull England were held 2–2 by plodding Austria, at Boras, while in Gothenburg, Garrincha and Pele tore Russia's defence to pieces. 2–0 hardly reflected the Brazilian superiority; 4–2–4 was buzzing at last.

England, Northern Ireland and Wales all had to play off. Only England lost, desperately 'blooding' Peter Brabrook and Peter Broadbent against the Russians, having enough chances to win, hitting a post, but falling to the only goal by Ilyin, in the second half, when McDonald's throw went to a Russian player.

Wales won a rough game against Hungary in Stockholm, in which Sipos was sent off for kicking Hewitt, and Terry Medwin got a cheeky winning goal, nipping in on a short goal-kick by Grosics to a defender to make the score 2–1. The Irish beat the Czechs by the same score after extra time in Malmo; two more goals for McParland.

But they had run out of steam and players. Their patched-up side, further wearied by a superfluous motor coach trip, fell in the quarter-finals to the French, 4–0 at Norrkoping. In Malmo, West Germany, with yet another goal by Rahn, overcame their eternal rivals Yugoslavia, while Sweden dealt confidently with Russia at Stockholm, with two goals in the second half.

Wales, in Gothenburg, put up a marvellous fight against Brazil, though the absence through injury of John Charles enfeebled their attack. The whole defence, however, was outstanding, with Jack Kelsey serene and sure in goal, Dave Bowen a fine captain, Mel Charles dominant in the air, and Mel Hopkins skilfully playing Garrincha. It was hard on the excellent Stuart Williams that Pele's late shot should have been diverted past Kelsey off his foot. Pele has called it the most important goal of his career.

On the same ground, Sweden reached unforeseen and unaccustomed heights of xenophobia in their semi-final against

5th WORLD CUP Switzerland, 1954				

Group 1

Yugoslavia	(1)1	France	(0)0	
Milutinovic				
Brazil	(4)5	Mexico	(0)0	
Baltazar, Didi,				
Pinga 2, Julinho				
France	(1)3	Mexico	(0)2	
Vincent, Cardenas		Naranjo, Balcazar		
(og), Kopa (pen)				
Brazil	(0)(1)1	Yugoslavia	(0)(1)1	
Didi		Zebec		

	P	W	D	L	F	A	Pts
Brazil	2	1	1	0	6	1	3
Yugoslavia	2	1	1	0	2	1	3
France	2	1	0	1	3	3	2
Mexico	2	0	0	2	2	8	0

Group 2

Hungary	(4)9	South Korea	(0)0	
Czibor, Kocsis 3,				
Puskas 2, Lantos,				
Palotas 2				
West Germany	(1)4	Turkey	(1)1	
Klodt, Morlock,		Suat		
Schaefer, Walter (O)				
Hungary	(3)8	W. Germany	(1)3	
Hidegkuti 2, Kocsis 4,		Pfaff, Hermann,		
Puskas, Toth		Rahn		
Turkey	(4)7	South Korea	(0)0	
Burhan 3, Erol,				
Lefter, Suat 2				

	P	W	D	L	F	A	Pts
Hungary	2	2	0	0	17	3	4
West Germany	2	1	0	1	7	9	2
Turkey	2	1	0	1	8	4	2
South Korea	2	0	0	2	0	16	0

Play-off

West Germany	(3)7	Turkey	(1)2	
Morlock 3, Walter (O),		Mustafa, Lefter		
Walter (F), Schaefer 2				

Group 3

Austria	(1)1	Scotland	(0)0	
Probst				
Uruguay	(0)2	Czecho-	(0)0	
Miguez, Schiaffino		slovakia		
Austria	(4)5	Czecho-	(0)0	
Stojaspal 2, Probst 3		slovakia		
Uruguay	(2)7	Scotland	(0)0	
Borges 3, Miguez 2,				
Abbadie 2				

	P	W	D	L	F	A	Pts
Uruguay	2	2	0	0	9	0	4
Austria	2	2	0	0	6	0	4
Czechoslovakia	2	0	0	2	0	7	0
Scotland	2	0	0	2	0	8	0

Group 4

England	(2)(3)4	Belgium	(1)(3)4	
Broadis 2, Lofthouse 2		Anoul 2, Coppens,		
		Dickinson (og)		

Switzerland	(1)2	Italy	(1)1	
Ballaman, Hugi		Boniperti		
England	(1)2	Switzerland	(0)0	
Mullen, Wilshaw				
Italy	(1)4	Belgium	(0)1	
Pandolfini (pen), Galli,		Anoul		
Frignani, Lorenzi				

	P	W	D	L	F	A	Pts
England	2	1	1	0	6	4	3
Italy	2	1	0	1	5	3	2
Switzerland	2	1	0	1	2	3	2
Belgium	2	0	1	1	5	8	1

Play-off

Switzerland	(1)4	Italy	(0)1	
Hugi 2, Ballaman,		Nesti		
Fatton				

Quarter-finals

West Germany	(1)2	Yugoslavia	(0)0	
Horvat (og), Rahn				
Hungary	(2)4	Brazil	(1)2	
Hidegkuti 2, Kocsis,		Santos (D) (pen),		
Lantos (pen)		Julinho		
Austria	(5)7	Switzerland	(4)5	
Koerner (A) 2, Ocwirk,		Ballaman 2, Hugi 2,		
Wagner 3, Probst		Hanappi (og)		
Uruguay	(2)4	England	(1)2	
Borges, Varela,		Lofthouse, Finney		
Schiaffino, Ambrois				

Semi-finals

West Germany	(1)6	Austria	(0)1	
Schaefer, Morlock,		Probst		
Walter (F) 2 (2 pens),				
Walter (O) 2				
Hungary	(1)(2)4	Uruguay	(0)(2)2	
Czibor, Hidegkuti,		Hohberg 2		
Kocsis 2				

Third place match: Zurich

Austria	(1)3	Uruguay	(1)1	
Stojaspal (pen),		Hohberg		
Cruz (og), Ocwirk				

Final: Berne 4.7.54   Attendance 55,000

West Germany	(2)3	Hungary	(2)2	
Morlock, Rahn 2		Puskas, Czibor		

West Germany: Turek; Posipal, Kohlmeyer; Eckel, Liebrich, Mai; Rahn, Morlock, Walter (O), Walter (F) (capt), Schaefer

Hungary: Grosics; Buzansky, Lantos; Bozsik, Lorant, Zakarias; Czibor, Kocsis, Hidegkuti, Puskas (capt), Toth (J)

Referee: Ling (England)

Leading scorers: 11—Kocsis (Hungary)
6—Morlock (West Germany),
Probst (Austria)
5—Hugi (Switzerland)

Germany, putting their cheer-leaders on the pitch to whip up a thundering chorus from the crowd, while at the same time banning the German cheer-leaders from the running track.

The Germans, ruthlessly tough against Yugoslavia, now found themselves on the receiving end; though Juskowiak was sent off in the second half for foolishly kicking Hamrin, who rolled about melodramatically. It did not prevent him scoring later, a wonderful individual third goal for his team.

The German team had recovered totally from the ravages of jaundice, and the numerous defeats which followed its 1954 World Cup success, and now had a splendid new leader in Uwe Seeler. It was from his cross that Schaefer volleyed a goal to give them the lead, against the play. Five

minutes later, when Skoglund scored from a sharp angle, Sweden equalised after a move in which Liedholm certainly controlled the ball with his hand.

Three minutes into the second half, the score still 1–1, Juskowiak stupidly kicked the elusive Hamrin, was sent off, and the balance tipped. A dreadful foul by Parling on Fritz Walter, playing so well, tipped it

time, wrecked the French defence, a pity for, prior to that, Fontaine had equalised a second-minute goal by the brave, thrusting Vava. But in the second half, plied by Didi's clever passes, Pele gave Brazil three more goals, Didi having restored the lead with a typical, swerving, long-range shot. A late goal by France's skilful inside-left, Piantoni, was cold consolation.

So to the final, George Raynor had forecast that if the Brazilians fell a goal behind, they'd 'panic all over the show'; yet though Liedholm picked his way through to score in four minutes, they did nothing of the sort. An official ban on using cheer-leaders on the pitch led to a curiously silent Swedish crowd, and the hostile atmosphere the Brazilians had feared was absent.

Two superb runs by Garrincha turned the tide. Each time his pantherine swerve and acceleration left Parling and Axbom standing, making two goals for the inrushing Vava and giving Brazil a 2–1 lead at half-time.

In the second half, Brazil took over, playing sublimely creative football. Pele scored two astonishing goals, one after a cool piece of jugglery over his head in the penalty area, surrounded by defenders, the other with a powerful header. Zagalo, the tireless left-winger, got the other, after which he knelt in tears. For Sweden, Simonsson, breaking through the always suspect middle of the Brazilian defence, got the second; but the mighty Santoses, Djalma (playing his first game of the

Far left: Goalkeeper Jack Kelsey in action for Wales during the principality's proudest footballing hour, the 1958 World Cup finals when Wales reached the quarter-finals.

Centre: *Billy Wright is sandwiched by Brazil's Vava and goalkeeper Colin McDonald who manages to punch clear during a group game in the 1958 World Cup. By drawing 0–0, England became the only team to prevent the Brazilians' from scoring.*

Above: Sweden's inside-right Gunnar Gren shoots during the 1958 final against Brazil.

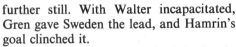

further still. With Walter incapacitated, Gren gave Sweden the lead, and Hamrin's goal clinched it.

The Brazil–France semi-final in Stockholm was also blemished, though Brazil did play beautiful football, with **Pele** a precocious 17-year-old in his most supple form. An injury to the elegant French centre-half, Bob Jonquet, eight minutes before half-

tournament) and Nilton, snuffed out the Swedish wingers. It was no match.

Despite their brave showing, the status of the four Home Countries within world football continued to decline. No longer were England the most feared side in Europe, while the best in that continent had failed against the artists from South America in two of the three post-War World Cups. It was a trend which still had several years to run.

While England groped uncertainly with the switch from the traditional W–M formation to 4–2–4, attitudes in high office continued along the same narrow track. Winterbottom, a professional figure, thoughbeit a conscientious and studious coach, remained in charge and it was even suggested that he had the ear of many of the selection committee. Nevertheless the committee existed and the end product often became the camel of committee procedure rather than the thoroughbred of a single-minded selector.

And, as in the mid-point between the 1954 and 1958 World Cups, an encouraging series of results papered over the cracks in the system. Playing a fluent 4–2–4, with Robson and Haynes linking in midfield, Winterbottom's side arrogantly beat Spain 4–2 at Wembley in 1960 and later that season destroyed Scotland 9–3 and Mexico 8–0; a 3–2 win over Italy in Rome was another fine performance.

By beating Portugal and Luxembourg, England qualified for the 1962 World Cup finals, to be held in Chile, but none of the other British nations could emulate their achievements of 1958. Scotland lost a play-off in Brussels with Czechoslovakia, who were to prove impressive competitors in South America. West Germany topped Northern Ireland's group, despite a gallant hat-trick by Billy McAdams in a 4–3 defeat in Belfast, while Wales paid the price of losing at home to Spain, though their players had some consolation in providing warm-up opposition for Brazil and Mexico before the tournament began.

Despite an injury to the incomparable Pele, and the fact that their team had by and large remained unchanged for four years, Brazil retained the World Cup in Chile in 1962. The real protagonist of their

BERGMARK PELE (B)

PELE (A)

GUSTAVSSON   AXBOM

SVENSON

The goal that established 17-year-old Pele as a truly world class star, Brazil's third in the 1958 World Cup final. He caught the ball on his thigh, whipped it over his head, and volleyed it past the Swedish goalkeeper.

success was unquestionably their marvellous outside-right, Garrincha, whose two devastating bursts had previously turned the final against Sweden in 1958. Oddly, Garrincha, who was sent off the field and had his head cut open by a missile in the semi-finals, did not do very much in the final. But then, Brazil would never have reached it without him.

England, in the quarter-finals, were one of Garrincha's victims, for he was responsible for Brazil's three goals against them at Vina del Mar, splendidly scoring two of them himself, and creating the other with a shot that bounced off goalkeeper Ron Springett's chest.

The surprise team of the competition was Czechoslovakia who, although without their injured star striker Kucera, managed to win through to the final, and score the opening goal there against Brazil. Third place went to Chile, the hosts, who owed much to the rabid support of a crowd which became more partisan and cacophonous as match succeeded match. Perhaps Chile's finest performance was their win over Russia in the quarter-finals at Arica, one of those rare occasions when Yashin had an inadequate game. Chile marred their performance with the excesses of the Battle of Santiago against the Italians, but then, after all, they had won nothing

since the Pacific War a hundred years previously.

Whether Chile should have staged the World Cup at all was a highly controversial question. Europe had presented the 1958 tournament, so the 1962 World Cup had to be played in South America. Uruguay and Brazil had been hosts already, and Argentina's disaffection since the War virtually excluded her. Carlos Distborn, the Chilean FA's president, passionately put Chile's case, even though she was still reeling from a dreadful series of earthquakes. It was precisely because they had nothing, he insisted, that they might be given the World Cup.

His argument prevailed, though it cannot be said that Chile made a very impressive job of the tournament. True, they built a fine new national stadium in Santiago, but facilities elsewhere were poor and—no fault of theirs—prices of admission equally insanely high for a depressed population. England played up in the Braden Copper Company stadium in shabby Rancagua. The other two groups took place in exquisite Vina del Mar, whose sea-side ground was a gem, and by the border in remote, dry Arica.

Once again, almost incredibly, England travelled without an official doctor, and the result was that their centre-half, Peter Swan, fell ill and, after receiving the wrong

156

treatment, almost died.

By sharp contrast with 1958, England stayed not in a centrally-located hotel, but in the mountain fastness of Coya. Though it was a retreat much coveted by other countries, many of the English players felt cut off and isolated.

England's group included Argentina, Bulgaria and Hungary. After Argentina had won a very hard game with Bulgaria by a goal from Facundo, their right-winger, England began their programme badly—losing 2–1 to the Hungarians.

The English performance was characteristically drab. Bobby Moore had just come into the team, in England's 4–0 win over Peru in Lima, but although he showed temperament and great promise, he and Ron Flowers, both big, blond and essentially defensive, tended to duplicate one another at wing-half. The team again pivoted around Johnny Haynes in midfield but by now Haynes and his strategy—the long ball through the middle, the crossfield pass to the right-wing—were too well known to foreign opposition. Even though Bryan Douglas and the fluent Bobby Charlton could do fine things on the wings, England lacked the ability to surprise the opposition.

The Hungarians deserved to win. In the blond Solymosi, at right-half, they had the most elegant player on the field, while Florian Albert, the young centre-forward whose superb individual goal won the game, was not far behind him. Tichy's famous right-foot gave Hungary the lead from long range, exposing Springett's vulnerability to such shots. Ron Flowers equalised from a penalty, and then Albert scored.

Against Argentina, England did much better. A tall, strong guardsman of a centre-forward, Alan Peacock of Middlesbrough, came into the team, used his head well, and stood up bravely to the violent tactics of Navarro, Argentina's notorious centre-half. Bobby Charlton, in magnificent form on the left wing, scored England's second goal with a low, right-footed shot. Flowers having given them the lead with another penalty. In the second half England got a third goal through the erratic but brilliant Jimmy Greaves, who was later to say: 'There's some good teams here that are playing bloody rubbish, because they're frightened to get killed.' Argentina's only goal came from the tempestuous Sanfilippo, though Springett swore he would have had the shot if Sanfilippo had not miskicked.

Hungary then thrashed the Bulgarians 6–1, three goals going to Albert, and concluded with a goalless draw against Argentina. Centre-half Meszoly gave a faultless

exhibition, much admired by the watching England players.

This put Hungary top of the group, and their 0–0 draw with Argentina confirmed that as a final position. England's own last game was a miserable goalless performance against Bulgaria, which could not, like Hungary's, be excused by the fact that they fielded numerous reserves. Once during the game, little Ivan Kolev, in splendid form at inside-left, shredded the England defence and almost made a goal—a goal that would have eliminated England. But they sur-

6th WORLD CUP Sweden, 1958

Group 1

West Germany	(2)3	Argentina	(1)1
Rahn 2, Schmidt		Corbatta	
N. Ireland	(1)1	Czechoslovakia	(0)0
Cush			
West Germany	(1)2	Czechoslovakia	(0)2
Schaefer, Rahn		Dvorak (pen), Zikan	
Argentina	(1)3	N. Ireland	(1)1
Corbatta 2 (1 pen),		McParland	
Menendez			
West Germany	(1)2	N. Ireland	(1)2
Rahn, Seeler		McParland 2	
Czechoslovakia	(3)6	Argentina	(1)1
Dvorak, Zikan 2,		Corbatta	
Feureisl, Hovorka 2			

	P	W	D	L	F	A	Pts
West Germany	3	1	2	0	7	5	4
Czechoslovakia	3	1	1	1	8	4	3
N. Ireland	3	1	1	1	4	5	3
Argentina	3	1	0	2	5	10	2

Play-off

N. Ireland	(1)(1)2	Czecho-	(1)(1)1
McParland 2		slovakia	
		Zikan	

Group 2

France	(2)7	Paraguay	(2)3
Fontaine 3, Piantoni,		Amarilla 2 (1 pen),	
Kopa, Wisnieski,		Romero	
Vincent			
Yugoslavia	(1)1	Scotland	(0)1
Petakovic		Murray	
Yugoslavia	(1)3	France	(1)2
Petakovic,		Fontaine 2	
Veselinovic 2			
Paraguay	(2)3	Scotland	(1)2
Aguero, Re, Parodi		Mudie, Collins	
France	(2)2	Scotland	(0)1
Kopa, Fontaine		Baird	
Yugoslavia	(2)3	Paraguay	(1)3
Ognjanovic, Rajkov,		Parodi, Aguero,	
Veselinovic		Romero	

	P	W	D	L	F	A	Pts
France	3	2	0	1	11	7	4
Yugoslavia	3	1	2	0	7	6	4
Paraguay	3	1	1	1	9	12	3
Scotland	3	0	1	2	4	6	1

Group 3

Sweden	(1)3	Mexico	(0)0
Simonsson 2,			
Liedholm (pen)			
Hungary	(1)1	Wales	(1)1
Bozsik		Charles (J)	
Wales	(1)1	Mexico	(1)1
Allchurch		Belmonte	
Sweden	(1)2	Hungary	(0)1
Hamrin 2		Tichy	
Hungary	(1)4	Mexico	(0)0
Tichy 2, Sandor,			
Bencsics			
Sweden	(0)0	Wales	(0)0

	P	W	D	L	F	A	Pts
Sweden	3	2	1	0	5	1	5
Hungary	3	1	1	1	6	3	3
Wales	3	0	3	0	2	2	3
Mexico	3	0	1	2	1	8	1

Play-off

Wales	(0)2	Hungary	(1)1
Allchurch, Medwin		Tichy	

Group 4

England	(0)2	USSR	(1)2
Kevan, Finney (pen)		Simonian,	
		Ivanov (A)	
Brazil	(1)3	Austria	(0)0
Mazzola 2, Santos (N)			
England	(0)0	Brazil	(0)0
USSR	(1)2	Austria	(0)0
Ilyin, Ivanov (V)			
Brazil	(1)2	USSR	(0)0
Vava 2			
England	(0)2	Austria	(1)2
Haynes, Kevan		Koller, Koerner	

	P	W	D	L	F	A	Pts
Brazil	3	2	1	0	5	0	5
England	3	0	3	0	4	4	3
USSR	3	1	1	1	4	4	3
Austria	3	0	1	2	2	7	1

Play-off

USSR	(0)1	England	(0)0
Ilyin			

Quarter-finals

France	(1)4	N. Ireland	(0)0
Wisnieski, Fontaine 2,			
Piantoni			
West Germany	(1)1	Yugoslavia	(0)0
Rahn			
Sweden	(0)2	USSR	(0)0
Hamrin, Simonsson			
Brazil	(0)1	Wales	(0)0
Pele			

Semi-finals

Brazil	(2)5	France	(1)2
Vava, Didi, Pele 3		Fontaine, Piantoni	
Sweden	(1)3	West Germany	(1)1
Skoglund, Gren,		Schaefer	
Hamrin			

Third place match: Gothenburg

France	(0)6	West Germany	(0)3
Fontaine 4, Kopa (pen),		Cieslarczyk, Rahn,	
Douis		Schaefer	

Final: Stockholm 29.6.58
Attendance 49,737

Brazil	(2)5	Sweden	(1)2
Vava 2, Pele 2,		Liedholm,	
Zagalo		Simonsson	

Brazil: Gylmar; Santos (D), Santos (N); Zito, Eellini, Orlando; Garrincha, Didi, Vava, Pele, Zagalo

Sweden: Svensson; Bergmark, Axbom; Boerjesson, Gustavsson, Parling; Hamrin, Gren, Simonsson, Liedholm, Skoglund

Referee: Guigue (France)

Leading scorers: 13—Fontaine (France)
7—Rahn (West Germany)
6—Pele (Brazil)

vived, finished second on goal average, and so qualified for the quarter-final.

In Group Three at Vina del Mar, where pelicans paraded on the rocks, mist rolled over the little stadium from the sea, and a uniformed samba band of students made music throughout each Brazilian game, the Brazilians did not have things all their own way. There was the polyglot Spanish team, under Helenio Herrera, Inter's manager, who had at first been expected to manage Italy. The team included Puskas, di Stefano (who did not or would not play, being or feigning injury, and none too happy with Herrera), plus Martinez of Paraguay and Barcelona. There were the Czechs, under the wily leadership of Rudolf Vytlacil, and with the famous half-back line of Pluskal, Popluhar and the gifted Josef Masopust. The rhythm might have been sedate, but Masopust and the lofty, Ianky Kvasniak guaranteed control in midfield. The fourth member of the group were the Mexicans; they would beat the Czechs, though no one was sure how hard the Czechs were trying.

Brazil, now under the management of Sao Paulo's Aymore Moreira, a less explosive character than Feola, lost Pele with a thigh strain after a couple of days and were virtually forced to modulate their 4–2–4 system into a 4–3–3. This was less a strategic than a tactical change, centred on the ability of Zagalo, their tireless left-winger, to cover the length of the whole left touchline, so that he was at once overlapping full-back and deep-lying outside-left. At centre-half, Mauro had taken the

captaincy from Bellini, while the little black Zozimo had succeeded Orlando at left-half. The famous partnership of Vava and Didi in midfield was resuscitated, for they had returned from service in Madrid to resume their positions.

In their opening game, Brazil beat Mexico 2–0 with goals from Zagalo and Pele, but the Czechs then held them to a 0–0 draw. Their third game, against Spain, was a thriller. Herrera gambled on a younger team with great success, Adelardo giving Spain a half-time lead. It was only the late brilliance of Garrincha, laying on two goals for Pele's young deputy, Amarildo, which gave Brazil a narrow victory. The Czechs, who had beaten Spain 1–0 in their opening match, accompanied Brazil into the quarter-finals.

In Santiago, the disgraceful brawl between Chile and Italy overshadowed everything else in Group Two. Trouble had been stirred up by unfavourable articles written about Chile by Italian journalists, but how far the reaction was genuine, how far it was deliberately exaggerated to create a climate in which the Italians could not win, remains obscure.

The tall, sonorous Ken Aston, who sent off two Italians, David and Ferrini, but missed the famous left hook with which Leonel Sanchez broke Maschio's nose, described the match as 'uncontrollable'. Later, the Italians accused the Chilean players of spitting in their faces from the start. Full of *oriundi*, South American born players, like Maschio, Sivori and Altafini (a Brazilian forward in the last World Cup) and deeply defensive, Italy went down 2–0 to the Chileans, drew drearily 0–0 with the hard Germans, and finally beat the Swiss 3–0 when it no longer mattered. West Germany, whose breakaway attacks led by Uwe Seeler were too much for the Chileans, led them into the last eight.

The Russians, at Arica, got there too, surviving a brutally hard game against Yugoslavia in which one of their full-backs had his leg broken. The Russians then beat Uruguay to qualify. Yugoslavia thrashed a now weary Colombian team 5–0 to earn their place in the quarter-finals.

Injury to Peacock meant that at the last moment England had to recall the disappointing Gerry Hitchens, then with Inter-Milan, as centre-forward against the Brazilians. But it was Hitchens who equalised after Greaves had headed against the bar, the irrepressible Garrincha having outjumped even the towering Maurice Norman to head the first goal from a corner. Springett's fine save from Amarildo, after Flowers had unaccountably passed across his own goal, make it the sadder that he should twice have been caught napping from long range in the second half, once when Garrincha diabolically curved in by the

right-hand post to make it 3–1.

The Yugoslavs for once got the better of their rivals West Germany in a fierce game in Santiago. Dragoslav Sekularac, their swarthy inside-forward, played well, as did Radakovic, the right-half, who scored the goal. It was four minutes from time when the little right-half, his head bandaged, smashed in Galic's pass to give Yugoslavia revenge for their defeat in the 1958 quarter-final.

Chile had to go up to Arica to play and beat the Russians; after which the streets of Santiago went wild with celebrations, cars honking the 'Viva Chile!' theme. Yashin had his second poor game, conceding a goal to Leonel Sanchez's free kick, then to a 35-yard drive by Chile's hard-shooting left-half, Eladio Rojas. Rojas was the Chilean engine in midfield, in partnership with the equally hard-shooting inside-forward, Toro.

The Czechs encountered the Hungarians at Rancagua, and won—thanks to Schroiff. His brilliant goalkeeping, plus a little help from the posts, enabled his team to hold out under tremendous pressure after they had scored early on through the tall inside-right Scherer in one of their very few breakaways.

Below: *The make-up of FIFA the game's controlling body. FIFA is split into six federations and the area of the world each federation represents is shown on the left. The four columns illustrate how unevenly power is distributed within FIFA. For example, seventy-five per cent of all players from countries belonging to FIFA are Europeans, while just six per cent are from Asia and Africa; Europe contains over fifty per cent of the professionals, Africa and Asia together only claim twelve per cent; yet the Afro-Asian block commands over half of the 140 votes in FIFA, while Europe can muster only 33. The apportioning of the 16 World Cup places among the six federations became a subject of contentious debate during the 1960s.*

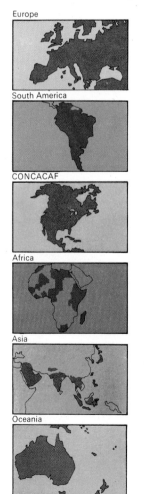

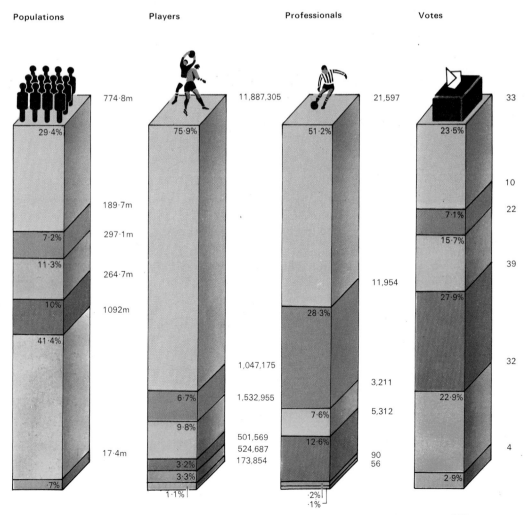

Top: *England's opening game in the 1962 World Cup finals was against Hungary in Rancagua. The handful of people who watched the match saw England get off to a poor start—losing 2–1.*
Here Johnny Haynes watches despairingly as his shot sails harmlessly over the Hungarian bar.
Above: *Referee Ken Aston decides that Italy's Ferrini should take no further part in the match with Chile.*
Italy not only lost the game 2–0 but also had David sent off as well.

Top: *In sharp contrast to the empty stand at Rancagua, Santiago is packed for the semi-final*
between hosts Chile and Brazil. Despite fanatical support,
Chile lost 4–2 and Brazil were the eventual winners.
Above: *The West Germans won Group 2, dropping only one point. That*
was in a dreary 0–0 draw with Italy, when even the opportunist
Uwe Seeler, in the second of his four World Cups,
flinging himself bravely to head for goal could not break the deadlock.

In the semi-finals, Brazil and the irresistible Garrincha majestically annihilated Chile. The goals Garrincha scored were wonderfully varied; a tremendous left-footer after nine minutes, another marvellous, leaping header from a corner that made it 2–0. Both showed talents which had lain unsuspected in 1958. Toro reduced the lead with a tremendous right-footed free kick, but just after the interval, the ever brave, aggressive Vava headed in Garrincha's corner. 3–1 down, Chile again came back into the game when Leonel Sanchez scored from a penalty, but the tireless Zagalo crossed for Vava to head another and seal the game.

The Czechs, those dark horses, won again, by no less than 3–1, beating the Yugoslavs at Vina del Mar before a mere 5000 (everybody was concentrating on the Santiago semi-final). Schroiff was again the Czech hero, and though they were weak on the wings, the Czechs nonetheless had most of the play and took the lead, through Kadraba. Jerkovic bustled through to equalise for Yugoslavia. However, two goals by Scherer, one a penalty, put the Czechs in their first World Cup final since 1934.

The match for third place out of the way —Chile won it 1–0 with a deflected shot from Rojas against an uninterested Yugoslav side—the stage was set for the final. The jog-trotting Czechs began beautifully when Scherer's clever diagonal ball put Masopust through for a pretty goal. Alas, Schroiff was doomed to a wretched game. He should have had Amarildo's equaliser from an 'impossible' angle, while late in the game he lost Djalma Santos' high lob in the blinding sun and dropped the ball for Vava to make it 3–1. Meanwhile, Amarildo, having a splendid game, had whipped past his man on the byeline in the second half to make the second Brazilian goal for Zito.

All in all, the Czechs had neither the pace nor the penetration to get through a Brazilian defence in which Nilton Santos looked cool as ice. Brazil, though slower than in 1958, had shown triumphantly that they were no one-man team; even if, at times, the one man who changed everything was Garrincha. He had put them on the hat-trick.

England returned from their fourth failure in four World Cups to compete in the newly formed European Nations competition. Their first tie, the home leg against France, ended in a dismal 1–1 draw. The low ebb of Chile had dropped even lower. And when the second leg took place in Paris early in 1963 Walter Winterbottom no longer acted as manager.

The selectors had stumbled upon a new name. Alf Ramsey, who watched the return Parisian debacle (England lost 5–2) with feelings approaching cold terror, had been but third choice as Winterbottom's replacement. He could not have taken over at a more demoralising point, but his single-mindedness and professional approach provided the perfect panacea, though many a toe that trod the carpets at Lancaster Gate was to be bruised by his tread.

By 1963, England had proved also-rans in international competition. The myth of pre-War invincibility had been shattered, particularly by the South American successes at world level and of course by Hungary. The need for a saviour was intense. It was time for Ramsey to walk on the water.

7th WORLD CUP Chile, 1962

Group 1

Uruguay	(0)2	Colombia	(1)1
Cubilla, Sasia		Zaluaga	
USSR	(0)2	Yugoslavia	(0)0
Ivanov, Ponedelnik			
Yugoslavia	(2)3	Uruguay	(1)1
Skoblar, Galic, Jerkovic		Cabrera	
USSR	(3)4	Colombia	(1)4
Ivanov 2, Chislenko, Ponedelnik		Aceros, Coll, Rada, Klinger	
USSR	(1)2	Uruguay	(0)1
Mamikin, Ivanov		Sasia	
Yugoslavia	(2)5	Colombia	(0)0
Galic, Jerkovic 3, Melic			

	P	W	D	L	F	A	Pts
USSR	3	2	1	0	8	5	5
Yugoslavia	3	2	0	1	8	3	4
Uruguay	3	1	0	2	4	6	2
Colombia	3	0	1	2	5	11	1

Group 2

Chile	(1)3	Switzerland	(1)1
Sanchez (L) 2, Ramirez		Wuthrich	
West Germany	(0)0	Italy	(0)0
Chile	(0)2	Italy	(0)0
Ramirez, Toro			
West Germany	(1)2	Switzerland	(1)1
Brulls, Seeler		Schneiter	
West Germany	(1)2	Chile	(0)0
Szymaniak (pen), Seeler			
Italy	(1)3	Switzerland	(0)0
Mora, Bulgarelli 2			

	P	W	D	L	F	A	Pts
West Germany	3	2	1	0	4	1	5
Chile	3	2	0	1	5	3	4
Italy	3	1	1	1	3	2	3
Switzerland	3	0	0	3	2	8	0

Group 3

Brazil	(0)2	Mexico	(0)0
Zagalo, Pele			
Czechoslovakia	(0)1	Spain	(0)0
Stibranyi			
Brazil	(0)0	Czechoslovakia	(0)0
Spain	(0)1	Mexico	(0)0
Peiro			
Brazil	(0)2	Spain	(1)1
Amarildo 2		Adelardo	
Mexico	(2)3	Czechoslovakia	(1)1
Diaz, Del Aguila, Hernandez (H) (pen)		Masek	

	P	W	D	L	F	A	Pts
Brazil	3	2	1	0	4	1	5
Czechoslovakia	3	1	1	1	2	3	3
Mexico	3	1	0	2	3	4	2
Spain	3	1	0	2	2	3	2

Group 4

Argentina	(1)1	Bulgaria	(0)0
Facundo			
Hungary	(1)2	England	(0)1
Tichy, Albert		Flowers (pen)	
England	(2)3	Argentina	(0)0
Flowers (pen), Charlton, Greaves		Sanfilippo	
Hungary	(4)6	Bulgaria	(0)0
Albert 3, Tichy 2, Solymosi		Sokolov	
Argentina	(0)0	Hungary	(0)0
England	(0)0	Bulgaria	(0)0

	P	W	D	L	F	A	Pts
Hungary	3	2	1	0	8	2	5
England	3	1	1	1	4	3	3
Argentina	3	1	1	1	2	3	3
Bulgaria	3	0	1	2	1	7	1

Quarter-finals

Yugoslavia	(0)1	West Germany	(0)0
Radakovic			
Brazil	(1)3	England	(1)1
Garrincha 2, Vava		Hitchens	
Chile	(2)2	USSR	(1)1
Sanchez (L), Rojas		Chislenko	
Czechoslovakia	(1)1	Hungary	(0)0
Scherer			

Semi-finals

Brazil	(2)4	Chile	(1)2
Garrincha 2, Vava 2		Toro, Sanchez (L) (pen)	
Czechoslovakia	(0)3	Yugoslavia	(0)1
Kadraba, Scherer 2 (1 pen)		Jerkovic	

Third place match: Santiago

Chile	(0)1	Yugoslavia	(0)0
Rojas			

Final: Santiago 17.6.62
Attendance 69,068

Brazil	(1)3	Czechoslovakia	(1)1
Amarildo, Zito, Vava		Masopust	

Brazil: Gylmar; Santos (D), Santos (N); Zito, Mauro, Zozimo; Garrincha, Didi, Vava, Amarildo, Zagalo

Czechoslovakia: Schroiff; Tichy, Novak; Pluskal, Popluhar, Masopust; Pospichal, Scherer, Kvasnak, Kadraba, Jelinek

Referee: Latychev (USSR)

Leading scorers: 4—Albert (Hungary)
Ivanov (USSR)
Sanchez (Chile)
Garrincha (Brazil)
Jerkovic (Yugoslavia)
Vava (Brazil)

THE EUROPEAN GAME
Europe 1955-1976

'Hail Wolves—Champions of the World', screamed the headlines one grey December morning in 1954. Wolverhampton Wanderers had recovered from a two-goal deficit to beat Honved of Budapest, a significant event maybe, but hardly justifying such an outburst of British chauvinism.

Much of the euphoria stemmed from the make-up of the Hungarian team. Puskas, Kocsis and four others had been in the national side which had twice slaughtered England, scoring thirteen goals, in the previous thirteen months. But Wolves had been favoured by conditions and had had

more incentive than their opponents (who were simply on a European jaunt), and had survived a number of goal-mouth escapes earlier in the game. While British eyes viewed the result through rose-tinted spectacles, more objectivity was revealed elsewhere in Europe.

The most far-sighted reaction came from France. In the daily sports paper *L'Equipe*, the editor, Gabriel Hanot, decried the over-reaction of the English. He wrote: 'We must wait for Wolves to visit Moscow or Budapest before we proclaim their invincibility. There are other clubs of international prowess, notably Milan and Real Madrid

Below: *The mystique of Moscow Dynamo when they toured England in October 1945 provided a magnetic attraction for crowds totally unused to contests against European club sides. For the first game of the tour, an estimated 100,000, the largest attendance ever at an English club ground, crammed into Stamford Bridge. The final total was never recorded as the gates were broken down. Chelsea and Dynamo drew 3–3.*

to name but two. . .' Prophetic words.

Hanot's opinion had no emptiness. The next day the paper devoted much space to outline plans for a European tournament, in which patriotic boasts could be put to the test. It was not an original thought; there had already been international competitions like the Mitropa Cup before the Second World War which featured the leading club sides in Austria, Czechoslovakia, Hungary, Yugoslavia and later Switzerland, Italy and Rumania. And after the War France, Italy, Spain and Portugal played one another for the Latin Cup. But *L'Equipe*'s plan provided for the whole of Europe, and Gabriel Hanot called for the support of the European Union of Football Associations.

This campaign from France originated an entirely new era in football. Not only did EUFA accept the proposal except for the name—EUFA preferred European Champion Clubs' Cup to Hanot's European Cup, which they wanted to keep for a national sides' competition—but in their acceptance they took a step which certainly cracked and even broke down much of the traditional insularity of top-class club football. Aided by the parallel development of floodlighting, which made practicable the extra fixtures which had to be played in midweek, the European Champion Clubs' Cup became a tremendous success—though officials might have been a little peeved that their lengthy nomenclature was immediately shortened into the European Cup.

As the European dream became reality, the commercial prospects of international club competition were not lost on the continent's leading participants. Before the end of the decade, the European Cup Winners' Cup and the Inter-Cities Fairs Cup had been instituted as spin-off tournaments, while in 1958 the first official contest between national sides, the European Nations Cup, began its life-span. Oddly, the actual name European Cup has never been utilised.

But for club football, the so-called European Cup itself has always been the blue riband event for which the prize, apart from the enormous silver trophy, is the prestige of being *the* most successful club side in the continent. And the first twenty years of its history provided some very salutory experiences for those nations who might have been expected to dominate —England (so fond of proclaiming its League as being the best in the world) with just one winner over that period, West Germany with only a single finalist before Bayern Munich's triumphs of 1974 and 1975, Italy with only the exploits of the two Milan clubs to cheer them; Eastern Europe

ES THE GREAT!

AD THE NELSON SPIRIT

By BOB FERRIER

AIN! AFTER SPARTAK, HONVED. WOLVES BEAT
NIGHT.

or a moment. Wolves beat Honved, champions of Hun-
est club side in the world, in one of the most glorious
een.

—furious speed, blinding skill, pounding power, super-
and something more.

It had, from Wolves, a strange,
scarcely describable bulldog spirit, the
Nelson spirit, that unquenchable moral
courage and faith in themselves that
now seems to be Wolves' copyright.

After the greatest first half I have ever
seen, in which the Hungarians played
brilliantly and proved themselves master
footballers, Wolves summoned up
apparently superhuman reserves of
strength and courage to grind Honved
into the Molineux mud.

It was a truly magnificent performance
in one of the greatest matches ever
played anywhere.

Now Wolves, who have clearly become
the Arsenal of the mid-century, can
rightly claim themselves club champions of the world.

Penalty Incident

The match turned on an incident four
minutes after half-time, when referee Reg
Leafe gave Wolves a penalty.

Left back Kovacs ran Hancocks off the
ball in the penalty area. To me it
merited nothing more than an indirect
kick for obstruction.

The decision horrified Honved, but not
Hancocks, who hammered the goal at fiery
pace past Farago to make the score 2–1.

Molineux was a morass of mud. Surely
the Hungarian artistry would be drowned
in it, but it took them five minutes to
refute that . . . only ten minutes to
score. Mathos tried to cross a ball which
hit Flowers. The referee said "foul."
Puskas took the free kick and there was
Kocsis, best header of a ball in football,
sending it true and bullet-like past
Williams.

And two minutes later, Kocsis was
sending centre forward Mathos through
on a brilliant pass to hit a screaming,
swerving shot past Williams.

Defeat Spurned

But with a majesty that spurned de-
featism, Wolves plunged into furious
attack. Farago made fabulous saves from
Hancocks, Broadbent, Swinbourne, Wilshaw, Smith and Flowers from all angles.

Then came Hancocks's penalty goal
Wolves were back in the game with a
bang and Honved failed temperamentally,
often kicking wildly to touch

With fifteen minutes left, with Puskas
worried, the peak point of the drama was
reached.

Wilshaw made a long, determined
thrust down the left wing, crossed to
Swinbourne. The young centre forward's header beat Farago all the way.
Within two minutes, Shorthouse sent
down the wing to Smith, a perfect pass
inside, and then a blistering shot from
Swinbourne.

What a golden double for Wolves!
With these results, Wolves have made
English football once again a power in
the world game.

game like it

says PETER WILSON

suitably
eparted
nt and
Volver-
e to
pres-
as low
ty-five

defence
a k l v
There

ing no
ly no
d been

he ball
jersey
th the
a split
e kick.

e the
panc

stations for the Hun-
garians

The football was not so
good as it had been, but
Honved never got their
domination back again and
were guilty of the most
childish attempts at time-
wasting.

It was like two strong
men trying to grip each
other's hands hard enough
to make the other beg for
mercy.

And suddenly you
realised that it was the
Hungarians who were
wriggling and shifting
and trying to get out of
the hold.

And for the first time
you hoped, you thought—

no, you KNEW . . . THAT
THE WOLVES HAD GOT
'EM.

The equaliser came from
Swinbourne's head but the
back-room architects had
been Wilshaw and Slater.

And before you could get
your breath back, or the
sweat out of your eyes—
yes, despite this raw,
clammy night you were
sweating now—Swinbourne
had done it again.

There was still nearly
ten minutes to go and with
less than two Honved
nearly—oh! so very nearly
—equalised through Csibor

But somehow you
couldn't believe that
these titanic Wolves
could lose it now.

I may never live to see a
greater thriller than this
And if I see many more as
thrilling I may not live
much longer anyway

in vain.

home.

scores the winner.

Interval chat by Cullis
—then team are inspired

AFTER-THE-MATCH
quotes:

STAN CULLIS,
Wolves' manager: "We
played better than
against Spartak. We
had to. The match was
the most exciting I have
ever seen. I had a chat
with Billy Wright at half-
time, and, after that, he
and the rest of the team
were inspired."

BILLY WRIGHT,
Wolves' captain: "It was
good to gain revenge for
England's defeat at
Wembley . . . it was a
wonderful achievement
by a wonderful team."

DENIS WILSHAW:
"It was the greatest
game in which I have
ever played."

GUSTAV SEBES:
Hungarian Deputy Minis-
ter of Sport: "We were

beaten. That is all there
is to know."

Chelsea's match with
Red Banner, the Hun-
garian club, tomorrow
WILL be televised. The
Football League had ob-
jected because of the
effect on attendances at
two F.A. Cup replays.

Milan, who play West
Ham tonight, arrived at
London Airport last
night. Manager Vittore
Purricelli said: "It
doesn't matter if we lose.
What is important is
that the football should
be good."

Left: *The chauvinistic
headlines that helped spawn the
European Cup. Reacting to
such boastful claims about the
status of Wolverhampton
Wanderers after their defeats
of Moscow Spartak and
Honved of Budapest, the
French sports paper* L'Equipe
*proposed a European
competition to settle the
arguments. EUFA accepted the
idea and the European Cup
was born.*

could gloat only of the achievement of Partizan Belgrade, losing finalists in 1966.

Retrospective analysis gave considerable authority to the argument that European competition of the very highest calibre suited the top teams of nations whose players did not face the unrelenting demands of a highly competitive league programme—Spain, Portugal, Holland and and even Scotland provided extremely successful teams who could gear themselves towards a European Cup tie in the reasonable certainty that the fixture was not wedged between two high-pressure games in their own leagues.

If France lit the blue touch paper of the European Cup, it was Spain who provided the explosion—in the exhilarating shape of the football of Real Madrid. The champions of Spain became champions of Europe for the opening five years of the competition—a record that surely will stand for all time. Certainly they had advantages; for one they emerged triumphant from a field of just sixteen clubs who explored the first European experience in the initial contest of 1955–56; in the 1975–76 version 32 clubs set out on that road. For another they enjoyed the advantage of a system in Spain which permitted and encouraged foreign players in club teams. Argentinians, Brazilians, Frenchmen, and Hungarians would find their places alongside the most talented Spaniards.

Yet, despite the glossy overtone of a club purchasing success, Real Madrid built their European Cup sides with an extremely shrewd business sense. Their key player, the hub of their every move and arguably the greatest player of his generation, was the Argentinian Alfredo di Stefano. Yet the deal which brought di Stefano from Bogota's Los Millionarios for a mere £10,000 was the equivalent of securing Johan Cruyff in his heyday on a free transfer. Even di Stefano's splendid achievement of scoring in each of his first five European Cup finals fails to encapsulate his overall value to Real.

Later Real emphasised their nose for a sound deal when they obtained the services of the same Ferenc Puskas who had taunted England and, indeed, every other country he had played against—for nothing. Puskas had been on yet another Honved tour when the 1956 revolution had broken out in his homeland; he had stayed on in the West, virtually out of football, almost penniless and very overweight, until Real gambled on an approach and were warmly rewarded.

The first European Cup tie was played on 4 September 1955 between Sporting Club Lisbon and Partizan Belgrade; just

Above: *Another example of the patriotic fervour which greeted Wolves' win over Honved, and which was heightened by the inclusion in the opposition of names like Puskas, Kocsis, Czibor, Boszik, Lorant and Budai who had taunted England at Wembley.*

European Champion Clubs' Cup Winners

Glasgow
Celtic
1967

Manchester
United
1968

Feyenoord
Rotterdam
1970

Ajax
Amsterdam
1971, 1972

AC Milan
1963, 1969

Internazionale Milan
1964, 1965

Benfica Lisbon
1961, 1962

Real Madrid
1956, 1957, 1958,
1959, 1960, 1966

four days later Real set out on a European adventure in which they would not lose an aggregate tie for five years and in which the champagne of their football would intoxicate a continent.

There was a panache about that initial year which would fade as the European Cup grew in size and therefore prestige. One hundred and twenty seven goals were scored in a mere twenty nine games, and as a reward to those Frenchmen whose inventive campaigning had provided the stimulus the final was staged in Paris. Forty thousand people paid around £20,000 to watch the game—many of them attracted by the presence of Reims but others in curiosity at this new departure. All left the stadium well aware of the status

Above: *The first 17 winners of the European Cup; most striking is how often the winners came from countries with relatively few top-class clubs.*

victims of this new need to travel across the continent.

After Real had raised high their second trophy, beating Fiorentina with goals from di Stefano and the fleet-of-foot left-winger Francisco Gento, Manchester United mounted another challenge. A 3–3 draw in Belgrade against the Red Star club ensured their place in the semi-final for the second successive year. But arguably the most tragic piece of football history unfolded when the plane which took off from Belgrade never reached Manchester. It lay shattered on the outskirts of Munich Airport, crashing on take-off after a re-fuelling stop. Amid much personal tragedy England lost a team capable of stopping the march of Madrid and also the few hopes of a successful World Cup in Sweden that year.

Eight players died—Roger Byrne, Tommy Taylor, Duncan Edwards, David Pegg (all England internationals). Geoffrey Bent, Eddie Colman, Mark Jones and Liam Whelan. Two more—Jackie Blanchflower and Johnny Berry—never played again. United also lost their secretary, Walter Crickmer, trainer, Tom Curry, and coach, Bert Whalley. Among the other dozen fatalities were eight newsmen.

United inevitably lost an emotional semi-final to AC Milan, after an inspired but all too narrow win in the home leg. And the Italians provided sufficient defensive resilience to hold Real goalless for an hour of the final in Brussels. Moreover they counter-attacked to take the lead, but di Stefano cast his shadow again to equalise, and after another exchange of scores Gento shot the extra-time decider.

In 1959 in Stuttgart Real chalked up victory number four—again beating Reims though Raymond Kopa, the stylish forward who had led the Reims attack in 1956, had by now been signed by Real. He did not score—Mateos and di Stefano were the marksmen in the 2–0 victory—nor was his stay with the club to be prosperous. Like another supreme artiste, the Brazilian Didi, he did not gell with di Stefano. The Argentinian gave short shrift to those who challenged his authority and they were quickly out of the team and the club. It might have been a similar path for Ferenc Puskas, who had been used to conducting his own orchestras for Honved and Hungary, but Puskas exhibited an astuteness which ensured his survival.

In his first season with Real, he had hardly endeared himself to di Stefano; indeed the pair raced neck and neck for the leading scorer's title, a claim di Stefano regarded as a right. In the last game Puskas

of Real Madrid.

Fortified by the partisan crowd, Reims led by two goals before di Stefano embroidered his own design on the game. He scored to begin a recovery which only faltered when the French champions led again at 3–2 but which climaxed in a winning goal by inside-forward Rial for Real. The new trophy had begun its annual pilgrimage to Madrid.

In 1956, Manchester United became the first of the Football League clubs to compete—the previous season the League had banned Chelsea's participation claiming to fear fixture congestion. England was just one of several new nations to send forward their champions as the umbrella of the Cup began to widen. United excelled, putting ten goals past Anderlecht in a stunning early round performance, but could not overcome Real in the semi-final where di Stefano's expertise proved too much for the precocious promise of the Busby Babes—promise that was never to be wholly fulfilled as eight players became

Far left: *The widening of horizons for European football and for Real Madrid. Jonquet (left) and Munoz, the captains of Reims and Real, undergo the formalities at the start of the first European Cup final. Real won a fluctuating game 4–3 in front of 40,000.*

Left: *Denis Viollet, a survivor of Munich, scores in Manchester United's 2–1 win over AC Milan in the first leg of the 1957–58 European Cup semi-final, United's first European tie after the tragedy. United lost the return 4–0 and had to wait ten years before becoming the first English club to win the trophy.*

raced through on his own, dribbled round the goalkeeper, but scorned the open goal —instead rolling the ball across for di Stefano to score. The gesture accepted, the two individuals became a pair and masterminded a Real performance in what was to become the definitive European Cup final.

Real's opponents in 1960 were Eintracht Frankfurt, who had announced their pedigree by scoring six times in *each* leg of the semi-final and in doing so ended the hopes of Rangers appearing in a home final, which was to be played at Glasgow's Hampden Park. In their semi-final Real had, thoughbeit temporarily, halted the rise of their local rivals Barcelona and it was as if those two electric ties had sharpened the edge for the final.

The enormous crowd in that vast stadium (127,621—the largest for a European final) were to see a match in which every move would remain etched on their memory. Eintracht contributed three exciting goals, the first from Kress giving them a stunning lead; Real replied with seven, four for Puskas and three for di Stefano, all the products of marvellous team-work in which the left-foot shooting of Puskas and the generalship of di Stefano were unrivalled. The match provided a perfect climax to the first five years of the competition and indeed, as it transpired, to the reign of Real.

For a quirk of the draw paired Real, who qualified as holders, and Barcelona, as Spanish League champions, in the first round of the 1960–61 tournament. The pretenders to the throne earned a 2–2 draw in Madrid with a last-minute penalty awarded by English referee Arthur Ellis and converted by Suarez. And amid fervour in the second leg Barcelona defended desperately but scored twice against a single reply from the right-winger Canario. The Kings were

dead, but Barcelona were not to ascend to the throne.

Remarkably the history of the European Cup falls into distinct geographical phases and though Real, with a home-produced team of whom only Gento of the old guard remained, were to rise again briefly and win a sixth title in 1966, the Spanish era had ended. Nonetheless, the Iberian flavour remained. Barcelona, inspired by the Hungarian triumvirate of Kocsis, Czibor and Kubala, did reach the final but the trophy slipped through their fingers—or more specifically the fingers of their goalkeeper Ramallets who made two severe errors— and went to the Portuguese champions Benfica.

Even the Lisbon club was surprised at its success, but the following season Benfica produced consistent flair and imagination to prove themselves very worthy followers in the footsteps of Real. Now strengthened by the inclusion of an elastic forward from Mozambique, Eusebio, they faced a challenging defence of their trophy in the semifinal against Tottenham Hotspur, England's double champions of League and Cup. After a 3–1 win in Lisbon they defied and denied Spurs in an atmosphere that had the popular papers renaming the London club's ground 'White Hot Lane'.

In the final they faced all the experience of Real Madrid, and in a spectacular night in Amsterdam trailed 3–2 at half-time to a hat-trick from Puskas. But the masters of the fifties were by now an ageing side and that night belonged to youth as Eusebio inspired a Benfica recovery and then with his own boots gunned down the illustrious opposition. But a year later he was to experience the pain of defeat as Benfica lost a third consecutive final to AC Milan and two goals from the Brazilian Jose Altafini

In their own stadium Real Madrid defend against Fiorentina in the 1957 European Cup final. Real retained the Cup 2–0.

—after Eusebio had given the holders the lead. The European Cup had entered its Italian phase.

It was an era which gave little credit to the competition. In 1964 and 1965 Internazionale of Milan outdefended their rivals and became champions of Europe with the miserly total of 16 and 15 goals in the respective seasons. In Suarez, Mazzola and Jair, the Brazilian forward, they possessed players of outstanding offensive ability, but coach Helenio Herrera built Inter's success on defensive discipline, organisation and cynical play. In the 1964 final they actually scored three times—two from Mazzola—to underline Real Madrid's failing battle with the passage of time; Puskas and di Stefano were playing in their ultimate final. But a more characteristic Italian victory came the following year; in their own San Siro stadium they met Benfica with the odds heavily stacked in their favour. But, leading through a Jair goal, they refused to budge from their cautious approach—even when the Portuguese lost their goalkeeper Costa Pereira. The inevitable 1–0 victory did the European game a great disservice.

After the revamped Real Madrid had won in 1966, Great Britain had its brief but memorable moments of ascendancy, Scotland providing a side to become the first non-Latin winners. Jock Stein's Celtic were the very antithesis of Inter-Milan—a team which pieced together infinite varieties of

attacking play; if Wallace, Chalmers and Lennox were strong running strikers and Auld and Johnstone elusive creators, the goals were equally likely to arrive from left-back Gemmell, centre-half McNeill or wing-half Murdoch.

The 1967 final had all the ingredients of melodrama. Celtic, everybody's favourites because of their attacking philosophies, met the respected but unloved Inter in Lisbon where many of the neutrals had bitter memories of Benfica's defeat in Milan two years earlier. Inter had their dream start, scoring from a penalty in the opening minutes and sat back for their familiar and expert defence of a one-goal lead. But Celtic's unrelenting pressure finally revealed a flaw: Gemmell equalised and then Chalmers touched in a Murdoch shot. Optimism had triumphed over cynicism.

The brief reign of the British continued for just one more season. Manchester United, too, succeeded with enterprising values, but their's was more than a triumph for eleven men; it became a monument to the devastation of Munich ten years earlier. Benfica reached the final again, and, as in 1965, were unfortunate enough to face a team in its own land. But the Wembley crowd were silenced when Graça equalised a header from Bobby Charlton and bellowed their relief as Stepney plunged at Eusebio's feet to thwart a seemingly certain winner. But once George Best had fashioned a super individual goal, United ended extra time in a convincing flourish with goals from Kidd and Charlton. A classic match and an emotional victory.

By now the balance of power had begun another shift. In thirteen seasons Holland had provided not one semi-finalist; now her leading teams, Ajax and Feijenoord, were to figure in the next five years with increasing impressiveness. Once more it was an instance of clubs with relatively easy League programmes arriving fresh and wholly committed to a European challenge, though there can be no minimising the talents of Cruyff, Neeskens and Keizer of Ajax and the likes of Israel and Van Hanegem from Feijenoord.

Ajax lost the 1969 final to AC Milan after scoring prolifically throughout the earlier rounds, and then retired to watch Feijenoord become the first Dutch winners, though their winning goal over Celtic came from a Swede, Ove Kindvall. Celtic's performance was a great disappointment. But Ajax were to become the team of the seventies in much the same manner as Real Madrid in the fifties. In an intensely competitive arena they strung together a hat-trick of victories—over Panathinaikos, managed by Ferenc Puskas, 2–0, over Inter Milan by the same margin, with Cruyff at the height of his powers scoring both goals, and then in a disappointing final over Juventus by a solitary goal.

Inter's progress to the 1972 final was one of the most remarkable in the history of the tournament. They lost an early game 7–1 to Borussia Monchengladbach, Boninsegna having been hit by a Coca-Cola can and Corso being sent off for kicking the referee. Their protest about the Coca-Cola can was upheld and they drew a replay in Berlin to go through. Not content with this, there followed all the other escapist variations available to non-winning teams.

In the quarter-finals Inter went through on away goals against Standard Liege, in the semis on penalties after two goalless draws against Celtic. 'Dixie' Deans was the Glaswegian's culprit. Inter managed to avoid having to toss a coin, but observers were forced to ask themselves whether (and if so, why) the European gods were smiling on this most negative of sides. They got no sympathy from Ajax in the final, however.

Ajax deserved their triumphs. They fielded a team of all-round players in which the defenders possessed such complete skills that they were never embarrassed or inhibited to find themselves in creative positions or at the fulcrum of an attacking move. The Amsterdam side in full cry became a stimulating sight with Cruyff the di Stefano of his era, yet the team had learned how to defend after their 4–1 caning in the 1969 final and they conceded only two goals in six semi-finals, and none in three finals, during those hat-trick years.

But in 1973 Ajax lost in the first round and Cruyff spread his wings to join Barcelona, for an astounding £922,000. And the following year West Germany had only its second finalist. In Brussels Bayern Munich, with eight West German internationals, a Swede and a Dane, trailed to Atletico Madrid until the very last minute of normal time when the central defender Schwarzenbeck equalised with a long low drive. Bayern accepted the reprieve, survived extra time and stormed through the replay two days later with two goals each from Hoeness and Müller. Their brinks-

Against the backcloth of the new Atomium in Brussels, AC Milan took Real Madrid to extra time in the 1958 European Cup final. Indeed, the Italian champions had twice led during the first ninety minutes, but first di Stefano and then Rial equalised. Gento's winner in the extra period brought the Spanish side their hat-trick of wins.

manship remained the following year when they survived a controversial disallowed goal and a confident penalty appeal to score twice against Leeds United. The Leeds supporters, in a mindless expression of their disappointment, wrecked areas of the Paris stadium and the immediate environs, disgusting behaviour which resulted in EUFA banning Leeds from European competition for an unwelcome period.

Violence off and on the field had become a sorry feature of the first twenty years of European tournaments, particularly as the prizes to be gained by victory and the prices to be paid in defeat grew greater and greater. But much of the sourness surrounded the Inter-Cities Fairs Cup which became littered with unpalatable incidents during a history beginning as a competition for cities staging international trade fairs and developed into a money-spinning contest which brought retitling to European Fairs Cup, in 1966, and then EUFA Cup, in 1971.

The first competition, started in 1955, took three years to complete; the second spread over two years. London entered a composite side, while the city of Birmingham was represented by the players of Birmingham City. Indeed, the Midlands club featured rather unpleasantly in the early acrimony; by 1961 eight of their players had been sent off against foreign opposition, a record which owed as much to a lack of acceptance of the British aggressive style of play as to any calculated physical violence.

Although the tournament was to become dominated by English clubs in its later years it would not have been surprising if clubs had opted out after some of the in-

timidation of the sixties. Chelsea featured in the prime example. At Stamford Bridge in 1965 they had achieved a creditable first round first leg win against AS Roma 4–1, an achievement marred only by the sending-off of Eddie McCreadie for retaliation, and a gradual increase of sourness during the game.

By the time Chelsea reached Rome for the return, the Italian press had drummed up hostility with reports which described the Chelsea players as 'killers'. The home supporters, inflamed at such news, journeyed to the ground prepared to cause trouble, and when the Chelsea party made their routine pre-match inspection of the playing surface they were pelted with rubbish—a reception which was repeated with even more uproar when they reappeared in their playing kit. No practice balls had been provided for their warm-up, and when they approached the Roma players for one the request was aggressively denied.

In the match itself, Chelsea faced not just the threat of maiming tackles but also of more debris—two players were in fact laid out by flying bottles. In the stand the rest of the party endured a succession of indignities, culminating in the bursting over them of balloons filled with urine. After a courageous goalless draw had been obtained, the team coach was smashed by Roma fans as it left the ground. Roma were banned from Europe for two years.

In unquestionably the most exhilarating European final, at Hampden Park in 1960, Real won their fifth successive crown.
Right: *Kress climaxes a flowing move to give Eintracht a lead in the 20th minute.*
Above right and far right: *Alfredo di Stefano, at the peak of his powers, scoring two of his three goals in the match. Ferenc Puskas claimed Real's other four in the 7–3 extravaganza.*

In another Anglo-Italian battle, the players of Lazio and Arsenal slugged punches at each other by the road side at the end of a post-match banquet in Italy. The feud continued into the second leg when five Italian players were booked at Highbury. And Lazio were in trouble again in the same competition when Ipswich ran the gauntlet of their players and their crowd in 1973. Fortunately, they suffered heavily from another ban for they were denied a place in the European Cup after winning the Italian championship.

Barcelona won the first final, beating a London side which contained players from Arsenal, Spurs, West Ham, Chelsea, Brentford and Fulham, dominating 6–0 at home after drawing 2–2 at Stamford Bridge. And they continued to dominate England with a comfortable win over Birmingham to retain the trophy. The Latin domination of the early years of the European Cup was

Above: *In 1963 Wembley staged its first final of the European Cup. Then Benfica, the champions of Portugal, lost to AC Milan and to two goals from their centre-forward Altafini.*

Right: *Sandor Kocsis turns away after scoring one of his four goals against Wolves at Molineux in the 1960 European Cup quarter-finals. Barcelona annihilated the Football League champions 9–2 on aggregate and brought to the surface the first serious doubts about the quality of English football. Previously, Manchester United had more than held their own in Europe.*

also reflected in the results in the Fairs Cup.

Birmingham were again beaten finalists in 1961, losing to Roma. And as the competition swelled its numbers and became an annual football battle (in more than one sense) there were wins for Valencia in 1962 and 1963, Real Zaragoza in 1964, and Barcelona in 1966. Major opposition came in the first significant challenge from the Iron Curtain nations; Dynamo Zagreb lost the final in 1963 but won in 1967, while Ferencvaros beat Juventus in 1965.

Zagreb's win came over Leeds United who reached their first final at the outset of ten successive European campaigns which only came to a halt with the sad events of Paris in 1975. Hampered by domestic commitments, Leeds never quite obtained the rewards they promised—notably in 1970 when they charged at three titles, the European Cup, the League and the FA Cup. Amid an orgy of fixture congestion and crippling injuries they faded from the League race, lost to Celtic in the European Cup semi-final, and then were left empty-handed when they lost to Chelsea in the FA Cup after dominating the first leg, which became Wembley's first drawn final.

The Leeds of the mid-sixties was a tough, unappreciated side in which the manager, Don Revie, did not dissuade his players from a resolute physical approach in the heat of the battle. Nor indeed were many

tears shed outside Yorkshire when Leeds appeared to be making a habit of coming second. Yet such an attitude ignored the superb team play of Revie's squad which revolved around the confidence and perception of Collins, Giles and Bremner in midfield—three diminutive men who knew enough about self-defence to ensure that their skills would not be swamped by any opponents seeking to kick them out of a game. Leeds United came of age in Europe and from the experiences, not always pleasant, gained on their travels they be-

Above: *In the 1966–67 final of the European Cup Winners' Cup, played at Nuremberg, Rangers defended solidly against the local favourites Bayern Munich. But the Scottish club finally fell to a winner in extra time scored by Roth and thus failed to complete a dramatic Glasgow double, Celtic having won the European Cup.*
Left: *In 1969, Ajax of Amsterdam gave Europe a foretaste of what was to come by reaching the European Cup final. Though they lost 4–1 to AC Milan in Madrid, they were to return as winners in 1971, 1972 and 1973.*

Right: England's unhappy run in the European Cup was again emphasised in the 1970–71 competition when Everton lost to unfancied Panathinaikos. But the Greek champions revealed their qualities, under the management of Ferenc Puskas, by reaching the final where they lost by two goals to Ajax.

Below right: A missed chance by Peter Marinello contributes to another English defeat as Arsenal go out to Ajax in 1972.

The European Cup failures of the better Football League clubs were one of the most remarkable features of its first two decades—particularly in the light of so many English successes in the minor competitions. Many League champions failed at the penultimate hurdle—Manchester United in 1957, 1958, 1966 and 1969, Spurs in 1962, Liverpool in 1965, Leeds in 1970 and Derby in 1973. But only two, Manchester United in 1968 and Leeds in 1975, actually made the final. The Mancunians' record is quite remarkable—they reached the semi-final stage on each of five attempts during a twelve-year spell.

came a unit of great skill and intense competitiveness.

In 1968 they began six years of English domination of the Fairs Cup by beating Ferencvaros, the only goal by Jones in the first leg being decisive, and they were to win again in 1971 on the away goals rule after scoring twice against Juventus in Turin. In the middle of that sandwich Newcastle United, with a more cavalier approach, and Arsenal joined the roll of winners. Both finals lacked nothing in drama. Newcastle obtained a three-goal advantage from their first leg against Ujpest Dozsa but in Hungary they had sacrificed two of those by half-time; but in

an incredible change of fortune Newcastle scored three times to take the Cup on a 6–2 aggregate. Captain Bobby Moncur scored three of the goals—a notable feat for a central defender.

Arsenal, however, did recover from a mauling away from home. Anderlecht, inspired by the Dutchman Jan Mulder, led 3–0 before a young substitute forward, Ray Kennedy, obtained a vital late reply. At Highbury, another youngster, Eddie Kelly, cut back the deficit, Radford equalised the aggregate and Sammels shot the winner.

As if to emphasise the English superiority *two* Football League clubs met in the 1972 final, the first under the heading of the EUFA Cup. And there was little of the European aroma about the two legs, in which Spurs beat Wolves largely thanks to a virtuoso performance by Chivers in the away match. Much more tension surrounded the following year's final when Liverpool beat Borussia Monchengladbach with more than a little help from the weather. The first leg at Anfield was abandoned early in the first half, but in that brief time Bill Shankly had spotted a weakness in the Germans' defence, and he included the tall Toshack when the game was replayed the following evening to exploit an uncertainty in the air. Toshack met all the high crosses and caused sufficient confusion for Liverpool to win 3–0 and, despite Gunter Netzer, they restricted Monchengladbach to two goals in Germany.

Borussia were to have their moment of satisfaction two years later when they contrived a masterful 5–1 win over Twente Enschede after being held on their own ground. It was a return to sanity following the 1974 final which had been ruined by the petulant and violent reaction of the Spurs supporters to their club's failure to beat Feijenoord. The name had been changed

but some of that early distastefulness provided by the Fairs Cup lived on. So did an increasing dislike of the traditionally fair-minded English supporters in Europe.

In chronology, the European Cup Winners' Cup became the third inter-club competition, though its status fluctuated with that of the Fairs Cup. In the mid-sixties it undoubtedly held the second rank to the European Cup, but later the larger fields and more lucrative purses of the Fairs trophy altered the balance. And whereas a tournament between the Cup winners of each European nation appeared a totally logical concept to English minds, it was not so elsewhere. Few other European nations feted and adored their knock-out competition like the English, and when the Cup Winners Cup was initially proposed in 1958 only six nations cocked an interested ear.

The following year a little campaigning raised that number to ten and on 1 August 1960 ASK Vorwaerts met Red Star Brno in the first tie. Only eight two-legged ties were played before Rangers qualified to meet Fiorentina in the initial final. But a Scottish win evaporated in the face of defeats both home and away to the Italians—a hat-trick of Latin wins in the first year of each of the three European tournaments. And the spice had a similar taste in 1962 when Atletico Madrid beat Fiorentina after a replay. But such little interest had been stimulated in Glasgow, where the first match had been held, that the city refused to stage the replay and it was not until the following September in Stuttgart that Atletico finally set their hands on the Cup.

Tottenham Hotspur became the first English club to win a major European competition in 1963 when a memorable five-goal display in Rotterdam thwarted Atletico Madrid's attempt to retain the

Above left: *Celebrations for Ajax after one of Cruyff's two goals which beat Inter Milan in the 1972 European Cup final.*

Above: *The clock shows that time is running out for Everton as the Panathinaikos players rejoice to a goal by Antoniadis which eliminated England's representatives in the 1970–71 European Cup competition.*

Above: *Brian Kidd and Shay Brennan are the Manchester United players who can only watch as Veron scores for Estudiantes in the second leg of the 1968 World Club Cup Championship. Both legs were fought out in an atmosphere of callousness and bad temper in keeping with the theme of this ill-conceived competition, which was effectively to die when Ajax later refused to take part, fearing for their players' limbs. Veron's goal clinched the tie for the Argentinians.*
Far right: *Allan Clarke of Leeds United gets in his shot despite the attentions of Franz Beckenbauer in the 1975 European Cup final. The night, which had begun so promisingly for Leeds, ended in disaster with a 2–0 defeat and a sickening display of violence from their fans. For Bayern it was part of a remarkable decade and the second of three consecutive European Cup finals. Bayern players—Maier, Schwarzenbeck, Beckenbauer, Breitner, Hoeness and Muller— also formed the core of the West German side which won the European Championship in 1972 and the World Cup in 1974.*

crown. But some of that year's spotlight fell on non-League Bangor City who found themselves in Europe as winners of the Welsh Cup. The part-timers caused a sensation when they beat mighty Naples 2–0 in North Wales, and, had the away goals rule then been in existence, they would have caused an enormous upset. But their 3–1 defeat in Italy earned only a playoff which ended in glorious failure at Highbury where Naples, exuding relief, scored a winner with only five minutes remaining.

Manchester United eliminated Spurs in the first round of the following competition and looked firm favourites to succeed them until they irresponsibly discarded a three-goal advantage over Sporting Lisbon; the Portuguese went on to beat MTK Budapest in the final in Brussels after a replay. But England had another winner in 1965 when West Ham United found a Wembley venue to their liking and beat TSV Munich in a classic display. Moore, Hurst and Peters unveiled the talents that were to enlighten the same stadium in a World Cup context twelve months later, but the goals went to a less heralded name, Alan Sealey.

Liverpool maintained the English challenge in 1966 but lost in the final in extra time to Borussia Dortmund and a freak goal from Libuda. And West Germany shaded Britain the following year, on their own territory; Roth's goal came in extra time and it gave Bayern Munich the margin of victory over Rangers. It was a bitter blow for the Glasgow club in a year in which Celtic won the European Cup and

all three major Scottish titles.

The British interest faded in 1968, although unheralded Cardiff City came within finger-tips of reaching the final. After beating Shamrock Rovers and NAC Breda, they triumphed over Moscow Torpedo in an epic tie; after winning 1–0 at Ninian Park they faced a 3000 mile trek to the easterly, un-European outpost of Tashkent where they held the Russians to one goal and a play-off. In Augsburg a goal from Norman Dean put the Welsh club into the semi-finals and to a dreadful anti-climax. A 1–1 draw in Hamburg seemed to be a large step towards the final but in Cardiff poor goalkeeping allowed the Germans victory. But two goals for AC Milan from Kurt Hamrin, the Swedish World Cup star of 1958 who had scored for Fiorentina in the very first Cup Winners' Cup final, put paid to Hamburg.

Politics intervened in 1969 when the European Cup and the Cup Winners' Cup had their first rounds re-drawn in the light of the Russian invasion of Czechoslovakia. But the beleagured nation still provided the winner of the Cup Winners' Cup when a first half burst from Slovan Bratislava just defeated Barcelona. The following three years belonged to Britain.

Only 10,000 watched in Vienna in 1970 as Manchester City beat Gornik Zabrze with goals from Neil Young and a Francis Lee penalty, indicative of the lack of interest in the competition. But more than four times that number saw Chelsea draw 1–1 in Athens in 1971 with a Real Madrid side which still contained Fancisco Gento. Many of the London supporters had to leave on their charter flights before the replay took place, but Chelsea scored twice in the first half through Dempsey and Osgood and held on to win.

And in 1972 Rangers finally laid hands on the trophy, beating Moscow Dynamo amid such wild scenes of celebration that the Russians objected and Rangers eventually received a temporary European ban. The fervour was understandable. The supporters had endured the apparent abolition of their hopes in the second round when they had beaten Sporting Lisbon on the away goals rule but were made to face a penalty play-off (which they lost) by an unthinking referee; eventually an official ruling put Rangers through. And then the supporters had to face two nail-biting ties against Torino and then Bayern Munich. Stein and Johnston (twice), were the scorers in the final.

The British run ended with a characteristic stroke of ill-luck for Leeds United who were thwarted and eventually beaten, more by some sinisterly inept refereeing than by

AC Milan; after a final gesture of frustration Norman Hunter was sent off and the referee was later banned by his national association. But Milan themselves were the losers in 1974 when East Germany, through FC Magdeburg, won its first European trophy. And the stock of Eastern Europe had never been higher than in 1975 Dinamo Kiev, whose side was also the Russian national team, beat Ferencvaros in an exhilarating display in which their forward Oleg Blochin stood comparison

Opposite: *Mick Jones forces in the solitary goal which beat Ferencvaros and won Leeds the 1968 Fairs Cup.*
Top: *Neil Young of Manchester City scores the first goal in the 2–1 triumph over Gornik Zabrze in the 1970 European Cup Winners' Cup final.*
Above: *Manchester United play in Dublin against Waterford in the 1969 European Cup.*

Newcastle beat Ujpest Dosza of Hungary in the 1969 Fairs Cup final with goals from a most surprising source. Defender Bobby Moncur scored twice in the first leg at St James' Park and Newcastle had a three-goal lead to take to Hungary. And when Ujpest had pulled back two of them in the first half in Budapest, it was Moncur who scored again in the opening minute of the second period. Ujpest were shattered and Newcastle added two more goals to win the Cup 6–2 on aggregate.

with any of the great names thrown forward by twenty years of European competition.

For Russia it was a rare sweet moment at club level in Europe, though as a nation they had competed with great commitment in the European Nations Cup (later to be retitled the European Championship). In Paris in July 1960 they had become the first recipients of the new international trophy with an extra time victory over Yugoslavia, while four years later they had narrowly lost to Spain in the intense partisan atmosphere of Madrid. Fourth in 1968, when Italy overcame Yugoslavia with home advantage in Rome, they reached the final again in 1972 only to be well beaten by a West German side more at its peak then than in the winning of the 1974 World Cup. In the whole period, the Russians had

actually lost only two European Championship games—the 1964 and 1972 finals. In 1968 they went out to Italy only on the toss of a coin after a goalless draw.

After twenty years, European competition had become an accepted fact of football life. If it had occasionally been a party to unpleasant, even horrible, sentiments and acts far removed from the spirit of competition, it had more than proved its value in offering the very best of top-level tournaments. 'Getting into Europe' had produced a new challenge for ambitious clubs across the continent; succeeding in it brought riches in cash and prestige. More than that it put an end to the idle boasts of patriotic newsmen whose reports so upset Gabriel Hanot in 1954. Wolves have yet to be champions of Europe, let alone the World!

ILLUSION AND DISILLUSION
England 1945-1976

The laws and the overall structure of English League football have changed little in the thirty years since the Second World War. One or two minor variations to be sure—substitutes, three-up three-down, 92 clubs in the League rather than 88. Superficially the most revolutionary change must have been the abolition of amateurism in 1974, and yet its real effect has been minimal. The same men play for the same teams in the same leagues. So all has remained calm? Not at all. Changes have, in fact, been dramatic and it is a very different game in the second half of the 1970s from those far-off days of the boom years of the late 1940s.

Surprisingly, the major changes are really the result of happenstances off the field—an affluence that brought television and the motor car to nearly every household, and the lifting of the maximum wage paid to players being the most pro-

Below: The impact of Munich; crowds watch in a Manchester street on the evening of 11 February 1958 as the coffins of those who died in the plane carrying English champions Manchester United pass by.

Right: *Vain defence by a Millwall back fails to stop Tommy Lawton, the Notts County centre-forward, breaking through at The Den. Lawton's . transfer to County, reported to be for a record £20,000 in 1947, caused a sensation. At the time Lawton was still the England centre-forward while County were struggling at the lower end of the Third Division South. His arrival did all that County hoped it would do, with packed gates week after week and some remarkable results such as crushing victories over Horsham 9–1, Exeter 9–0, Ipswich 9–2 and Newport 11–1. Lawton was to appear four more times for England while playing in the Third Division.*

minent. It was a period of fluctuating fortunes—optimism for perhaps a dozen years, barely dented by the trauma of the national team's defeats against the USA in 1950 and Hungary in 1953, followed by a period of steady decline relieved only by the twin emotional peaks of England's World Cup win in 1966 and Manchester United's European Cup, two years later and ten after Munich. And if, by the mid-1970s, this decline in interest appeared to have been halted, it had not happened soon enough to keep more than a dozen clubs in the black in any single season.

As in all periods, there were definitive teams and memorable moments, particularly with the Manchester United of Law, Best and Charlton, fortuitously confirmed in the memory by that game against Benfica at Wembley in 1968, and the earlier United team, killed at Munich, whose potential was never tested and thus remains a what-might-have-been. Tottenham probably came closest to United with two fine teams at the start of the 1950s and 1960s, the latter being the best one season side of them all (then without the later acquired Greaves) in their double year of 1961. Leeds, with their strange collection of runners-up awards (five League, three FA

Cup, one League Cup, one European Cup, one European Cup Winners' Cup, one Fairs Cup by 1976) totally outweighing their successes, must rate next—despite their sadly stifling influence, shared with Liverpool and others, during the second half of the 1960s.

Totally memorable games are fewer in the domestic context—Milburn's hat-trick against Portsmouth in the 1952 FA Cup quarter-final, Blackpool's Cup win of 1953 (though not by virtue of the quality of its football), Manchester United's last League game before Munich, 5–4 at Highbury, the League Cup successes at Wembley for Third Division Queen's Park Rangers and Swindon Town, and Sunderland's emotional run to the Cup final and ultimate success in 1973.

Less significant in the final analysis are so many features which seemed important at the time—Arsenal's dramatic but uninspiring double, a string of unmemorable Cup Winners' Cup and Fairs Cup successes for English clubs, and the years of rewarded perpetual motion by Liverpool. There were the sad and sorry declines of Sheffield Wednesday and Aston Villa, the demise of New Brighton, Accrington, Gateshead, Barrow and Bradford Park Avenue, and

the gradual withdrawal of support from not only the Third and Fourth Division clubs—throwing into real doubt the wisdom of the abolition of the old dual Third Divisions—but also from the minor leagues and now 'defunct' amateur sides.

Most critics of English football in the 1970s have, often vehemently, argued that the game has declined since the Second World War, without being absolutely precise about the meaning of the term. 'Decline' is, after all, a relative expression but it is generally taken to mean that far fewer people watch, and are interested in, the game. The most difficult post-War phenomenon to explain is probably not why attendances have generally got smaller, but why they reached such a dramatic peak in the late 1940s. In 1950 there was no serious expectation that the week-in, week-out packed crowds would remain faithful forever. It was very obviously an unusual time—with football a rare diversion for the mass of people living through rationing and austerity. Assuming times got better, then the options open to everyone were going to widen.

It is too easy to forget that football has to be placed in a much wider social context. Changing habits of work, leisure and domestic life affect football no less than anything else in Britain. In the past thirty years there have been some dramatic social changes (the virtual universal possession of television sets and motor cars to name just two which need to be considered here) and the face of football has been inevitably changed along with almost everything else.

On the most superficial level, just as the introduction of Saturday half-day working gave football such a boost in the 1870s, so its disappearance had a clearly damaging effect. The traditional Saturday in so many towns, particularly in the North and Midlands, during the 1930s and 1940s was a morning's work, a pub lunch and the local football ground (be it soccer or rugby league). A man at home on a Saturday morning is surely less likely to make a specific journey to a football ground on a Saturday afternoon than one already out and with his workmates by lunchtime. It is also worth remembering that so many of the major clubs still have their grounds in central factory areas (Manchester United, Derby County and Sheffield United being very good examples) while few (Crystal Palace being a rare case) are located in the suburban areas which hold the bulk of the population today.

Above: *Peter Doherty scores Derby County's vital second goal in the 1946 Cup final against Charlton Athletic. This was the first of the post-War Cup competitions and is the only one ever to have been played on a two-legged basis until the semi-final. Derby won 4–1 with three goals coming in extra time. For Charlton there was some consolation when they returned the following year to defeat Burnley 1–0 for their only major honour.*

Above: *Days long gone; an early post-War crowd at an Accrington Stanley game.*

Probably even more important has been the shift of emphasis in domestic life to the more 'cellular' or single family unit throughout the country. This is most evident in a simple physical way—the disappearance of the terraced working class areas in the centres of our large cities (Moss Side in Manchester, Scotland Road in Liverpool, St Ann's Well Road in Nottingham) and their replacement by the semi-detached private and council estates on the outskirts. Private ease of transport, socially dominating television, increasing affluence and greater national emphasis on 'home comforts' have all helped break down the sheer interdependence of the old communities—and it was this shared lifestyle of the men-folk (work, pub, football —among so much more) that gave the game most of its grass-roots support. Nowadays a man is just as likely to accompany his wife shopping to the local town centre on a Saturday afternoon as go to 'the match'— a situation which was almost unthinkable twenty years ago.

The most important difference of all between the 1940s and the 1970s may be even simpler—an extension of choice. In 1946 there really was very little to do on a Saturday afternoon; even shopping held little appeal at a time of rationing and minimal spare cash. Since then the alternatives have multiplied thousandfold—from personal leisure interests such as sailing or fishing, through to domestic pursuits such as greenhouses or do-it-yourself. Even at the most mundane level, it is worth remembering that simply driving out to visit friends or watching television on a Saturday afternoon were not available to ninety-five per cent of the population back in the 1940s. Brian James of the *Daily Mail* is undoubtedly correct when he says: 'What needs to be explained is not why football has lost so many spectators, but what is the magic ingredient that has caused it to retain so many for so long?'

Notwithstanding any of these basic 'external' factors, it is still natural to look within the game—to 'internal' changes for an explanation of the very real decline in attendances and the more subtle fall in interest over the last few years. It is arguable, of course, that interest is now much greater, that far more people are exposed to and aware of football. Their awareness, however, comes from the possession of a television set rather than Saturday afternoon pilgrimages.

The facts are straightforward and indisputable. In the 1940s, overall Football Leagues attendances rose to a peak of 41,271,424 in the 1948–49 season. Since then they have steadily declined to around the 25 million mark today. There was only one hiccup in this progression, just after England's World Cup win, when attendances rose slightly for a brief period. The immediate post-War 1940s was such an exceptional period in English history that it can be dismissed as the baseline from which the level of attendances and interest ought to be considered. Much more serious for the game than the absolute drop in numbers since 1950 is the fact that, like a shore being eroded by the sea, the decline (up until the mid-1970s at least) has been so steady over a period when the population has been rising. The reasons that can be given for these trends are legion, but the most important can be classified under three headings—money, mobility and the media.

The abolition of the maximum wage in 1961, after the George Eastham case, brought the whole question of the status of professional footballers into the public arena and was perhaps the single most important event of the whole period.

Eastham wanted to leave Newcastle United. The club refused to let him go, arguing that he was the key to their midfield, and were simply following the Football League's regulations—under which a player was beholden to his club until *they* wished to transfer *him*. The system had no basis in law—it survived because it had never been challenged. Eastham changed all that.

It is worth stressing that Eastham was not fighting for more money or for the abolition of the maximum wage—but 'retain-and-transfer' and the maximum wage had lived together and were to die together. Jimmy Hill and Cliff Lloyd, chairman and secretary of the Professional Footballers' Association, were able to take the initiative offered by Eastham's dispute with the League. They won because of an acknowledged mood of change—the League realised it stood no chance of winning a lawsuit on the issue and, at long last,

Below: *The way that Lancashire football in the 1960s became a tale of two cities. In the first season of the new decade, 1970–71, over 3,409,000 fans passed through the turnstiles of the 'big four', Liverpool, Everton and the Manchester duo. The ten other League clubs that were then in pre-reorganisation Lancashire, Barrow (who were later thrown out of the League), Blackburn, Blackpool, Bolton, Burnley, Bury, Oldham, Preston, Rochdale and Southport attracted only 1,978,000. In that season, receipts from programme sales at Everton exceeded gate returns at Barrow.*

saw that it was fighting adversaries who would take matters that far. The maximum wage (which was only £12 per week as recently as 1956–57) was abolished in 1961, but the Eastham case was not settled until June 1963 when Mr Justice Wilberforce declared retain-and-transfer to be 'an unreasonable restraint of trade.' Oddly, the less resisted abolition of the maximum wage has had far more effect on the game than the end of retain-and-transfer.

saw that it was fighting adversaries who would take matters that far. The maximum wage (which was only £12 per week as recently as 1956–57) was abolished in 1961, but the Eastham case was not settled until June 1963 when Mr Justice Wilberforce declared retain-and-transfer to be 'an unreasonable restraint of trade.' Oddly, the less resisted abolition of the maximum wage has had far more effect on the game than the end of retain-and-transfer.

In the former case the results were startling. Within months Johnny Haynes became Britain's first £100-a-week footballer. The three greatest British goalscorers of the era—Denis Law, Jimmy Greaves and Joe Baker—soon returned from Italy where they had gone in pursuit of wages commensurate with their crowd-drawing power. And, of course, clubs having to pay out these wages got poorer. There was no more money coming in at the gate—Bobby Charlton was still Bobby Charlton whether he earned £20 or £200 per week—but there was a lot more going out in players' wage packets and salaries are usually the largest part of any club's expenditure. It took some time for the inevitable result to work through the system.

First admission prices started to rise. This has often been cited as a prime reason for declining crowds, but the few surveys conducted suggest this is unlikely to have had more than a marginal effect.

There has never been any obvious reluctance to pay more money for a good seat and the entrance fee still remains only a part of the whole cost of watching a game. Travelling to the ground, particularly for away games, costs at least as much as admission for many spectators. Even at today's prices, football remains good value compared with the cinema, theatre or other spectator events.

Increased wage bills have had a vital effect in causing clubs to cut their playing staffs. Several larger clubs (most noticeably Carlisle, even while playing in the First Division, and Portsmouth) cut their staffs so dramatically that they only fielded one professional side, making up their teams with apprentices or even amateurs.

For the clubs in the lower divisions the abolition was a tragedy. In 1958 the Third Divisions North and South had been rearranged into Third and Fourth. This increased costs—most obviously travel—automatically. But while a Fourth Division club could only pay a player the same as a First Division side (in theory at least) there was still a hope of keeping some better players. But with the maximum wage gone there was no hope—the good players went anyway, and even the moderate ones demanded far more than the average Third Division side could reasonably afford. It seemed absurd that the League could survive with ninety-two full-time professional clubs for much longer, and yet most hung on, millstones around the neck of a surely

Opposite page: Two of the reasons most often mentioned as responsible for the decline in attendances at first class football matches over recent years.
Opposite top: Televised games, in this case a League Cup tie between West Ham United and Sheffield United, was the area of greatest debate within the game. Paradoxically, the strongest fears were not for the clubs which were regularly featured in televised matches, but rather for the teams in the lower divisions who were never fortunate, or unfortunate, enough to appear on a Saturday night or Sunday afternoon.
Opposite bottom: Hooliganism has probably only had a small effect on overall attendances, but was nonetheless a growing problem for clubs, police and spectators in the early 1970s. After Manchester United's last First Division game at the end of the 1973–74 season, when their match with Manchester City had to be abandoned following a crowd invasion, United erected barriers to prevent spectators at their infamous Stretford End ever gaining access to the pitch again. Manchester City were awarded the game in one of the handful of instances where the League has allowed a result to stand despite a match not running its full course.
This page: A more convincing demonstration of the negative effect televised football may have on attendances occurred during the 1969 Home International Championship, all of which was televised live. On a wet night at Hampden Park, less than 8,000 fans turned up to see Scotland play Northern Ireland, not a particularly attractive fixture at the best of times but hardly appealing at all in the rain rather than beside a warm fire. Critics argue that live games, which the television companies would prefer, must be less damaging to weekly attendances than the more subtle dangers of recorded highlights, which often fail adequately to represent the whole ninety minutes of the game.

HOT **OXO** A BEEFY DRINK
MADE IN A MOMENT

Above: *Memories from the Third Division North of 1948. Within fifteen years both Gateshead and Accrington Stanley had left the League, Gateshead unexpectedly being thrown out to make way for Peterborough in 1960 and Accrington leaving of their own volition in 1962. Ten years earlier, in March 1952, this fixture, at Gateshead's Redheugh Park, had the unwelcome distinction of attracting the lowest attendance —484—ever recorded in an English first class match played under normal conditions.*

drowning system. Indeed in the thirty years following the Second World War only Accrington Stanley were forced into real bankruptcy—though many sides remained more or less insolvent for much of the time.

By 1976 (when the combined losses of the League clubs added up to £10 million) wholesale changes in the system were not only being advocated but even seemed to have a serious chance of being adopted. Part-time clubs in the lower divisions appeared one near-certainty sometime during the rest of the decade.

Few clubs were helped, either, by the steady rise in transfer fees. Alan Ball became the first player to be transferred between English clubs (Blackpool to Everton) for over £100,000 in 1966. Martin

Peters the first for £200,000 between West Ham and Spurs in 1970, and Bob Latchford the first £300,000 in 1974 moving from Birmingham to Everton.

Prices continued to rise. Stoke City paid £350,000 (the highest fee ever paid for a player in English football) for Peter Shilton from Leicester and £250,000 for Alan Hudson of Chelsea in the same year, 1974. Derby County paid what may turn out to be the last really big fee ever in November 1975 for Leighton James from Burnley for £300,000. By this time, however, the spiral had long since ceased. Prices had declined to a more manageable if not necessarily more practical level.

On the one hand clubs simply could not afford to pay the prices asked. On the other many were becoming convinced that the way to success was a competent manager and a young, carefully groomed team in the manner of Bobby Robson's Ipswich or Don Revie's original Leeds. There was no lack of examples of sides unable to buy themselves success—Everton and Manchester City (in Malcolm Allison's latter days) at the higher levels, Crystal Palace, Aston Villa and Manchester United during their attempts to prevent decline. And there were other factors.

In 1975 the League and the Professional Footballers' Association were discussing proposals that would allow players to negotiate their own contracts and would establish a formula for 'transfer of registrations' based on the player's age, the division he was playing in and his annual salary. This would limit the highest fee to not much more than a third of what Stoke paid for Peter Shilton and the proposals were discussed in the face of two simple facts. One was practical, that the system had run away far beyond the clubs' ability to control it, in the sense that they had to ask high fees that virtually no one could afford to pay, while few clubs ran at a profit. In any season it is unlikely that more than a dozen of the League's ninety-two clubs end up in the black, and the days are long gone when the likes of Tottenham would buy a player at the end of the season to reduce their profit and thus their tax liability (absurdly buying players is tax deductible, improving grounds—even for safety reasons—is not). The other reason, connected with new contracts, was simply that players themselves were striving for contractual freedom which would end the current transfer system.

At the time some clubs, notably Chelsea with the millstone of their new stand and a seven figure debt, were so overdrawn that, had they been any other business but a football club, bankruptcy proceedings

ASSOCIATION FOOTBALL

Queen in brawl at Palace

By ALBERT BARHAM : Crystal Palace 1, Blackpool 0

The satisfaction of Crystal ~lace's latest victory, which ~~~~~ ~ight up the table, ~~~~~ ~ight at Sel- ~~~~~ ~meful free-

seen of Rowe or Hutchison, whose play has attracted a numger of rival managers. Palace might well have had three goals so hard pr~~~~

equaliser when Suddick too advantage of a misplaced pass McCormick and lobbed the b over Jackson's head, only for it ~ whisked away. This was ~ment for Blackp~~ ~for

could not have been far away. Indeed Luton, surviving on 10,000 crowds, admitted late in 1975 that they were an astonishing £700,000 in debt and had to sell their best player, Peter Anderson, to Antwerp for £60,000. It is interesting that, at this time, their income from gate money covered neither their loan interest nor their wage bills. Many clubs had mortgaged their grounds as a means of raising capital. Thus the dramatic collapse in property prices in the mid 1970s, coupled with the restrictive Community Land Bill added yet another major headache for those grappling with financial survival.

The other long-term reason for the negotiations between League and PFA is explained in the Anderson transfer—that Britain is now a member of the Common Market in which free movement of labour is theoretically allowed. In the mainland market countries, free movement (of

varying degrees) was already the norm by 1975. And the League decided, with unusual foresight, to prepare their own plans, hopefully before another Eastham case forced them to do so anyway.

With costs rising, and attendances falling, attempts were naturally made to bring more money into the game. One such way was the creation of more competitions. These proliferated in the 1960s, parallel with the growth of European football, and were encouraged by football's desire to find sponsors but unwillingness to sell the plums—the FA Cup and the League. Alan Hardaker's own baby, the League Cup, was the most prominent. But there were others of a rather lesser nature—the Texaco, Watney, Anglo-Scottish and Anglo-Italian Cups to name just four which added to an already tightly packed fixture list. Effects were interesting.

The League Cup was a sickly infant—

Above: *The press also has its part to play in entertaining and informing the public, although it is often accused of taking its role either too seriously or too flippantly. The Guardian tends to be rather more whimsical than its competitors, as here in reporting some of Gerry Queen's antics at Selhurst Park* **Bottom:** *Reg Lewis scores the first of his two goals for Arsenal in the 1950 Cup final against Liverpool, cleverly converting Jimmy Logie's perfect through pass.*

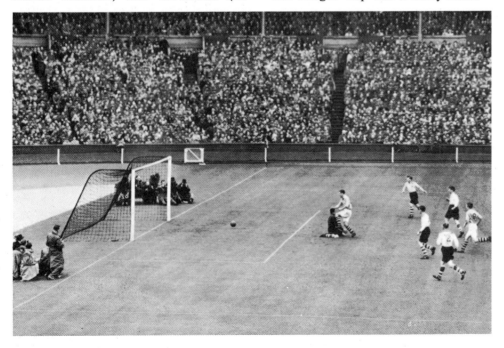

voted in at the League's AGM in 1960 by a majority of only 15. Several of the major clubs avoided it at its inception and it was not until the final moved to Wembley that any real enthusiasm was generated. Even then, the regular appearance of clubs from lower divisions in the later stages (three Third Division Wembley finalists between 1965 and the 1975 final—which was itself an all Second Division affair) became a virtually unremarked feature.

League Cup attendances suffered as badly as any, including those in the two minor European competitions, which were inspiring less enthusiasm in England by 1976, but at least it survived. Other competitions eventually succumbed—or looked set to do so—unloved and certainly unmourned. They may have had a small beneficial effect on the balance sheets of those clubs which partook, but, on the other hand, it is likely that they contributed in the long run to the wholesale decline in attendances.

Again the point is subtle. A very large proportion of football's followers goes week in, week out. Attendance is a ritual but, like church going, if the ritual is once broken it faces more wholesale harm. If the fan who never misses a League or Cup game decides, one Wednesday evening, that he simply cannot be bothered to see his side play Albion Rovers in the Anglo-Scottish

Cup or Oldham Athletic in the Texaco Cup, or even Keflavik of Iceland in the EUFA Cup, then it is not such a large step to deciding Stockport County in the third round of the FA Cup or even Birmingham City in the League one Saturday do not justify the effort. Once the habit is broken, real selectivity is probably not far behind. And with increasing affluence adding the motor car to nearly all family households, football has seen the traditionally limited working man given mobility.

In essence, this has altered the concept of the 'local' club. The classic case was Bolton Wanderers who, unexpectedly, under Jimmy Armfield and Ian Greaves regained some of their old status in the mid-1970s. Nevertheless, it is still actually easier and quicker to travel to Old Trafford from some parts of Bolton and watch Manchester United than it is to go to Burnden Park and see Wanderers. The network of motorways that had criss-crossed the country by the early 1970s threw up large numbers of comparable, if not so extreme, cases. Anyone living in Lancashire, Cheshire, Derbyshire or even parts of Yorkshire could, if they wished, regard Manchester United as their 'local' side. The motor car and motorways had put Old Trafford within two hours range of over 10 million people; and they came, but at the necessary expense of their local side.

WALKER

TAYLOR

MILBURN

FARM

WALKER

TAYLOR

MILBURN

Newcastle United were the Cup team of the 1950s, taking the trophy three times between 1951 and 1955. Jackie Milburn, at centre-forward, was their most celebrated player and his goal against Blackpool in the 1951 final (this page) is one of the most famous of all Cup goals scored at Wembley. Ernie Taylor back-heeled the ball to Milburn, who hit it left-footed past Blackpool's keeper George Farm with astonishing and literally unstoppable force.
Opposite page: Milburn scored a less characteristic goal in the first minute of the 1955 final against Manchester City, rare because it was with his head. City performed a relatively common Cup final feat by returning the next year to defeat Birmingham City 3–1.

Rangers and Celtic had been having a similar effect in Scotland for years.

All this has become intimately tied up with another factor—the media. Television, newspapers and magazines have all played their part in dramatising the bigger clubs at the expense of the smaller. And there remains a considerable area for debate (possibly the most important in the game today) around television's effect on

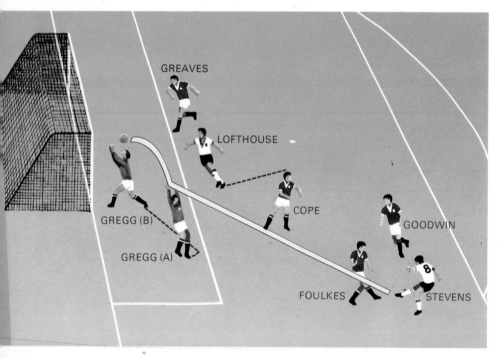

the game—a debate that reached heated argument in 1974 when the Football League and the television companies very nearly failed to come to an agreement over the weekly broadcasting of matches.

There are relevant points on both sides. Certainly the edited highlights style of presentation is guilty of altering the basic components of a ninety-minute game—in that goals do not appear at regular intervals, the slick inter-cutting of the camera provides a much closer insight than the view from the terraces, and as yet there are no facilities in the stadia for viewing replayed incidents in slow-motion. The

hour-long packages produced by Match of the Day and its Independent equivalents are glossy but distorted products, which may discourage potential spectators at grounds from leaving their armchairs on a Saturday afternoon.

But the television companies can legitimately counter by pointing to the fact that it is the football authorities which condition the style of the edited programme. Both BBC and ITV have searched for a plan which would enable regular *live* matches to be screened; but as yet the League and the FA, mindful of the effect that type of programming would have on the attendance of other matches played at the time of the broadcast, have rejected the proposals. And who can blame the television editors, restricted in the amount of the game they can show, for selecting the most exciting portions of the game. Would the public want it otherwise?

Almost as important is the continual focusing of the cameras on the very best teams in the country. Not only does this play its part in the polarisation of football towards a few select teams at the expense of the lower divisions, it ignores the considerable entertainment that exists in the Third and Fourth Divisions. The contract between the Football League and the television companies does specify that a small number of Third and Fourth Division games must be screened, but in fact television executives tend to regard these fixtures as necessary evils to be got over and done with early in the season when their viewing figures are at their lowest. The system is so orientated towards the top of the First Division that the arm-chair viewer can see perhaps the highlights of a third of the League programme of Manchester United or West Ham without moving from his fire-side.

Television rightly claims that it is putting millions of pounds into the game for the right to show matches, and in doing so is giving millions of pounds of free advertising to the club which gives an attractive performance in a televised match. For example the constant televising of George Best, Bobby Charlton and company in the sixties certainly helped attendances at Old Trafford and nothing has changed the truism that fans will flock to see a winning team. People came from miles around to see the stars that television helped to create. But this constant focusing on a few has been at the expense of the lower divisions which, in their producing and educating of young players, are vital factors in the chain which creates the 'Super-Club.'

To many younger fans football is in danger of becoming Leighton James, Colin Todd and Kevin Keegan. It is possible that the local Fourth Division side, even if only a few miles away, is as remote from 'today's' football as Alex James or Alan Morton. The need for coexistence between television and the clubs is obvious—and solutions must be available, just as in the United States, where the American version of professional football annually receives (at 1976 prices) over $80 million for the right to televise games.

If television, greater mobility and the abolition of the maximum wage could all be said to have contributed to falling support for clubs in the lower divisions, if

not necessarily the higher, the position may be reversed on another of the game's failures—hooliganism. While this has not always been confined to matches involving major clubs, it is normally associated with the First Division in England and Rangers and Celtic in Scotland.

Like television, the causes and effects of crowd misbehaviour are open to a considerable degree of dispute, but it is clear that hooliganism is not caused by football, rather that football matches provide a rare stage for a much wider social phenomenon. It is argued, however, that hooliganism on the terraces is basically associated with misbehaviour on the pitch. This is clearly non-provable, for while instances can be quoted to show there can be a coincidence, far more show the reverse—the fact that many arrests are made before games begin for instance.

And while no one can reasonably deny that hooliganism must dissuade some spectators from attending potentially troublesome matches, it is interesting that those clubs whose games are most readily associated with crowd violence (Celtic and Rangers in Scotland, Manchester United and Chelsea in England) have never lacked for supporters at home or drawing power away, nor have had any reason to suppose that the reputation of their fans has done them any lasting harm.

On the all-important field of play, however, it is surely possible to isolate two strands which have contributed to a decline in attendances, if not support, for

Opposite page: *Two consecutive finals, two appearances by Manchester United, two controversial goal-keeping incidents.*
Bottom left: *Peter McParland collided with Ray Wood (left) early on in the 1957 final, breaking the goalkeeper's cheekbone, and then went on to score two goals and thus take the Cup back to Villa Park.*
Top and bottom right: *In 1958 there was a new United team which had fought its way from Munich to a remarkably emotional final. Bolton Wanderers were already leading 1–0 when their centre-forward Nat Lofthouse charged goalkeeper Harry Gregg, a survivor of the crash, and forced both ball and keeper into the net. The charge would certainly not be allowed today, but at the time it secured Bolton's victory.*
Below: *Stan Cullis leaves Molineux having been sacked as Wolves manager in September 1964. He had taken the club to two FA Cups and three League Championships since the War.*

Munich, the most emotional, traumatic and arguably significant event in post-War English football.

Right: *Matt Busby addresses his team in Belgrade just before their last match, a European Cup quarter-final tie against Red Star.*

This page centre: *The United team line up before that 3–3 draw in the Yugoslavian capital.*

From left to right: Duncan Edwards (died), Eddie Colman (died), Mark Jones (died), Ken Morgans, Bobby Charlton, Dennis Viollet, Tommy Taylor (died), Bill Foulkes, Harry Gregg, Albert Scanlon and Roger Byrne (died).

This page bottom: *Back in Manchester a week and a half later with Assistant Manager Jimmy Murphy still trying to get a team together 54 minutes before the kick-off of a Cup tie with Sheffield Wednesday, United's first game after Munich. He is shaking hands with Stan Crowther (centre), just purchased from Aston Villa, for whom he had played against United in the previous year's Cup final. Crowther, having signed, went straight into the team and was given a unique FA dispensation to play for two clubs in that year's competition.*

Opposite page top: *Lord Burghley, the BEA Elizabethan airliner which was carrying the Manchester United team when it crashed after refuelling at Munich Airport.*

Opposite page bottom: *Ten years after; Matt Busby, who only just survived Munich, embraces the other two survivors still with United, Bill Foulkes and Bobby Charlton, at the end of United's European Cup final victory over Benfica in 1968.*

SASTAVI TIMOVA

CRVENA ZVEZDA

Beara

Tomić   Zeković

Mitić   Spajić   Popović

Borozan   Šekularac   Toplak   Tasić   Kostić

Rezerve: Durković, Cokić i Stojanović

Glavni sudija: KARL KAJNER
(Austrija)

Pomoćne sudije: ROMAN i KINELT
(Austrija)

Scanlon   Viollet   Taylor   Charlton   Morgans

Edvards   Jones   Colman

Byrne   Foulkes

Gregg

MANCHESTER UNITED

Next Home Match
1st DIVISION
United v NOTTS. FOREST
22 Feb. Kick-off 3-0 pm

Shirts Red   **MANCHESTER UNITED**   Knickers White

Youth International Match
ENGLAND v GERMANY
Wednesday, 12 Mar
Kick-off 7-30 pm

.... 2 3

.... 4 .... 5 6

R .... 7 .... 8 .... 9 .... 10 11

Referee:
A. Bond, London
Kick-off 7-30 pm

FOOTBALL GREEN PLEASE

Linesmen:
F. Wain, Bakewell
Red Flag

F. P. Clarke, Coventry
Yellow Flag

L

FINNEY 11   **FROGGATT** 10   **SHINER** 9   **QUIXALL** 8   **WILKINSON** 7

O'DONNELL 6   **SWAN** 5   **KAY** 4

JOHNSON 3   **MARTIN** 2

RYALLS

Team changes
will be
indicated by
loudspeaker

Shirts Blue and White Stripes **SHEFFIELD WEDNESDAY** Knickers Black

Team changes
will be
indicated by
loudspeaker

the game in England. One is the lack of success of the England international side in the past thirty years (with the 1966 World Cup shining through as a startling exception) coupled with similar failings of English clubs in European football, and the second is surely the tactical changes that have affected the 'entertainment value' of the game.

Entertainment value is, of course, an almost impossible factor to quantify. It is usually illustrated by goal scoring statistics although a goalless draw can, of course, be as exciting as a ten goal classic (the scoreless 1970 FA Cup semi-final replay at Villa Park between Manchester United and Leeds was arguably one of the best of all post-War Cup games played in this country). Nonetheless, goals scored must illustrate some element of 'attack mindedness' if nothing else and they do provide interesting statistics.

Even as late as the 1960–61 season seven League clubs managed to score 100 goals in the season, excluding cup matches. Double winning Spurs got 115, Fourth Division Peterborough scored 134, and Chelsea, though twelfth in the First Division with only 37 points, still managed 98. Things changed rapidly. Not since the 1963–64 season has a First or Second Division club scored 100 goals in League matches. That year, Southampton got exactly 100 to finish fifth in the Second Division, though Leeds won the title with a mere 71. By 1971 Liverpool were able to finish *fifth* in the First Division with a total of 42 goals scored—exactly one per game! They conceded just 24 and with one more point would have finished third. Similarly Liverpool (again) and Derby came respectively second and third in 1973–74 with 52 goals each.

The League's decision from the 1973–74 season to promote and relegate three rather than two clubs probably accelerated rather than softened this trend. One third of the way through the season, it was no exaggeration to say that half the First Division clubs were looking to avoid the relegation zone rather than have any more commendable ambitions. The result was the inevitable search for the away point with two men up front and a tight defence. Some clubs even started to be criticized for playing that way at home. The tactical changes of the period are covered elsewhere, but their effect on the game had, bluntly, been essentially defensive.

It was increased perceptions of the European and world games that had the major effect on English football, essentially adjusting the balance even further towards defence. The influential factors are numer-

ous, but one or two are worth isolating. Firstly, there was the adoption of Brazil's 4–2–4 (later 4–3–3) formation first apparent in the 1958 World Cup finals.

Rather more important was European football. It took only a handful of European Cups to produce a 'defend away, attack at home' mentality among most entrants. In this sense, the two-legged ties were an unfortunate though, from the financial point of view, necessary evil.

It was not long before English clubs began bringing these tactics back home. It

Opposite page: *Before and after; the upper team sheet is from the game against Red Star Belgrade, the lower from the programme for the first post-Munich match, against Sheffield Wednesday at Old Trafford.*
Above: *The greatest of the English post-War goalscorers, Jimmy Greaves, relaxing after a game. On his right is Spurs and Wales winger Cliff Jones.*

is, after all, not such a great logical jump from defending in depth at San Siro, Milan, on a Wednesday evening to doing the same thing away at Anfield or Elland Road the following Saturday afternoon.

Thus the defence-minded away side—particularly from the lower half of the division—became predominant. The tactic was even accepted; solid packed defence becoming a virtue in the absence of anything more praiseworthy. In effect it only confirmed what everyone knew—that it is easier to plan defence than attack. Forwards need those elusive skills which cannot always be programmed; defenders cannot be skill-less, but systems can be devised to protect goalmouths and this is where the emphasis was placed throughout the 1960s. It is interesting that those areas where attacks could be planned—essentially from set piece moves—began to represent a greater and greater percentage of the total goals scored in the League. This confirmed not only the ability of clubs to 'coach by numbers' in attack, but also the competence of defenders to control 'open' play.

Opposite top: *A man who needs no caption, George Best, in the green of Northern Ireland, evading a tackle by Peter Storey.*

Opposite below: *Another of the era's more significant figures, George Eastham, whose courage in taking legal action against the Football League brought to an end not only the retain-and-transfer system but was also the inspiration for the abolition of the long-standing maximum wage. Eastham ended his playing career, as here, in Stoke City colours. He scored the winning goal in the 1972 League Cup final against Chelsea, a particularly apposite event for Eastham as it was the first goal he had scored for three years.*

This page: *The man who could never give the game up; Bill Shankly rests at the end of the line during a Liverpool team picture at the start of the 1964–65 season. Liverpool were reigning League Champions and were to win the FA Cup that year. Liverpool's style and success has characterised the English game in the 1960s and 1970s and they, with Leeds, have been the dominant team of the period. But despite domestic success, they have always found headway difficult to make in Europe, and have come to epitomise what has been critically judged to be poor and retrogressive in the domestic game since 1970. Shankly surprised most observers by retiring after Liverpool's Cup win in 1974 and handing over the management to his deputy, Bob Paisley. His success in taking Liverpool to a record ninth Championship in 1976 was generally regretted outside Merseyside. The other three contenders—QPR, Manchester United and Derby—had all contributed rather more originality to a season which, at long last, saw a perceptible upswing in interest and spectator appeal. Liverpool did, however, perform noticeably well in the EUFA Cup, particularly in defeating the Barcelona of Cruyff and Neeskens in Spain.*

Some clubs, most notably Derby County using the place kicking skills of Alan Hinton, won titles because of their ability to score from set piece situations while others lost them because of the absence of comparable preparation. Nor was attacking play encouraged by the benevolence shown by referees to 'overenthusiastic' tackling from defenders. A brief 'referees revolution' in the early 1970s did help reduce some offences—notably the tackle from behind—but it lost steam and still left ball players often too badly treated.

Ramsey stands head and shoulders above other English tacticians of this period by his ability to adapt and mould talent below the best (both at club and international level) into truly successful outfits. His use of Jimmy Leadbetter as a withdrawn left-winger was remarkable at a time when numbers were still supposed to mean something and, added to the battering ram of Phillips and Crawford, produced an unstoppable one season wonder at Ipswich. The East Anglian side succeeded by surprise rather than by skill. Having just been promoted from the Second Division in 1961, their particular talents had not been open to scrutiny by the premier clubs (most still in awe of Tottenham's magnificent double-winning side and thus nonplussed by Ramsey's totally different functional formation) and they came through as complete jokers in the pack.

On a wider stage, Ramsey's selection of the barely known Hurst to act in his club role as England's target man was even more remarkable in the face of a country wholly committed to the genius of Jimmy Greaves. But others saw what Ramsey saw. West Ham's Ron Greenwood provided Ramsey with the core of the World Cup winning side; it should not be forgotten that West Ham players captained the winning side and scored all four goals in the final; each played, and was picked for, his club role.

Almost forgotten now is the Leicester City of Matt Gillies and Bert Johnson which had considerable success in the early 1960s with a version of the fluid 'total football' which the Dutch side in the 1974

A catalogue of disasters for Leeds United and Don Revie (above) who watches his side lose their last game of the 1971–72 season at Wolverhampton and thus miss yet another chance of the double. They needed only to draw this game to match Arsenal's double of the previous season.

Above right: *Ray Crawford heads one of his two goals in the fifth round FA Cup tie at Colchester in the 1970–71 season. The Fourth Division club caused one of the greatest of all Cup upsets by winning the game 3–2.*

This page bottom: *Jim Montgomery's remarkable save from Peter Lorimer during the 1973 Cup final, when Second Division Sunderland became the first non-First Division side to win the FA Cup since 1931. Leeds were unlucky enough to lose three FA Cup finals in the space of eight years. In 1965 they took Liverpool to extra time, in 1970 Chelsea to a replay and lost in extra-time despite dominating both games, and in 1973 came Sunderland and Montgomery.*

World Cup later came to epitomise. Leicester were unfortunate enough never to win anything, though they did establish some sort of record by reaching and losing four FA Cup finals in the space of two decades.

Even lowly Crystal Palace, managed by Dick Graham, achieved some remarkable successes by the simple expedient of changing numbers on players' backs. This

patently irrelevant act threw better sides into confusion for a while and put observers in mind of Harry Johnston's inability to cope with Nandor Hidegkuti's roving number nine in the Hungarian debacle of 1953. Graham once threatened to number his players in alphabetical order, claiming that numbers did not matter anymore, but it was not until the 1966 World Cup, when centre-forwards wore 22 and goalkeepers

14, that the British public was able to comprehend (if not accept) that number 11 was not necessarily there to run up and down the left touchline for 90 minutes.

Chapman, and all the vestiges of his great side and the decade in which it had dominated, were long gone on 31 August 1946 when League football reopened after the Second World War. It was a different world from the depressed, fearful years of that terrible decade, but there was one reminder of the 1930s for the fixture list was identical to that with which the League had opened on 26 August 1939. The latter season had lasted for just three games and, for the record, Blackpool were leading the First Division with the only hundred per cent record when the whole programme was abandoned.

August 1946 was not strictly the first post-War first class football. There had been a strange 1945–46 FA Cup competition, played on a two-legged basis for the one and only time. As a result Charlton became the only side ever to reach a Cup final after indisputably losing an earlier game; Fulham beat them 2–1 in a third round match but Charlton won on aggregate by taking the other leg 3–1.

The Cup final, when Charlton met Derby, was also memorable; the ball burst after the referee, in a pre-match discussion, had strangely said the chances of it doing so were a million to one. To take the coincidence further, the ball burst during Derby's

League game with Charlton the next week and also during the 1947 Cup final—when Charlton beat Burnley 1–0. Shoddy materials were blamed rather than the hard shooting of the Charlton forwards. Bert Turner, Charlton's half-back, also became the only player to score for both sides in a final, which Derby eventually won 4–1.

Less than a decade later Derby were to lose 6–1 at home to non-League Boston United in a second round cup tie which must rank as the greatest giant killing feat of all time. Derby were to come back into prominence in the 1970s with the mercurial Brian Clough in charge. They won two extremely tight League championships, those of 1972 and 1975, after becoming the biggest spenders in the League during that period and thus established, surprisingly enough, a post-War record (two Leagues and one FA Cup) as good at the time as that of Leeds United.

The 1946–47 League season was a triumph. Grounds were packed, entertainment was unlimited. Clubs chopped and changed teams to find winning combinations—Third Division Hull City used a record forty-two players in the season! It was also the longest season in history. Midweek matches were banned for a time to save fuel, and then the terrible late winter of 1947 came, bringing with it wholesale cancellations. As a result the season ended on 14 June, with the 1947–48 games starting just seventy days later.

This page: The most disputed goal of the 1970s occurred during a League game between Leeds and West Bromwich Albion at Elland Road towards the end of the 1970–71 season. Tony Brown comes away with the ball while the Leeds players appeal that Colin Suggett (right) is offside. Even Brown stopped, but the referee, Ray Tinkler, while acknowledging that Suggett was in an offside position, claimed that he was not interfering with play. Brown restarted his run, passed the ball to Jeff Astle, also seemingly in an offside position, and West Bromwich scored and won the game 2–1. Leeds were later to argue, with some justification, that this patently inconsistent refereeing decision cost them two League Championships. In 1970–71 an extra point would have given them the Championship from Arsenal. The crowd invasion which followed the awarding of West Bromwich's goal caused Leeds to have to play their first four home matches of the following season away from Elland Road. They won none of these games.

203

McFAUL

OWEN

RADFORD (B)

RADFORD (A)

The 1940s were good times for League clubs. Attendances kept rising, to a peak of 41,271,424 in 1948–49, and it was not only League clubs that benefitted. That season the Amateur Cup final was first staged at Wembley and attracted 95,000. Four years later it was almost as difficult to get a ticket for the Amateur Cup final as for the FA version. That was the year of Pegasus's 6–0 crushing of Harwich and Parkeston and, even more romantic, of the Matthews' Cup final.

This strange, almost legendary, event remains the ultimate final—Stanley Matthews' supposed last chance of a major honour (in fact he was still playing League football a decade later). Blackpool had lost two earlier finals (1948 to Manchester United—a classic this—and 1951 to Newcastle United) and the whole nation, minus a few souls living in the vicinity of Bolton, wanted the Seasiders to win. Their remarkable recovery in the last twenty minutes from 3–1 down to win 4–3 has tended to obscure some of the realities. Most praiseworthy was Stan (the 'other Stanley') Mortensen's hat-trick—the only one in a Cup final this century—and the game also provided the highest aggregate of any Wembley Cup final. Worthy of similar note was Bolton's perverse tactical failing in leaving Matthews, in the second half, facing an injured half-back and a full-back suffering from cramp.

Poor Bolton. Just five years later they were back at Wembley and this time it is possible that not even their own supporters would have minded if they had lost. This was arguably an even more emotional game—with a Manchester United risen phoenix-like from the ashes of Munich providing the opposition. Nearly twenty years later Munich provides an emotional rallying point unique in the modern game, rendering United less a football club than an article of faith. They are, of course, the most prominent of the post-War English sides—having won the League in 1952 (after coming second in four of the previous five seasons), 1956, 1957, 1965 and 1967, the Cup in 1948 and 1963 and, of course, the European Cup in 1968.

But, more than that, they were the side of George Best, Bobby Charlton, Denis Law, Johnny Carey, Tommy Taylor, Roger Byrne and the incomparable Duncan Edwards. So many of the most memorable moments over the past thirty years of English football revolve around United—the 1968 European Cup final at Wembley, the 1957 and 1958 Cup finals with their contentious charges on two United goalkeepers, Ray Wood (by Peter McParland) and Harry Gregg (by Nat Lofthouse), the

5–4 victory at Highbury in the last game before Munich, and the most emotional game in the whole history of English football, the first game after the disaster when a scratch United side (Stan Crowther had been signed from Aston Villa fifty-four minutes before the kick-off) beat Sheffield Wednesday 3–0.

Matt Busby, taking over a second rate club (they had been in the Second Division for most of the 1930s) with a bombed out ground, had created three great sides. The first, Cup winners in 1948 though unable to use their own ground, he half inherited and moulded; the second, to die at Munich in 1958, he created from scratch; the third, he invested in and led to the ultimate triumph at Wembley in 1968.

Even in decline they could not stay out of the headlines. The 'he's back—no he's not' George Best saga was still continuing in 1976, having begun as long ago as November 1972 when, at 26, he first announced his retirement. It would be unfair to say that Best dragged United down with him, but he was always the most publicised factor. Having lived off his genius, United found it difficult to live without it. Best's reputation, if not the man himself, lay like a great cloud over Old Trafford, from under which successive managers Wilf McGuinness and Frank O'Farrell could never escape—especially with Busby ever present in the background. Half way through the 1973–74 season goalkeeper Alex Stepney was United's leading scorer with two penalties, and they were inevitably condemned to the Second Division, if only for a season.

Meanwhile the nation's press continued to trumpet that George Best was becoming a bore, that no player was bigger than his club or the game—and simply by their attention arguably proved the opposite. Best was a great loss to the game, the one man who could add 10,000 to any gate, and probably the cleverest player ever to emerge in the British Isles. He was arguably denied his true place in the game because he was Irish and thus never had the chance to perform on the ultimate stage of the World Cup.

At the other end of the hierarchy, the League added four clubs on to bring it up to current strength in 1950 and in itself this provided an interesting story. At the annual general meeting four new clubs— Colchester United, Gillingham, Scunthorpe and Lindsey United and Shrewsbury Town —were admitted, two each to both sections of Division Three. The election of Scunthorpe to the Northern group was one of the strangest quirks of post-War football. On the first ballot Shrewsbury were elected

easily but Workington and Wigan Athletic tied for second place. Rather than just a straightforward vote between the two tied clubs, the League took it into its corporate head to organise another ballot—and Scunthorpe defeated both of their seemingly stronger opponents. Workington replaced New Brighton the following year but, twenty-five years on, Wigan are still trying to gain entry to the League.

Meanwhile Portsmouth experienced a brief moment of glory by winning two successive championships and giving the game the classic 'Pompey Chimes' ('Play up Pompey, Pompey play up') while Arsenal justified the 'lucky' tag yet again by winning the 1950 FA Cup without even leaving London. To be fair, in 1971 and 1972 they reached successive Cup finals without having a single home draw either year. The former was, of course, the year of their double—so different in style and appeal from that of north London neighbours Tottenham ten years earlier, but equally valid in its time.

Leeds must rank as Manchester United's greatest rivals for the premier spot in post-War English football, although they did not emerge as a potent force until as late as 1964, when Don Revie took them to the Second Division championship. Since then their record has been astonishing and they have had the most consistently successful decade in the history of post-War English football. Only Aston Villa in the 1890s and Arsenal in the 1930s can claim to better it.

Over the eleven seasons between 1965 and 1975 Leeds' League positions have been 2,2,4,4,1,2,2,2,3,1,9. In 1965 and 1970 they were runners-up in both Cup and League and in 1972 just one goal away from the double when Wolves beat them 2–1 in the final match of the season. During this period Leeds ranged from the depths of their cynical, defence orientated and sometimes even brutal early years, to the delights of the 1973–74 season when it was not until their thirtieth League game that they suffered defeat. Jimmy Armfield, taking over after the disastrous if comic forty-four day interregnum of Brian Clough, seemed set to continue the pattern despite the club's showing in the European Cup final of 1975.

Liverpool, since their promotion in 1962, have been the other club which has always been there at the top of the division, but they have rarely had the charm of Leeds to compensate for their less attractive, if non-stop, style. Liverpool, under Bill Shankly, were the arch advocates of the continual motion 'he'll run his legs off for me' game. They were never great goalscorers; in the five seasons from 1969 to 1974, a period when they did not fall below fifth in the First Division, they managed 295 League goals, an average of less than 60 a season. More than any of the other leading English clubs, Liverpool have tended to be exposed by able European sides. Ajax, in crushing them 5–1 in Amsterdam, Bayern Munich in playing a tight and clever defensive game, and Red Star Belgrade, by their delightful skills, made Liverpool look an inflexible, unimaginative side by comparison. To be

Opposite: *The two men most often advocated for the creative midfield role in the England side of the mid-1970s, Alan Hudson of Stoke City (standing) and Trevor Brooking of West Ham United. England team manager Don Revie rarely appeared to agree with his myriad of amateur advisers.* **Below:** *Celebration and retribution for a young Manchester United fan at Old Trafford before the barriers were put up.*

Above: *Another favourite of the crowds but not, seemingly, the England team manager, was Leeds United forward Duncan McKenzie, one of the few unarguably original and gifted forwards in the English game in the mid-1970s. Here Liverpool's Tommy Smith intervenes in a Leeds' attack.*

fair, they played much better in defeating a thrilling Borussia Monchengladbach team in the 1973 EUFA Cup final and winning the same competition after defeating Barcelona and improving Bruges in 1976.

Those two years also saw a combination of arguably unrelated events catch the public eye. In the space of four years, three Second Division clubs reached the Cup final and two, Sunderland in 1973 and Southampton in 1976, won the trophy. Whether this was of significance or merely a statistical curiosity was unclear.

Southampton's road to their first Wembley final was undoubtedly the easiest of any post-War finalist. They played only one First Division side (Aston Villa, against whom they equalised in the last minute) and, astonishingly, drew a Fourth Division side in the quarter-final (Bradford City) and Third Division Palace in the semi. But there was no disputing the quality of their win over Manchester United in the final, Bobby Stokes' goal leaving yet another young, much heralded United side, as in 1957, without the double they had threatened. The Saints' win put them on a par with the other great Wembley shock winners —Blackburn in 1928, Portsmouth in 1939, Villa over United in 1957 and Sunderland in 1973.

Coinciding as it did with the change to 3-up, 3-down, this arrival of Second Division influence appeared to contradict the growing belief in the inevitability of a 'super-league' of Liverpools and Arsenals.

Actually, Sunderland's defeat of Leeds was an act of a different nature in the

1973 Cup final; an astonishing, emotional, sentimental and sad affair with Second Division Sunderland rendering Leeds runners-up once again. It was memorable not so much for Ian Porterfield's first half goal, but for Jim Montgomery's astonishing save from Peter Lorimer's close range thunderbolt in the second half. At that moment the whole ground knew that Leeds were yet again going to come second. Very much the story of a long decade and one which saw massive doubts cloud over the English game.

Still to come as Sunderland carried the Cup back up the A1 was the three day week, with its power restrictions forcing midweek games to be played in the afternoon, fuel difficulties causing travel problems and reducing attendances, England's departure from the 1974 World Cup and 1976 European Championship, and an economic depression which was to blow as ill a wind over football as any other part of the economy.

In 1976 even mighty Leeds were only covering three quarters of their £800,000 outgoings from gate receipts, but such a successful club had little difficulty in making up the difference. Nonetheless, those inside and outside the game, from bank managers to the armchair fan, were at last being forced to ponder that there was no law which decreed that England and Wales could support 92 professional clubs or, at a much more basic level, that the man-in-the-street must watch a football match on Saturday. The rest of the 1970s would be an interesting period.

THE RISE AND FALL OF SIR ALFRED RAMSEY
The World 1963-1976

On 27 February 1963, England played their first international football match under the managership of Alf Ramsey. On Mayday 1974 the Football Association issued a statement confirming that the now knighted Sir Alf Ramsey had been sacked. In those eleven years England had taken part in 113 internationals, losing just seventeen. A reputation had been revived, a World Cup won, and another reputation had been lost.

The era of Alf Ramsey had the most profound effects on domestic football. Alone he completely altered the balance of power inside the Football Association; his broom swept clean the remaining cobwebs of the amateur age. He wore a mantle of professionalism that had been previously ignored, even frowned upon, at Lancaster Gate. And his thoroughness in preparation, allied to considerable tactical acumen,

Overcome with emotion Jack Charlton slumps to his knees at the sound of the final whistle at the end of extra time in the 1966 World Cup final. Just as Alf Ramsey had prophesied three years earlier, England were world champions.

Geoff Hurst, who did not win a place until the quarter-final, became a national hero with a hat-trick against West Germany—the first ever scored in a World Cup final.
Top: *He equalises Haller's goal with a downward header from Bobby Moore's free-kick.*
Centre: *Hurst's disputed second goal—the shot on its way to the underside of the bar.*
Above: *Hurst's third goal, in the final moments of extra time—the focal point of everyone in the ground except Alf Ramsey, who admiringly watched the pursuing Overath.*

sprung from a very recent history of catastrophes a succession of England teams that, for a time, put the mother country back at the top of the international pile.

From the start Ramsey had clearly worked out his priorities. His players were to be his single-minded concern. Officialdom, the press, public relations, protocol, even etiquette were areas of very secondary importance. If such attitudes brought forth little popularity, Ramsey remained unmoved; time with his players was precious. He saw little value in attending cocktail parties or press conferences. At best they became necessary evils where his appearances were timed to an absolute minimum.

Some of his social discomfort stemmed from his background—he came from the working-class London suburb of Dagenham. His clipped speech bore the manner of elocution lessons (which he always denied taking) and he was never at ease away from his players. But his convictions lacked nothing in courage, although there was often an absence of subtlety in the way he presented them. Having achieved a major coup in abolishing the long-standing Selection Committee for international matches, so that he picked his own England teams, he hardly ingratiated himself with the ever-present FA officials by declaring that the only real use of such gentlemen on England tours was that they saved him from having to attend cocktail parties!

As a manager, it should not have been surprising that he placed a high value on the character, fitness and dedication of his players. In his own playing career, which began at Southampton and continued successfully for Tottenham Hotspur and England, he had turned himself into a particularly constructive full-back. Hour after hour he had spent on the training-ground practising the absolutely basic skill of kicking, until he became a master of the precise pass over any distance.

In his managerial infancy at Ipswich, he had built a solid edifice where there had seemed to be no bricks. His Ipswich Town side swept from the Third Division to the League Championship, with a collection of local players bolstered by a couple of cheap signings and some reactivated veterans—all welded into a totally functional unit by Ramsey's discipline, perception and dedication.

He brought the same qualities to bear for England. His aim was to turn the international side into a true team instead of being merely a collection of highly talented individuals who turned up unprepared for half a dozen games a season. And the players responded to his approach. While Ramsey, especially in the later years of his reign, became an oft-criticized figure, there were no dissenting voices from the players. Sadly, he revealed only to them the real warmth of his character, while the rest of the country became used to the critical debates of his failures first in public relations, later on the field.

In 1963 his impact was immediate. In a shambolic display, the England he had inherited collapsed 5–2 to France and were eliminated from the European Nations Cup (later the European Championship) in the first round—a tournament won the following year by Spain. Yet by the summer he had fashioned a squad that had improved enough to beat Czechoslovakia 4–2 in Bratislava, East Germany 2–1 in Leipzig and Switzerland 8–1 in Basle. Tactically his side played in 4–2–4 formation with Terry Paine and Bobby Charlton acting as marauding wingers.

Charlton, in his book *Forward for England*, gave an instance of the changes Ramsey had wrought: 'Before the tour I had always looked on practice games before a big match on the continent as pretty light-hearted affairs. The goalkeeper often played as a forward and somebody like me, who fancies himself as a goalkeeper, went between the posts. This is what every footballer would do if it was left to him, but it isn't the Ramsey order of things. We are not allowed to have a ball to start with but have to familiarise ourselves with the ground. If I am playing on the left-wing I have to run up and down my side of the field, getting the feel of the turf beneath my feet, and then go and study the area around the corner flags. Most of the continental grounds have a track running around them and I had found that in the past, through running over the mound, I had been put off or lost my run up when taking corners . . . when I ran on to the field at Bratislava to play against Czechoslovakia I felt as if I knew the ground as well as any in England . . .'

Ramsey also used the opinions of his players by allowing them a voice at team talks—occasions which, in the past, had been lectures rather than discussions. It was a much-appreciated change of style. Yet Ramsey never allowed contempt to be bred from familiarity, an attitude typified by his disciplining of the young Bobby Moore for transgressions while England were touring North America in the summer of 1964. Both men ultimately benefitted from the crossing of swords with a resulting mutual respect which was to serve England so well for the rest of the decade.

With the 1966 World Cup to be staged in

Top: *England began the World Cup in disappointing fashion—a 0–0 draw against the containing defence of Uruguay.*
Centre: *Goalkeeper Gordon Banks and his defenders provided the cornerstones of the home team's ultimate triumph.*
Above: *Portugal's Eusebio scores a penalty against Russia, one of his nine goals.*

Above: *The diminutive Herr Kreitlein, the West German referee, faces controversy and the tall Argentinian Rattin in the quarter-final of the 1966 World Cup. Sent off by Kreitlein, Rattin refused to leave the field and the game was held up for eight minutes before he eventually departed.*
Above right: *Ramsey was incensed by the physical intimidation shown by Argentina, and after the match he referred to their players as 'animals'. At the final whistle he ran on to the pitch to prevent George Cohen (right) and other England players from swapping shirts with their opponents.*
Far right: *Pak Doo Ik watches his shot beat Albertosi to create the sensation of the 1966 competition—North Korea's 1–0 victory over Italy.*

England, Ramsey was not burdened by the worry of qualification. And while Scotland (to Italy), Wales (to Russia) and Northern Ireland (to Switzerland) were faltering in their bids to qualify for the finals, the England manager could devote his entire attention towards structuring a side for that event. Ramsey predicted an England success, the country chuckled, and the rest is, of course, history.

The most significant foundation stone was laid in Madrid in December 1965—just six months away from the finals.

Against the then champion nation of Europe, Ramsey opted for the practical. He tightened the rather loose defensive belt of 4–2–4 by using an extra man in midfield at the expense of an outright attacker. The focal point of the switch was Bobby Charlton, withdrawn from the wing to play in a deeper vein alongside a robust tackler in the slight, but ultra-competitive, Nobby Stiles and the deft, history-making, George Eastham. The Spaniards bewilderment at facing such a system was akin to that Ramsey (playing in his last international) and his colleagues must have felt when they

met the Hungarians at Wembley twelve years earlier. And England, despite losing Joe Baker (who had opened the scoring) with a thigh injury, beat Spain at a canter 2–0.

Ramsey's squad for the World Cup began to take shape—particularly in defence. In goal Gordon Banks had rightly established his claims ahead of Springett and Waiters; his agility and composure were to prove major factors in the months ahead. At right-back George Cohen, a fitness fanatic, could attack with a flourish and was to become the classic overlapping full-back while the breed was still in its infancy. His partner, the stylish Ray Wilson, added poise and balance to the defence. Jack Charlton, Bobby's older brother, but his junior in international experience, provided an uncomplicated centre-half whose strength in the air was invaluable, as were his regular goals from corner-kicks.

But the key defender was Ramsey's captain Bobby Moore—already a player of world class. Utterly composed on the ball, a resolute tackler and a magnificent distributor, he possessed a razor-sharp awareness and his speed of thought set him apart from others, even at the exalted heights of the international game. Tall, blond and handsome, with a touch of arrogance, he almost strode from the pages of schoolboy fiction. In consecutive years he had lifted trophies at Wembley for his club West Ham—the 1964 FA Cup and the European Cup Winners' Cup in 1965.

Elsewhere positions remained open to several candidates. Stiles, limited as a creative player but a lion in the tackle, seemed to be a strong candidate in midfield; in the end, gap-toothed and extrovert, he was to become the symbol of England's triumph. Charlton, an enigma for much of his career, was still a gamble in midfield, but was probably to play at his best in 1966; meanwhile Eastham, the exuberant young Alan Ball, the stylish Martin Peters from West Ham all competed for a place.

Paine, Callaghan, and Connelly were the leading contenders in Ramsey's quest for orthodox wingers. And as out-and-out attackers, the willing Roger Hunt, who toiled unselfishly in the team cause, was cast very much in Ramsey's mould. Less so was the prolific but individualistic Jimmy Greaves, England's best post-War goal-scorer; both seemed likely to play rather than another hard-working striker, Geoff Hurst, a third offspring of the successful West Ham side.

Pieces of Ramsey's World Cup jigsaw were still dropping into place during the tour he had organised as an immediate run-in to the tournament. Ball's enthusiastic skills seemed to outweigh his problems of temperament and clinch his place, while Hurst's chances faded when his ball control failed the test of a bumpy Copenhagen pitch eight days before the competition was to start. England duly took residence in the Hendon Hall Hotel and watched their rivals arrive.

Ramsey had promised from the first, 'We shall win the World Cup', though no home team had done so since Italy in 1934, and, despite a switchback of changing fortunes, he was to make good his boast.

Besides England's triumph, it was the World Cup of Brazil's surprising downfall —a cautious team of veterans falling heavily at Everton to the Hungarians and Portuguese. It was the tournament, too, of the astonishing North Koreans, the most remarkable of all outsiders, who conquered the Italians, frightened the Portuguese, and became the toast of the Middlesbrough crowd. The 1966 World Cup was also the true watershed in the career of Jimmy Greaves, a career which thereafter slid on into anti-climax, having been denied its ultimate stage. It saw, too, the further

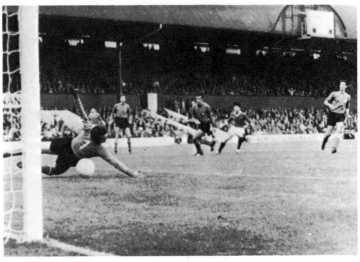

8th WORLD CUP England, 1966

Group 1

England	(0)0	Uruguay	(0)0
France	(0)1	Mexico	(0)1
Hausser		Borja	
Uruguay	(2)2	France	(1)1
Rocha, Cortes		De Bourgoing (pen)	
England	(1)2	Mexico	(0)0
Charlton, Hunt			
Uruguay	(0)0	Mexico	(0)0
England	(1)2	France	(0)0
Hunt 2			

	P	W	D	L	F	A	Pts
England	3	2	1	0	4	0	5
Uruguay	3	1	2	0	2	1	4
Mexico	3	0	2	1	1	3	2
France	3	0	1	2	2	5	1

Group 2

West Germany	(3)5	Switzerland	(0)0
Held, Haller 2 (1 pen),			
Beckenbauer 2			
Argentina	(0)2	Spain	(0)1
Artime 2		Pirri	
Spain	(0)2	Switzerland	(1)1
Sanchis, Amancio		Quentin	
Argentina	(0)0	West Germany	(0)0
Argentina	(0)2	Switzerland	(0)0
Artime, Onega			
West Germany	(1)2	Spain	(1)1
Emmerich, Seeler		Fuste	

	P	W	D	L	F	A	Pts
West Germany	3	2	1	0	7	1	5
Argentina	3	2	1	0	4	1	5
Spain	3	1	0	2	4	5	2
Switzerland	3	0	0	3	1	9	0

Group 3

Brazil	(1)2	Bulgaria	(0)0
Pele, Garrincha			
Portugal	(1)3	Hungary	(0)1
Augusto 2, Torres		Bene	
Hungary	(1)3	Brazil	(1)1
Bene, Farkas,		Tostao	
Meszoly (pen)			
Portugal	(2)3	Bulgaria	(0)0
Vutzov (og), Eusebio,			
Torres			
Portugal	(2)3	Brazil	(0)1
Simoes, Eusebio 2		Rildo	
Hungary	(2)3	Bulgaria	(1)1
Davidov (og),		Asparoukhov	
Meszoly, Bene			

	P	W	D	L	F	A	Pts
Portugal	3	3	0	0	9	2	6
Hungary	3	2	0	1	7	5	4
Brazil	3	1	0	2	4	6	2
Bulgaria	3	0	0	3	1	8	0

Group 4

USSR	(2)3	North Korea	(0)0
Malafeev 2,			
Banischevski			
Italy	(1)2	Chile	(0)0
Mazzola, Barison			
Chile	(1)1	North Korea	(0)1
Marcos (pen)		Pak Seung Jin	
USSR	(0)1	Italy	(0)0
Chislenko			
North Korea	(1)1	Italy	(0)0
Pak Doo Ik			
USSR	(1)2	Chile	(1)1
Porkujan 2		Marcos	

	P	W	D	L	F	A	Pts
USSR	3	3	0	0	6	1	6
North Korea	3	1	1	1	2	4	3
Italy	3	1	0	2	2	2	2
Chile	3	0	1	2	2	5	1

Quarter-finals

England	(0)1	Argentina	(0)0
Hurst			
West Germany	(1)4	Uruguay	(0)0
Held, Beckenbauer,			
Seeler, Haller			
Portugal	(2)5	North Korea	(3)3
Eusebio 4 (2 pens),		Pak Seung Jin, Yang	
Augusto		Sung Kook, Li Dong	
		Woon	
USSR	(1)2	Hungary	(0)1
Chislenko, Porkujan		Bene	

Semi-finals

West Germany	(1)2	USSR	(0)1
Haller, Beckenbauer		Porkujan	
England	(1)2	Portugal	(0)1
Charlton (R) 2		Eusebio (pen)	

Third place match: Wembley

Portugal	(1)2	USSR	(1)1
Eusebio (pen), Torres		Malafeev	

Final: Wembley 30.7.66
Attendance 93,000

England	(1)(2)4	West Germany	(1)(2)2
Hurst 3, Peters		Haller, Weber	

England: Banks; Cohen, Wilson; Stiles, Charlton (J), Moore (capt); Ball, Hurst, Hunt, Charlton (R), Peters.

West Germany: Tilkowski; Hottges, Schnellinger; Beckenbauer, Schulz, Weber; Held, Haller, Seeler (capt), Overath, Emmerich

Referee: Dienst (Switzerland)

Leading scorers: 9—Eusebio (Portugal) (4 pens)
5—Haller (West Germany) (1 pen)
4—Beckenbauer (West Germany)
Hurst (England)
Porkujan (USSR)

The agony of defeat. Eusebio weeps at the end of the road for Portugal in 1966—at Wembley against England in the semi-final. Eusebio's penalty, which had reduced the score to 2–1, was the first goal conceded by England in the competition and the semi-final had been an exhilarating occasion. Portugal were cheered in defeat by spectators who had thrilled to the quality of their attacking football. Forgotten, though, was the brutal manner in which the Portuguese, in particular defender Morais, had eliminated Pele and Brazil earlier in the tournament.

twilight of the Argentinians, who had substituted force for their traditional finesse, and who would later be dismissed in a word by Sir Alf Ramsey; 'animals'.

Brazil recalled their 1958 manager, Vincente Feola, who in turn brought back his 1958 half-backs, Orlando and Bellini, to join their fellow veterans, Djalma Santos and Garrincha. Tostao, at 19, was just beginning to emerge; Pele was still formidable, but seemed to be in poor physical and mental shape.

England, back from their successful tour, on which Greaves had looked very sharp, opened the football with a tiresome draw against Uruguay at Wembley. The Uruguayans, under the canny managership of Ondino Viera, packed their *catenaccio* defence, produced a few dazzling moments from Pedro Rocha, and held the unimaginative England attack at bay without too much trouble. Not until the semi-final and final would England really take wing. Meanwhile there were unexciting victories to come over Mexico, even more defensive than their South American neighbours, and France—the only game which moved Ramsey to rebuke his team's performance. But then at least the players knew that everything possible was being done for them, instead of feeling themselves slighted

by a remote hierarchy. This time, too, there was at long last a team doctor, the excellent and robust physician, Dr Alan Bass, who was also firmly in charge of the anti-doping arrangements.

The other three qualifying groups were played in the North East, where Russia, Italy, Chile and the amazing North Korea made up Group Four, the Midlands, where Argentina, West Germany, Switzerland and Spain competed, and Lancashire, where at Everton and Old Trafford Brazil, the holders, Hungary, Bulgaria and Portugal played.

The Swiss made a disastrous beginning against West Germany at Sheffield, not least because two stars, Kuhn and Leimgruber, broke bounds and were suspended. Germany, with Franz Beckenbauer attacking splendidly and scoring twice, and Helmut Haller, the blond inside-forward, contributing two more, annihilated them 5–0. Then Argentina, subjecting the key Spanish schemer, Luis Suarez, to some crude treatment, beat Spain 2–1, both goals being scored by their fine centre-forward, Luis Artime, splendidly supplied by Ermindo Onega.

At Everton, Brazil began well enough against Bulgaria, though Zito was unfit. Pulverising free-kicks by Pele and Garrincha won them the game despite Yakimov's clever dribbles for the European side. Yakimov's team-mate, Jetchev, badly mauled Pele with little let or hindrance from the English referee, Jim Finney. Finney's colleague, George McCabe, would prove an even more permissive referee in the Portuguese game, when Morais savaged Pele well after the result was in the bag. Indeed, the Brazilians went home saying justifiably harsh things about English refereeing.

The North Koreans, tiny men pressure-trained in monastic seclusion in an army barracks, showed nothing to frighten anyone against Russia, who beat them comfortably 3–0, while Italy, who had shown fine recent form under little Edmondo Fabbri, their manager, laboriously beat Chile 2–0 at Sunderland.

England went on to meet Mexico and to score, at last, with a right-footed thunderbolt from Bobby Charlton, now their midfield general, and another from the faithful but much criticized Roger Hunt. Also in Group One, Uruguay beat France 2–1 at White City.

Against Mexico, Ramsey brought in the subtle and elegant West Ham player, Martin Peters, primarily an attacking right-half, but adept at stealing into dangerous positions near goal. Peters acted the part of a false left-winger. The orthodox wingers, Connelly, Paine and Callaghan, were all tried on the right flank and in turn discarded. But the defence, with Gordon Banks serene and gymnastic in goal, was awfully hard to beat.

Not so Brazil's. Against Hungary and the dazzling Florian Albert, playing something of a 'Hidegkuti', deep-lying role, it simply folded up. The Hungarians used the dominant Matrai as a sweeper and played only two strikers, the quicksilver Bene and the deadly Farkas. But when they broke, the Hungarians moved up at great speed.

Brazil had not lost a World Cup game for twelve years, since the Battle of Berne in 1954, also against the Hungarians, until that memorable night at Goodison. Under steady rain, against a Brazil deprived of the injured Pele, Hungary went ahead after only three minutes with a splendid goal by Bene, dribbling gloriously on the right, then cutting in. The nineteen-year-old centre-forward, Tostao, in his first World Cup match, equalised when Lima's free kick rebounded to him, but Albert and Hungary were in sweeping command. After half-time Albert and Bene gave Farkas the chance to score with a devastating right-footed volley, and Meszoly knocked in the final nail from a penalty.

Desperately Brazil made abundant changes for the decisive match against the Portuguese. The veteran Gilmar was succeeded by Manga, the tall goalkeeper nicknamed 'Frankenstein', who crossed himself nervously as he came on to the field. Seven of Brazil's team were playing their first ever World Cup game; and it told. Manga let them down after only fourteen minutes when he feebly punched out Eusebio's cross and Simoes, Portugal's brisk little winger, headed in. Next, Torres, the giant centre-forward, headed on the elegant Coluna's free-kick for the celebrated Eusebio to notch the second. The black inside-forward from Mozambique would be the tournament's leading goalscorer.

Morais' dreadful foul on Pele early in the second half lamed him, and with Pele went Brazil's last fleeting chance. Rildo did come up to score, but Eusebio whipped in Portugal's third after a corner and Brazil were out.

England's win against France, with two goals from Roger Hunt, was undistinguished. The result was encouraged by an injury to Herbin, and blemished by a controversial foul by Stiles on Simon. Officials of the FA insisted Ramsey drop him, Ramsey said he would rather resign, and the matter went by default.

Uruguay became the other quarter-finalists, by virtue, if that is the word, of an unbelievably dreary goalless draw against Mexico, at Wembley, where England were to play all their games. Foreigners who pursued the conspiracy theory, unearthing in that fact a dark plot to benefit England, ignored the fact that, had England not won their group but come second, they would have played quarter and semi-finals away from Wembley.

West Germany, having thrashed the Swiss, became absurdly cautious, using Beckenbauer ridiculously deep just as they would have him play against Bobby Charlton in the final. They drew an ill-tempered game against the provocative Argentinians at Villa Park 0–0, Albrecht, the Argentinian sweeper, being sent off. After that, a 2–1 win over the lively Spaniards, thanks to a remarkable goal by their big left-winger, Emmerich, guaranteed their quarter-final place.

Meanwhile, there were high jinks in the North East. Italy, playing without their 'brain', Gianni Rivera, lost 1–0 to Russia at Sunderland, going down to a second-half goal by the Russian right-winger, Chislenko. Worse was to come. The North Koreans, who had already held Chile to a draw, were growing in stature match by match. They were giving Italy as good as they got in front of a Middlesbrough crowd who spoke of them as 'us', when Bulgarelli tried to

The 1966 World Cup final produced two goals of immense controversy—West Germany's second goal in the last breath of the second half, which forced extra time, and England's third.
Above: *Wolfgang Weber slides in the German equaliser following a free-kick bitterly contested by the England players.*
Above right: *Schnellinger's arms are raised in ecstasy while Bobby Moore adopts a similar pose in a claim that the ball struck Schnellinger's hand before reaching Weber. The goal stood.*
Right and far right: *None of the many photographs taken of England's third goal prove conclusively whether Hurst's shot did bounce down over the line—as the linesman and subsequently the referee ruled—or on it as the Germans claimed. The bottom picture on the far sequence shows Roger Hunt turning away convinced that a goal had been scored; in the background the Russian linesman Bakhramov who seconds later signalled the goal. Was he in a position to see?*
Below right: *The diagram shows the move which put England 3–2 in front.*

216

foul a Korean, hurt his knee, and went off. Pak Doo Ik, North Korea's inside-left, then proceeded to score the historic goal which qualified North Korea, knocked out Italy and cost Fabbri his job and his players a tomato bombardment at Genoa airport.

The quarter-final produced two monstrosities of bad sportsmanship, one thriller and one mediocrity. England's match against Argentina fell into the first category.

From the start Argentina, captained by the huge, arrogant Rattin, paid less attention to playing the football of which they were capable than to obstructing England's players. England, who had left out Greaves on the grounds that he was still unfit (a source of some controversy), preferred the powerful West Ham striker Geoff Hurst, out of favour since that clumsy performance in Copenhagen.

Herr Kreitlein, a somewhat officious little West German referee, was taking Argentinian names in profusion almost from the start. At length, just before half-time, Rattin's insistent protests caused him to be sent off. For eight minutes he would not go, and the whole game hung in the balance. At length he slowly and sullenly went and the match dragged on, England finding it as hard as before to break through a tough, clever, ruthless defence. Roma in goal made one astonishing save from Hurst by the foot of a post, but could not stop the beautiful header from Peters' cross with which Hurst won the game, thirteen minutes from time.

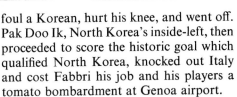

At Sheffield, dark doings; two Uruguayans, Troche and Silva, were sent off, while another one grabbed Haller by the genitals. Not that the Germans did not at times provoke their opponents, sometimes by histrionic reactions to their tackles. One down at half-time to a goal by the lively,

Below: *At the greatest moment of his career Ramsey gives no outward show of emotion. Geoff Hurst has just given England an invincible lead in the World Cup final. More extrovert are reserves Ian Callaghan (grey sweater) and Jimmy Armfield (red sweater), and trainer Harold Shepherdson. Reaching across is Les Cocker, later assistant to Ramsey's successor Don Revie.*

Opposite page: *Two more of the really memorable football faces and photographs.*
Top: *Alex James, key to the Arsenal midfield of the 1930s and ranking among the contenders for the title of Britain's best ever player, leaves three Manchester City defenders stranded at Highbury. Furthest left of the three is Matt Busby.*
Bottom: *Footballer of the Year Tom Finney takes an early bath at Stamford Bridge in 1954.*

blond striker Siggi Held, Uruguay's depleted team fell apart in the second half, when three more goals followed.

The thriller was at Everton, where the amazing little North Koreans, attacking brilliantly and imaginatively, were three

Ramsey was never more at home than with his players, in whom he inspired tremendous loyalty. Here the enjoyment of the England manager is quite apparent as he screens the ball from Colin Bell during a training session.

goals up in half an hour. Then Eusebio majestically took over. Running gloriously and controlling the ball superbly, he won the game for Portugal. He scored twice before half time, once from a penalty, and then twice after it, one of them another penalty. Augusto, a right-winger converted to a midfield man got a fifth against a now dispirited Korea. They were out, but their feats would long be remembered.

Hungary, plagued by bad goalkeeping in most of their games, could blame Gelei again for their mediocre defeat by Russia at Sunderland; a sad end after their brilliance against Brazil. Gelei was largely responsible for both Russian goals, while Bene alone scored for Hungary—Rakosi missing an open goal.

Of the two semi-finals, England and Portugal proved a masterpiece, Russia and West Germany a scandalous anti-climax. Even with Sabo limping and Chislenko—injured by Schnellinger and irate—sent off, the Germans could only squeeze through 2–1. Haller, after Schnellinger's fine cross-field pass—immediately following his tackle on Chislenko—and Beckenbauer, with a remarkable, swerving left-footed shot, got the goals. Porkujan replied with a late one for Russia.

Bobby Charlton, in compelling form, got both of England's goals against Portugal, and his performance arguably won the final as well as the semi-final. The Germans were so impressed by Charlton's abilities that Beckenbauer was eventually used in the final in an entirely defensive role to subdue the number nine, thus easing England's task considerably. England were, in fact, better value than their 2–1 victory over Portugal suggested. Nobby Stiles tackled Eusebio right out of the game, and there should have been several English goals before Bobby Charlton scored on the half-hour after Pereira could only block Hunt's shot. He hit a glorious, right-footed second, in perhaps his most memorable game ever, after Hurst's powerful run and pass eleven minutes from the end. Then Portugal pressed hard, Jack Charlton punched out Torres' header and Eusebio scored from the penalty, the first goal Banks had conceded in the tournament. Thereafter, England deservedly held out in a remarkably sporting game. The sight of almost every Portuguese player shaking Bobby Charlton's hand after he scored his second goal was unforgettable, as was the fact that no foul was conceded for the first half-hour of the game.

Portugal then beat Russia in the dullest of third-place matches, and the stage was set for the final between England and West Germany. The Germans, who had never managed to beat England, would have liked to replace their goalkeeper, Tilkowski, but Maier was unfit; ultimately they probably suffered from the fact.

It turned out to be a match of the highest drama. In the end, it was largely resolved by the extraordinary stamina, the endless running, of Alan Ball, but Alf Ramsey was scarcely wrong when he told the England players at the end of normal time that they would have to win it twice.

Germany took the lead after thirteen minutes when Ray Wilson headed a cross straight to Haller, who scored. Not since 1938 had the side which scored first won a World Cup final and this was to be no exception as Geoff Hurst, on whom Ramsey had gambled so wisely, skillfully headed in Bobby Moore's free kick six minutes later.

The third West Ham man, Peters, put England into the lead twelve and a half minutes from the end after Hurst's shot had been blocked in the goalmouth, and all seemed over. Instead, West Germany got a last-ditch equaliser. It was, if anything, a free-kick to England when Jackie Charlton and the irrepressible Siggi Held leapt together for the ball. But Germany were given it, Emmerich's drive ricocheted across goal, and Weber put it in.

So to extra time. Ball's incredible running down the right soon brought as its first reward a fierce shot off the underside of the bar by Hurst. Goal or not? The West Germans, with apparent justification on later viewing of the available film, claimed it was not, but the referee consulted his Russian linesman, who gave it. England were ahead 3–2, and there was a fourth to come when Hurst ran through a scattered German defence to score, with an accurate and powerful left-footer, his third; a personal record in a World Cup final.

As Geoff Hurst galloped clear to strike

But Ramsey could never relax in the company of the Press, and he was suspicious of journalists around the world. At this press conference in Mexico during the 1970 World Cup finals his unsmiling attitudes did not endear the England squad to local reporters. Public relations, and substitutes, were to remain his Achilles heels.

home that last shot, write his name in the record books and send a nation delirious ('the triumph of the common man, always assuming he can do something so uncommon as to score three goals in a World Cup final' wrote one commentator), Ramsey's reaction was typical of the man. As all around him Englishmen leapt into the air in ecstasy he sat unsmiling, watching the proceedings with outward dispassion. Later he admitted that he had been admiring the character and fitness of the West German midfield player Wolfgang Overath who had forced himself to chase vainly back, always a stride behind Hurst, as the last goal unfolded.

Typically, too, Ramsey the man was tightly ensconced in his shell when, as the celebrations continued the following day, he curtly informed two newspapermen, who had been staunch supporters throughout his reign, that he would not discuss the match because it was his day off. This was the same man who had been found watching a youth match while his players were celebrating Ipswich Town's remarkable League triumph.

Yet in shortly over three years Alf Ramsey had masterminded a remarkable upsurge—an achievement recognised by his knighthood if not by the paucity of his salary (for much of his time at the post he earned less than many First Division managers). But his success did not receive universal acclaim. His team was criticized as functional rather than exciting, that it lacked wingers; comments which undoubtedly hurt Ramsey and which ignored the fact that his was a great practical triumph in which he had utilised the only available materials he had to manufacture the finished product. Certainly, too, many of his detractors were those who had suffered from his continuing suspicion of the press. Nevertheless, even at the height of his triumph, there were those who were waiting with anticipation for the moment he fell from grace.

That process began, in reality, when the champions of the world could not establish a suitable claim in Europe. Qualification for the finals of the Nations Cup, now renamed the European Championship, depended on the results of the 1967 and 1968 Home Internationals. Scotland became the first country to beat the world champions when they won 3–2 at Wembley, though England suffered injuries on the day. Scotland duly became favourites to qualify, only to squander their advantage by losing 1–0 to Northern Ireland in Belfast. England picked up maximum points from matches with Ireland and Wales and thus needed a draw at Hampden

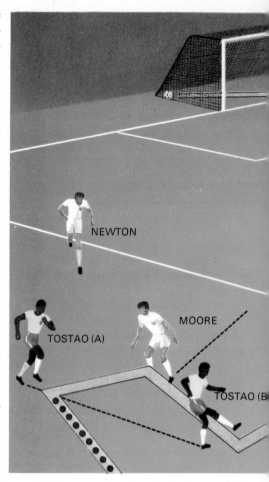

in February 1968 to reach the quarter-finals. Martin Peters gave England the lead, and though Cooke inspired a Scottish comeback and a goal for Hughes, Ramsey's England retained their discipline and composure and took home their point.

In the quarter-final, England again showed their quality by dethroning Spain, though they carried but a single goal lead to Madrid from the first leg. But another fine performance brought a 2–1 win with goals from Peters and Norman Hunter, who was playing in midfield. But when Italy, Russia and Yugoslavia joined England in the semi-finals the worm began its turn. In Florence Yugoslavia were England's opponents, and a 1–0 defeat was not the end of their disappointment. Alan Mullery, who had replaced Stiles as the defensive midfield player, was sent off, the first man ever to suffer that indignity wearing an England shirt. Though England were in vintage form to beat Russia in the play-off for third place, Ramsey's critics had turned up the volume on their mutterings. Italy beat Yugoslavia in a replayed final to wipe out some of the memory of their World Cup disappointment.

Ramsey had already begun his preparations for the defence of England's world title. Though this time he would not

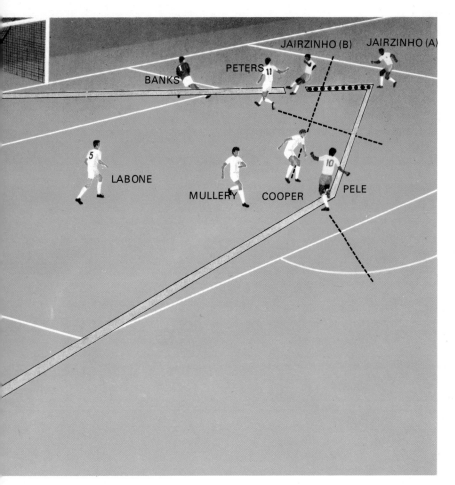

JAIRZINHO (B) JAIRZINHO (A)

PETERS

BANKS

LABONE

MULLERY COOPER PELE

prophesy an England win in the rarefied altitudes of Mexico, he insisted that the new squad was better equipped than that of four years earlier. In his thoroughness he arranged a tour of South America a year before the finals. A goalless draw in Mexico City was followed by an excellent 2–1 win in Uruguay and a 2–1 defeat in Rio at the hands of Brazil, who only looked convincing as England tired towards the close.

Of the 1966 side, the three players whom Ramsey had claimed as 'world-class' remained—Banks, Moore and Bobby Charlton, though the ageing Charlton would surely suffer in the heat of Mexico. Hurst, fortified by his achievements in 1966, had blossomed into an intelligent, dangerous goalscorer—a prototype striker of his age who was held up as an example by other managers (notably Bill Nicholson to Martin Chivers) for their own forwards to copy. Peters, another as gifted with the inside as the outside of his head, remained a pillar, though somewhat burdened by the tag pinned on him by Ramsey as a player 'ten years ahead of his time.' Stiles, though superseded by Mullery, would be included in the squad, perhaps as something of a talisman, the symbol of 1966 and all that. Jack Charlton had also lost his place, to

Brian Labone, but he, too, would be in Mexico as the Everton centre-half's understudy. Another inspirational figure of the World Cup win, the combative Alan Ball, seemed certain of his place, though his role had become wholly midfield rather than that of an auxiliary touchline player.

Ramsey had demanded loyalty in his players and returned it. Again the critics found ammunition; Ramsey's 'Old Guard' became a newspaper phrase with derogatory overtones. The clamour was for youth, typified by the talented but wayward Peter Osgood, who did make the final squad and played briefly as a substitute in the World Cup but who was to achieve little in the international arena. Ramsey placed such reliance on character that he tended to be suspicious of the erratic genius. At this time he clearly placed more value in the wholehearted but less gifted Jeff Astle, a centre-forward very much of the old school.

Apart from Mullery for Stiles, Cohen and Wilson had also been replaced—Cohen tragically retiring with a complicated knee injury; Keith Newton and Terry Cooper could both attack with verve, particularly Cooper, a converted outside-left. The willing Roger Hunt had also gone at his own volition, again after criticisms that totally ignored what he had unselfishly

Above left: *The goal with which Brazil beat England in the 1970 World Cup group encounter at Guadalajara. Tostao drew Moore away from the middle and when his cross reached Pele, left-back Terry Cooper had to make a challenge. Pele rolled the ball into the now vacant space on his right and the powerful Jairzinho arrived to score. England had played extremely well in defeat, and many believed that the holders could retain the trophy if they met Brazil again in the final. But quarter-final catastrophe against West Germany ended that possibility.*
Above: *Instead Brazil met Italy in the final, and Gerson (number eight) celebrates his goal which restored Brazil's lead at 2–1, on their way to a 4–1 success.*

NEWTON

MULLERY

MAIER

HURST

LEE

Playing 4–4–2 in Mexico in 1970, Ramsey's tactics relied heavily on his full-backs and midfield players contributing to the attack. Against West Germany in the quarter-final the philosophy worked superbly. England took a first-half lead with a move begun by Mullery in his own half, with the ball being switched to the overlapping Newton on the right. When the full-back's cross arrived in the goalmouth so did Mullery to flash the ball home.

contributed to the team cause, often at the expense of personal glory. Francis Lee, stocky and pugnacious, took Hunt's place.

The 1966 triumph had been based on a sound, stifling defence, and Ramsey took a further step in that direction by choosing to defend the World Cup in a 4–4–2 formation. In that decision he was considerably helped by the flair of his two full-backs, both of whom would have to shoulder an extra attacking burden in the exhausting Mexican conditions. Yet the switch in formation was not that far removed from the tactics of four years earlier. A 4–3–3 label had been pinned on the England side, though in fact only Hurst and Hunt were wholly committed to offence. Peters and Ball had both drifted between the roles of striker and midfield auxiliary.

There had been another change; World Cup football was now a thirteen-a-side game with the allowance for the first time of two substitutions. Ramsey, for all his thoroughness, was to find substitution a difficult ploy—not just in the World Cup of 1970 but much later in his career as

England manager. Some later argued that it was to be his fatal Achilles heel. But, that apart, England left for South America and a pre-finals tour of Colombia and Ecuador with a high degree of organisation as far as football was concerned, though again Ramsey's unease in peripheral matters was to make him a target for criticism.

Sir Alf Ramsey was determined, by his own admission, to win friends and influence people. He was to have his work cut out. His own concentration on football matters rather than press conferences was well-known to British journalists, but the foreign press found it totally unacceptable. Conflict between Ramsey and the foreign press was constant. If he had granted interviews between, say, twelve and two in the afternoon, then he saw that all interviews stopped at two.

The Mexicans completely disregarded Ramsey's restrictions. At two o'clock, for example, the Mexican TV camera teams would suddenly arrive, set up all their lighting and other equipment, and demand interviews. Ramsey, as he had explained he

PETERS

LEE

HURST

NEWTON

would, refused. With both sides intransigent, the situation deteriorated into a hostile stalemate. The Mexican press tried to get their own back. When England returned to the Mexican capital from South America, with their captain Bobby Moore detained on a trumped-up charge of stealing a bracelet, and Jeff Astle, the West Bromwich forward, plainly the worse for the voyage, the Mexican press described them as a bunch of thieves and drunks. On the day of the opening ceremony at the Aztec Stadium, when Mexico played Russia, the whole of the huge stadium erupted in a torrent of hatred when the Union Jack was carried round. It was by now quite clear that the English had for the moment taken the place of the detested North American *gringos*.

The case of Bobby Moore and the bracelet, which blew up in the notoriously raffish city of Bogota, Colombia, on the eve of the World Cup, showed all the signs of the classic 'frame-up'. Bogota is well known for such things; Moore was by no means the first celebrity falsely accused of

theft. In previous years it had happened, among others, to an opera singer and a bullfighter.

England were staying at the Hotel Tequendama when Moore and Bobby Charlton entered a shop in the hotel. They looked around the shop, the *Fuego Verde* (Green Fire) left, and sat outside on a bench. They were then approached by the proprietor and a shop girl and accused of stealing a diamond bracelet. Bobby Moore, against whom the charge was eventually brought, went on to play in Ecuador, but left the England team's plane and went into voluntary custody on his return to Bogota. After a few days under indulgent 'house arrest', he was permitted to join the England party in Mexico City. The absurd charges dragged on, despite one sordid revelation after another which indicated a crude plot against Moore, until ultimately they sank into abeyance. In the circumstances, it was astonishing that Moore should have a majestic World Cup; better even than that of 1966, when he was chosen the outstanding player.

England increased their lead with a similarly worked goal. Again Newton defied the heat and the rarefied atmosphere to stride forward down the touchline, and this time he directed his cross to the far post. There Martin Peters had timed his run to perfection on the blind side of the defenders and he slid in the goal. At this point England were so much in command that the dramatic turnabout seemed inexplicable.

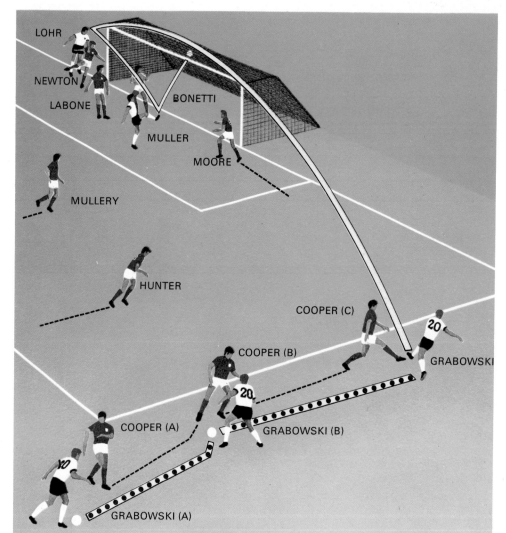

LOHR

NEWTON

LABONE

BONETTI

MULLER

MOORE

MULLERY

HUNTER

COOPER (C)

20

COOPER (B)

GRABOWSKI

COOPER (A)

20

GRABOWSKI (B)

20

GRABOWSKI (A)

In extra time West Germany exacted some revenge for their Wembley defeat in 1966 by completing a remarkable comeback. Goals by Beckenbauer and Seeler had pegged back the scores by Mullery and Peters, and Schoen used his substitutes to better effect than Ramsey.
Right: *It was one substitute, Grabowski, who particularly plagued England and he set up the winner. Lohr met his deep cross and turned the ball back for Muller to score.*
Below: *Muller beats Bonetti, a late replacement for the sickly Banks, as Moore watches the end of his dreams of lifting the World Cup a second time.*

Even at the time, let alone in retrospect, the Football Association's lack of foresight seemed incredible, especially after the experiences of the 1969 tour. A glib public relations man who handed the Mexicans the affectionate platitudes they craved could have saved infinite trouble. As it was, the night before the Brazilian match in Guadalajara, rancour and bitterness came to a crescendo, to the detriment of the English team. From late in the evening before the Brazilian game, Mexican fans, and perhaps a few Brazilians, began to gather, chanting, outside the Hilton Hotel, Guadalajara. It had seemed quite a little haven the previous year, on tour, with its comfortable rooms and its swimming pools; but that was before the World Cup hordes swept over the city, and tranquility disappeared. But then, as Sir Alf observed later: 'Wherever we'd gone in Mexico, they'd have found us.'

Round and round the hotel for hours on end, drove a convoy of motor cars, blowing their horns, while crowds of Mexicans gathered on the pavement opposite the hotel and chanted for Brazil. A line of police confronted them, but simply kept them at bay, doing nothing to disperse them, even though the clamour was kept up far into the night, and the English delegation made an official protest. It was evident that the authorities, too, shared the general hostility to the English party.

The object of the pro-Brazilians, or anti-English, was quite clearly to prevent the England players from sleeping, and in this they were only too successful. Several of the England men had to change their rooms in the middle of the night to escape the persistent clamour. In the circumstances it was amazing that they should last the ensuing game so well, losing a marvellous contest only by 1–0, and themselves missing a string of good chances; the most memorable was an open goal which fell to Jeff Astle and led to 'Astle's Miss' almost becoming part of the language.

Before the World Cup finals even began, there had been rather more serious violence in the shape of the 'Football War' between El Salvador and Honduras. These countries, already politically at loggerheads, had been drawn together in the Central American qualifying group. Honduras won at home 1–0, lost away 3–0, and were finally eliminated 3–2 by El Salvador in Mexico City after a dramatic extra-time winning goal. This served to ignite already smouldering passions on the border. There followed violence and bloodshed, the conflict lasted days, and there were an estimated 3000 deaths before peace was re-established. Alas, El Salvador's participation in Mexico was sheer anti-climax, for they lost all their games in the Mexico City group without even the consolation of scoring a goal.

El Salvador were not the only doubtful starters in the finals. The collective blackmail exercised on FIFA in the previous World Cup by the Afro-Asia bloc, who walked out in a body when they were not allowed more than one entrant, had its reward. They were now each permitted one entrant, which seemed grossly unjust to South America, let alone to Europe with its array of powerful international teams. In the event, the Moroccans, who won the African group, did well, but those who hoped the gallant little North Koreans, heroes of 1966, would represent Asia again, were disappointed. They withdrew on political grounds, refusing to meet Israel, who ultimately qualified, eliminating an improved Australia in their group's finals. Both Morocco and Israel acquitted themselves honourably, though neither won a game.

The scandal of kick-offs at noon was explained, though not excused, by the demands of international television; the European companies wanted to be able to show the games, so far as possible, live, bouncing the pictures by satellite. FIFA cravenly agreed, yet the biggest irony of all was that they did not profit much by their decision, the rights having been sold virtually for a song to Telesistema Mexicana, who had resold them at a huge profit.

Brazil, the eventual winners of the tournament, their third post-War success and all in the space of four tournaments, had their own difficulties to overcome before even making sure of their place in Mexico. They had appointed as team manager the slender, volatile journalist and ex-manager of Botafogo, João Saldanha. Some said that the controversial and voluble Saldanha was appointed simply to silence his trenchant criticisms. Be that as it may, he began in a blaze of goals and glory, Brazil sweeping through their qualifiying group, with their new centre-forward Tostao—he had played in the one World Cup game in 1966—a prolific success. Then Tostao suffered a bad injury to the retina of an eye, the team lost form, Saldanha unwisely locked horns with Pele, and out he went on the very eve of the final. He was replaced by Mario Zagalo, outside-left in the World Cup successes of 1958 and 1962, now also managing Botafogo. Tostao made a surprising recovery and morale was restored, but there was still no good goalkeeper, and the defence as a whole looked slack.

Above: *Nobby Stiles, mascot of England's 1966 World Cup win and key midfield ball winner for his club, Manchester United.*
Top right: *Pele had been in masterful form throughout the 1970 competition,*
once almost scoring from the halfway line, and here selling a unique dummy on the Uruguayan keeper Mazurkiewicz, who followed Pele and not the ball. Pele switched directions, shot, but the ball went just wide.
Above right: *Pele was denied another goal by this unbelievable save by Gordon Banks from the Brazilian's fierce downward header. Banks had raced across goal to turn the ball round the post.*
Centre right: *Nobby Stiles, the epitome of success in 1966, remained in the 1970 squad as something of a mascot.*
Below right: *The World Cup is won and Brazil's supporters set out for some unusual souvenirs.*

Italy, holders of the European Championship, were banking so heavily on the goalscoring Cagliari striker, Luigi Riva, that it seemed doubtful any man could carry so huge a burden. In the event, he could not, though they did reach the final.

The West Germans, who had found a fine new centre-forward in the stocky Gerd Muller, and had such distinguished survivors as Franz Beckenbauer and Wolfgang Overath from their 1966 World Cup final team, were expected to win their group in Leon, though no one knew whether Muller could be reconciled with the great veteran centre-forward, Uwe Seeler, persuaded by Helmut Schoen, West Germany's manager, to come out of retirement shortly before the finals.

In the event, the much criticized but not imperceptive Schoen put the two in the same bedroom, and made Muller the striker and Seeler a midfield player, with colossal success.

The curtain-raiser, played in intense midday heat at the Aztec Stadium, resulted in the dull, traditional opening goalless draw between Mexico and Russia; over-zealous refereeing by a West German anxious to go by FIFA's new book did

nothing to help matters.

These were the two teams which ultimately qualified in Group One. Belgium, who had done so well to qualify, fell apart, the team allegedly riven by quarrels over who wore whose type of football boot, and for what payment. Some wore Adidas, some Puma; some neither, to their chagrin. A similar contretemps in the Czech camp at Guadalajara, in England's group, led, on their return home, to the sacking of the team manager and long suspensions for almost all the players.

Yet to qualify, Mexico needed what many regarded as a disgraceful refereeing decision, when they were given a highly doubtful penalty, by which they beat Belgium.

In Guadalajara, Mr Loraux's permissive refereeing of England's match with the rough Rumanians made nonsense of all that had gone before in the opening game; Mocanu, the left-back, lamed at least two players, but England won with a crisp goal by Geoff Hurst. The Brazilians, with Pele and Jairzinho in marvellous form, accounted for the Czechs, after conceding the first goal. Perhaps they would have beaten England more comfortably had their splendid, left-footed, midfield star, Gerson, been available. As it was, both teams qualified.

In Group Two, Italy, riven by the furore over whether Gianni Rivera or Sandrino Mazzola should be the midfield general, and haunted by their North Korean defeat of 1966, defended ignominiously to qualify, squeezing through with a 1–0 win against Sweden, a goalless draw with Uruguay, and another with little Israel. Qualifying with just one goal scored was poor even by Italian standards. Only El Salvador of the sixteen teams scored less.

In Group Four, Morocco gave the West Germans a dreadful fright in their opening game at Leon, holding the lead until well into the second half before finally succumbing 2–1. Peru, under the old Brazilian star, Didi, were the revelation of the group, playing marvellously open, exciting football, inspired by the drive of Chumpitaz, and the control of their young black star, Cubillas. Bulgaria, by contrast, were a dour disappointment. But, as expected, the Germans won all their matches, and even the Peruvians were finally no match for Muller's fine finishing.

The advantage of playing at Leon— higher than Guadalajara—and Gordon Banks' illness (Banks' earlier save from Pele, one handed, was almost miraculous), helped Germany to beat England in an exciting quarter-final, a definitive game which will surely live in the memory of all who saw it. England, with Alan Mullery surpassing himself, both making and scoring their first goal, took a 2–0 lead, but the absence in goal of Banks, the vulnerability of Bonetti, and Ramsey's surprising substitution of Bobby Charlton and Martin Peters, swung the pendulum. Grabowski, brought on as substitute for Libuda, ran riot on the right wing, and Germany won 3–2 in extra time, Muller volleying the winner. Beckenbauer had scored the first and Seeler got the second with a backheader.

At Guadalajara, Brazil won an exciting game against the bright Peruvians. Rivelino, with an impressive left-foot, played nominally at outside-left but in reality dwelt largely in midfield and he got one of the goals for Brazil. Tostao scored two, and the powerful right-winger, Jairzinho, the other. Jairzinho was to become the first and, so far, only player to score in every game of a World Cup final series.

At Toluca, Italy at last came out of their shell, showing their full potential and thrashing Mexico 4–1; no refereeing decisions would come to the Mexicans' aid this time. Rivera, coming on instead of Mazzola at half-time, galvanised Italy's attack.

Group 1

Mexico	(0)0	USSR	(0)0
Belgium	(1)3	El Salvador	(0)0
Van Moer 2, Lambert (pen)			
USSR	(1)4	Belgium	(0)1
Byshovets 2, Asatiani,		Lambert	
Khmelnitsky			
Mexico	(1)4	El Salvador	(0)0
Valdivia 2, Fragoso,			
Basaguren			
USSR	(0)2	El Salvador	(0)0
Byshovets 2			
Mexico	(1)1	Belgium	(0)0
Pena (pen)			

	P	W	D	L	F	A	Pts
USSR	3	2	1	0	6	1	5
Mexico	3	2	1	0	5	0	5
Belgium	3	1	0	2	4	5	2
El Salvador	3	0	0	3	0	9	0

Group 2

Uruguay	(1)2	Israel	(0)0
Maneiro, Mujica			
Italy	(1)1	Sweden	(0)0
Domenghini			
Uruguay	(0)0	Italy	(0)0
Sweden	(0)1	Israel	(0)1
Turesson		Spiegler	
Sweden	(0)1	Uruguay	(0)0
Grahn			
Italy	(0)0	Israel	(0)0

	P	W	D	L	F	A	Pts
Italy	3	1	2	0	1	0	4
Uruguay	3	1	1	1	2	1	3
Sweden	3	1	1	1	2	2	3
Israel	3	0	2	1	1	3	2

Group 3

England	(0)1	Romania	(0)0
Hurst			
Brazil	(1)4	Czechoslovakia	(1)1
Rivelino, Pele,		Petras	
Jairzinho 2			
Romania	(0)2	Czechoslovakia	(1)1
Neagu, Dumitrache		Petras	
(pen)			
Brazil	(0)1	England	(0)0
Jairzinho			
Brazil	(2)3	Romania	(0)2
Pele 2, Jairzinho		Dumitrache,	
		Dembrovski	

England	(0)1	Czechoslovakia	(0)0
Clarke (pen)			

	P	W	D	L	F	A	Pts
Brazil	3	3	0	0	8	3	6
England	3	2	0	1	2	1	4
Romania	3	1	0	2	4	5	2
Czechoslovakia	3	0	0	3	2	7	0

Group 4

Peru	(0)3	Bulgaria	(1)2
Gallardo, Chumpitaz,		Dermendjiev,	
Cubillas		Bonev	
West Germany	(0)2	Morocco	(1)1
Seeler, Muller		Houmane	
Peru	(0)3	Morocco	(0)0
Cubillas 2, Challe			
West Germany	(2)5	Bulgaria	(1)2
Libuda, Muller 3 (1 pen),		Nikodimov, Kolev	
Seeler			
West Germany	(3)3	Peru	(1)1
Muller 3		Cubillas	
Bulgaria	(1)1	Morocco	(0)1
Jetchev		Ghazouani	

	P	W	D	L	F	A	Pts
West Germany	3	3	0	0	10	4	6
Peru	3	2	0	1	7	5	4
Bulgaria	3	0	1	2	5	9	1
Morocco	3	0	1	2	2	6	1

Quarter-finals

Uruguay	(0)(0)1	USSR	(0)(0)0
Esparrago		(Mexico City)	

Uruguay: Mazurkiewicz; Ubinas, Ancheta, Matosas, Mujica; Montero Castillo, Cortes, Maneiro; Cubilla, Fontes (Esparrago), Morales (Gomez).
USSR: Kavazashvili; Dzodzuashvili, Kaplichny, Shesternev, Afonin; Khurtsilava (Logofet), Muntian, Asatiani (Kiselev); Evryuzhikhin, Byshovets, Khmelnitsky.
Referee: vah Ravens (Netherlands).

Italy	(1)4	Mexico	(1)1
Domenghini, Riva 2,		Gonzales	
Rivera		(Toluca)	

Italy: Albertosi; Burgnich, Cera, Rosato, Facchetti; Bertini, Mazzola (Rivera), De Sisti; Domenghini (Gori), Boninsegna,

Riva
Mexico: Calderon; Vantolra, Pena, Guzman, Perez; Gonzales, Munguia (Diaz); Pulido; Valdivia (Borja), Fragoso, Padilla
Referee: Scheurer (Switzerland).

Brazil	(2)4	Peru	(1)2
Rivelino, Tostao 2,		Gallardo, Cubillas	
Jairzinho		(Guadalajara)	

Brazil: Felix; Carlos Alberto, Brito, Wilson Piazza, Everaldo (Marco Antonio); Clodoaldo, Gerson (Paulo Cesar); Jairzinho, Tostao, Pele, Rivelino
Peru: Rubinos; Campos, Fernandez, Chumpitaz, Fuentes; Mifflin, Challe; Baylon (Sotil), Leon (Reyes), Cubillas, Gallardo
Referee: Loraux (Belgium).

West Germany	(0)(2)3	England	(1)(2)2
Beckenbauer, Seeler,		Mullery, Peters	
Muller		(Leon)	

West Germany: Maier; Hottges (Schulz), Fichtel, Schnellinger, Vogts; Beckenbauer, Overath, Seeler; Libuda (Grabowski), Muller, Lohr
England: Bonetti; Newton, Labone, Moore, Cooper; Mullery, Charlton (R) (Bell), Ball; Lee, Hurst, Peters (Hunter)
Referee: Coreazza (Argentina).

Semi-finals

Italy	(1)(1)4	West Germany	(0)(1)3
Boninsegna, Burgnich,		Schnellinger,	
Riva, Rivera		Muller 2	
		(Mexico City)	

Italy: Albertosi; Burgnich, Cera, Rosato (Poletti), Facchetti; Bertini, Domenghini, Mazzola (Rivera), De Sisti; Boninsegna, Riva
West Germany: Maier; Patzke (Held), Schnellinger, Schulz, Vogts; Beckenbauer, Overath, Seeler; Grabowski, Muller, Lohr (Libuda)
Referee: Yamasaki (Mexico)

Brazil	(1)3	Uruguay	(1)1
Clodoaldo, Jairzinho,		Cubilla	
Rivelino		(Guadalajara)	

Brazil: Felix; Carlos Alberto, Brito, Wilson Piazza, Everaldo; Clodoaldo, Gerson; Jairzinho, Tostao, Pele, Rivelino
Uruguay: Mazurkiewicz; Ubinas, Ancheta, Matosas, Mujica; Cortes, Montero Castillo, Maneiro (Esparrago); Cubilla, Fontes, Morales
Referee: De Mendibil (Spain)

Third place match: Mexico City 20.6.70
Attendance 80,000

West Germany	(1)1	Uruguay	(0)0
Overath			

West Germany: Wolter; Patzke, Fichtel, Schnellinger (Lorenz), Vogts; Weber, Seeler, Overath; Libuda (Lohr), Muller, Held
Uruguay: Mazurkiewicz; Ubinas, Ancheta, Matosas, Mujica; Montero Castillo, Maneiro (Sandoval), Cortes; Cubilla, Fontes (Esparrago), Morales
Referee: Sbardella (Italy)

Final: Mexico City 21.6.70
Attendance 110,000

Brazil	(1)4	Italy	(1)1
Pele, Gerson,		Boninsegna	
Jairzinho, Carlos Alberto			

Brazil: Felix (Fluminense); Carlos Alberto (Santos), Brito (Flamengo), Wilson Piazza (Cruzeiro), Everaldo (Gremio Porto Alegre); Clodoaldo (Santos), Gerson (Sao Paulo); Jairzinho (Botafogo), Tostao (Cruzerio), Pele (Santos), Rivelino (Corinthians)
Italy: Albertosi (Cagliari); Burgnich (Internazionale), Cera (Cagliari), Rosato (AC Milan), Facchetti (Internazionale); Bertini (Internazionale), [Juliano (Napoli)], Mazzola (Internazionale), De Sisti (Fiorentina); Domenghini (Cagliari), Boninsegna (Internazionale), [Rivera (AC Milan)], Riva (Cagliari)
Referee: Glockner (East Germany)
Leading scorers: 10—Muller (West Germany)
7—Jairzinho (Brazil)
5—Cubillas (Peru)
4—Pele (Brazil)
Byshovets (USSR)

Right: *Beaten 3–1 at Wembley in the first leg of the European Championship quarter-final in 1972, Ramsey played only two front men in the second leg in Berlin. He included both Storey and Hunter as defensive midfield players. Here Storey provides a stranglehold on Muller just as England did on the West Germans; but the useless goalless draw meant only aggregate defeat.*

In Mexico City, another curious refereeing decision caused bitter contention, for the ball seemed almost certainly out of play when Uruguay's Cubilla crossed to make the only goal, against leaden Russia.

The tremendous drain on physical resources exerted by the Leon quarter-final had as much as anything to do with Germany's semi-final defeat by Italy, in Mexico City. The Germans, a goal down to Italy at half-time, equalised through Schnellinger in injury time, but when the brilliant Beckenbauer had his shoulder badly hurt in a ruthless Italian foul, their hopes vanished. There was a volley of goals in extra time, Rivera getting the last of them, to give Italy a 4–3 win. Sheer necessity had drawn Italy out of their defensive crouch, but they were to resume it with disastrous results in the final.

At Guadalajara, again, Brazil won an exciting semi-final against the Uruguayans. It was 1–1 at half-time, Felix's blunder—he was an oddly erratic goalkeeper for a World Cup winning side—giving Cubilla a goal. But it was to be no 1950. In the second half, Jairzinho and Rivelino, with that marvellous left foot, laid the persistent

Uruguayan bogey and took Brazil into the final.

There, Italy's tactics rebounded on them. They gave away an early goal to Pele's superb header, though equalised before half-time when Clodoaldo foolishly back-heeled and the excellent Boninsegna snapped up the chance; but, thereafter, Gerson was allowed to dominate the midfield.

Gerson himself put Brazil in front with a superb shot on the turn, and then the splendid Pele cleverly made goals for Jairzinho and Carlos Alberto. It was a triumph for attacking football. Despite the excellence of Boninsegna and Sandrino Mazzola, who was impeccable in midfield and always ready to drive forward, Brazil's determined attack gave Italy no chance.

Gordon Banks may have been the best goalkeeper, and may have made the finest save of the tournament, but Brazil simply did not need a great goalkeeper.

Bobby Charlton's appearance in the quarter-final against West Germany gave him his 106th cap, beating Billy Wright's record. Ramsey aimed to save him for the semi-final when he withdrew him from the game. But, in fact, as Charlton walked, somewhat perplexed, to the touchline he was leaving an international pitch for the last time. It is hard not to sense that moment as symbolic of the end of an era.

The first half of the new decade was a depressing time for England and the rest of the home countries, though Scotland were to enjoy a pocket of consolation in qualifying for, and doing themselves some justice at last, in the finals of the 1974 World Cup. It was only the third time they had competed in the final stages. But it was Ramsey's England once again which made the most progress in the next international challenge, the 1972 European Championship.

Scotland could not manage a goal or a point from their three away ties in Belgium, Portugal and Denmark. Wales did the double over Finland but could make little headway against Czechoslovakia or Rumania. Northern Ireland coped with tiny Cyprus but not Russia or Spain. But England came through unbeaten against Switzerland, Greece and Malta—though the group could hardly be classified as demanding.

With more than a sense of irony the draw for the quarter-final paired Ramsey with his old adversary Helmut Schoen. The first leg at Wembley was scheduled for 29 April—on a Saturday right at the heart of the climax to the Football League season. Ramsey had been battling for years for the release of key players from their clubs in time to prepare for important internationals. The clubs, with an understandable if perhaps short-sighted attitude, had shown and continue to show some reluctance to be totally co-operative. For seasons Ramsey, and, indeed, the various managers of Scotland, Wales, Northern Ireland and Eire had to make do and mend squads ravaged by withdrawals for injuries that seemed to clear up with great rapidity once the internationals had been played.

Now, as Ramsey faced West Germany, he was once again hampered. His first choice centre-half in his announced squad was Roy McFarland of Derby County, a club in the vanguard of the championship race; the reserve to McFarland was Larry Lloyd of Liverpool, raw and selected simply to gain experience of international atmosphere. Suddenly McFarland was withdrawn by Derby on the pretext of injury, yet two days later he played for his club and helped them to the League title. Country had lost to club again.

Ramsey did not gamble on Lloyd; instead he selected Bobby Moore to wear the number five shirt. With Norman Hunter alongside him both centre backs were of similar inclination, happier to mark space

and to cover. Neither was a man who regarded it as his role to go automatically for the ball in the penalty area. The move failed. West Germany took a first-half lead after Moore had been pressurised. Lee equalised but Moore tripped Held to concede a penalty from which Gunter Netzer scored, and then Muller continued the torment he had begun in Leon with a third.

England had been overrun in midfield where Ramsey had strangely, given his earlier record, not selected a player to win the ball. Mullery, a last-minute addition to the squad, was left as a substitute. Netzer, particularly, roamed Wembley at will and his perception and passing ability ran England into the ground with a display as good as any seen at Wembley since Hungary twenty years before.

For the second leg, Hurst was omitted. The news was broken to him on his car radio. Ramsey, so devoted to his players, showed an astounding lack of feeling in discarding a man who had run thousands of miles and withstood hundreds of tackles in his cause. He also returned to his basic principles for the second leg. Storey and Hunter, defensive strongmen, were drafted into midfield alongside Ball and Colin Bell; only two outright attackers, Martin Chivers and Rodney Marsh, began the game. England came back from Berlin with a useless 0–0 draw and a mass of criticism for their unsuccessful negative tactics.

Ramsey was by now a manager under

Right: *With England drawing against Poland and staring elimination in the face, Ramsey did not introduce a substitute forward, Kevin Hector, until the last two minutes of the game. Even then the Derby County forward very nearly bought salvation when this last-gasp header was cleared off the line.*

Far right: *The scoreboard at Wembley spells out the stark reality for an England side which needs to win to avoid elimination at the World Cup preliminary stages for the first time in history. But 17 October 1973 was to be a sad night for all, particularly Martin Chivers (left, attacking the Polish defence) who had a disappointing game which brought to an end his international career. Failure to qualify for the final stages also heralded the end of Ramsey's reign as manager, but Poland's subsequent performances in the finals mollified some of the despair about England's standing in world football. They overcame Argentina, Italy, Sweden, Yugoslavia and Brazil, only failing to defeat West Germany and finishing third. As well as having the two leading scorers in the final stages (Lato and Szarmach) goalkeeper Tomaszewski proved himself to be anything but the 'clown' he was dubbed by one English manager and even made two penalty saves—from Sweden and West Germany. Just as history may judge England's 1966 victory to be not quite the remarkable success it first appeared, so the record books might regard the 1970s to have been nothing like as bad as they seemed from the standpoint of 1976. And while it is a poor excuse for failure, England did have the misfortune to meet a West German side at its absolute height in the European Championship of 1972, a largely unknown Polish side in 1973 which nearly went on to win the World Cup and a rapidly improving Czechoslovakian side two years later in another European Championship.*

fire. His personality, which so often had produced a public image at best of reticence and at worst of rudeness, now started increasingly to work against him. Some of the more vitriolic newspapermen stood up in the press box at Wembley and openly cheered when West Germany scored. The knives were out and sharpened.

But he faced a vicious circle. No one recognised a greater need than he for the rebuilding of the England side, but the time the system gave him to do it was, to say the least, limited. After the return with West Germany, England played the home internationals—during which they sank to even further depths in losing at home to Northern Ireland and a goal from their player-manager Terry Neill. Then the fixtures allowed just one more international after the close season before the trail of World Cup qualification loomed up for the first time in Ramsey's reign. England were paired with Wales and Poland and the away tie at Ninian Park was scheduled for 15 November 1972. On 11 October, England met Yugoslavia but club demands meant that Ramsey could not field anything like his chosen eleven. Of the side that met Wales only Moore, Ball, Bell and Storey had played against the Yugoslavs. Unimpressively, Bell's goal lifted Ramsey over the first World Cup hurdle.

Worse followed in the return at Wembley; Wales led through John Toshack only for Hunter to save face with a spectacular thirty-yard equaliser; in the final analysis the draw was to be of no use to either side. Wales beat Poland in Cardiff to further their own chances, particularly when England crumbled in Katowice at the start of a

summer tour. Defensively orientated again, with only Chivers and Allan Clarke as attackers, England played with composure in a cauldron of excitement but gave away two very bad goals. A free-kick was deflected past Shilton for the first and then in the second-half, with England showing clear signs of recovery, Bobby Moore was caught in possession and Lubanski ran through to score. Tragedy.

When Wales lost by three goals in Katowice, in a match of violence and vendetta with Hockey being sent off, England had to beat Poland at Wembley to qualify for the finals. Ramsey elected to go into the game without his captain, who had been dropped by West Ham earlier in the season, though Moore sat behind Ramsey on the substitutes' bench. And ironically it was a mistake by his replacement, Hunter, which turned the game away from England. Ramsey's side had thrown away a series of chances when Hunter was caught in possession on the half-way line and Domarski finished the breakaway with a scoring shot.

Clarke finally did equalise with a penalty but England's finishing continued to be cruelly wasteful. Ramsey once again demonstrated his uneasy use of extra players by delaying the arrival of a substitute forward, Hector, until the dying moments. Even then Hector might have provided the most dramatic of salvations, only for his last-gasp header to strike a defender on the line and stay out. Such was the margin between success and a desperate failure.

Hector played for England just once more—also as sub against Italy—a sadly short career. In truth,

England did not lose their place in the finals at Wembley against Poland, but at Katowice and in that draw against Wales. A point in either game would have put them through. It is also worth noting that the Poland game was a magnificent spectacle, an excellent game of football, fraught with emotion, tense and undecided to the very last second. Like the quarter-final defeat at Leon four years earlier, it saw football at its best, an England side deserving of massive support—and tragic, traumatic defeat.

Within a month England had lost at home again—1–0 to Italy with a goal three minutes from time, even though Bobby Moore had been recalled for his 108th and last international. 'Alf's final humiliation', screamed the headlines from the popular press.

Ramsey took the blow on the chin and remained standing. But his pleas to be given more time with his players to solve the problems fell on deaf ears, particularly

at the Football League. His attempt to organise a get-together for his squad prior to the Poland match was destroyed by a League ruling that all his selected players should play for their clubs four days before the crucial World Cup tie. The preparation for international matches in the seventies was symptomatic of a problem almost as pathetic as those which Ramsey had faced at the start of his term of office.

A look at the international fixture list emphasised Ramsey's problems. After the Italy game, it was almost six months until England met opposition again, and then rebuilding began with the blooding of five new caps for a friendly in Portugal. But even if given the opportunity of sowing new seeds, Ramsey was not going to be given the chance to cultivate them. On 14 February 1974, an enquiry had begun internally at the Football Association to investigate the standing of England in international football, a position which

233

maybe should have been clear to all.

On 1 May the announcement was made from Lancaster Gate: 'Following meetings, a unanimous recommendation was submitted to the executive committee that Sir Alf Ramsey should be replaced as England team manager. This recommendation was accepted unanimously by the executive committee.' Ramsey, like many a football manager, had been punished for failure. Yet there prevailed the thought that one or two toes that had been trodden on heavily when Ramsey had taken over at Lancaster Gate had rejoiced in the opportunity to kick back.

Ramsey led England through 113 matches, 69 of which were won, 27 drawn and 17 lost—the equivalent of a League team scoring 61 points in a 42-match season. But international competition is not a League and Ramsey had paid the price for falling short of those big prizes which his own 1966 success had led the English public to expect.

Joe Mercer became a caretaker manager through the 1974 home internationals and a summer tour during which England provided opposition for nations warming up to contest the 1974 World Cup finals in West Germany—a tournament in which Scotland were to be Great Britain's only representatives. And while the nation sat back to view the games in Munich, the Football Association announced that Don Revie, fresh from Leeds' magnificent twenty-nine-game unbeaten run at the beginning of the 1973–74 season, would be the new England team manager.

Scotland had had their own managerial problems. They had taken a large pace towards qualification by beating Denmark home and away under the auspices of Tommy Docherty. But when Manchester United intelligently persuaded Docherty to become their manager, Willie Ormond had been brought in as his replacement. Ormond endured a 5–0 home defeat against England in his baptismal match, but pieced together a side just good enough to beat Czechoslovakia at Hampden Park and so go through. Indeed Scotland lost an early goal but hit back with responses from Jim Holton and Joe Jordan. With England and Wales cancelling each other out, Scotland became the only domestic survivor when Northern Ireland inexplicably lost in Cyprus.

Ormond's squad could have hardly gone through a more sensational approach to their first World Cup since 1958. There was open bickering about the money players were, or were not, making from commercial ventures. And rumours about a lack of discipline were substantiated when Jimmy

Left: Scotland alone represented Great Britain in the 1974 World Cup finals, but were eliminated at the Group stages. Having drawn with Brazil and beaten Zaire, inferior goal difference meant that they needed to beat Yugoslavia to go forward into the second round. Instead despite putting much pressure on Maric, the Yugoslavian goalkeeper, they could only draw 1–1, and though remaining the only unbeaten team, Scotland went out of the competition.

Johnstone, somewhat the worse for wear, had to be rescued in the early hours adrift in a small boat in the Firth of Clyde near the side's training camp. And when Johnstone, for a second time, and Bremner, the captain, were fined for further misbehaviour only days before the World Cup began, hopes for Scotland's success were hardly enhanced.

The 1974 World Cup was organised with Germanic efficiency—a computer had even selected the dates for the games to be fitted into what was supposed to be the driest period of the year. In fact the whole competition took place under darkened skies and often in teeming downpours. But on the field West Germany proved to be the most efficient team, though certainly not the most attractive, and became the first holders of the new World Cup.

The Germans, of course, retained the nucleus of their excellent European Championship squad of two years earlier. Maier, Schwarzenbeck, Beckenbauer, Breitner, Hoeness and Muller had all been in that side (though Netzer was missing) and had also been the core of the Bayern Munich who had defeated Atletico Madrid and so won the 1974 European Cup final. All this plus playing the final on their own Munich ground finally proved too much for the Dutch, who had provided much of the competition's adventure while their hosts struggled to get into their groove.

The rain fell heavily as Brazil and Yugoslavia started yet another World Cup with a goalless draw. Scotland, together with Zaire, shared Group Two with these two nations, but Ormond's side never recovered

from only beating the Africans by two goals, from Lorimer with a characteristically violent volley and Jordan with a soft header. The Yugoslavs showed less inhibition in putting nine past Zaire, essential scoring with goal difference a factor in the event of a tie. The Zaire coach, overruled from Kinshasa where a more open 'African' game was demanded and led to the nine-goal debacle, resigned.

That same night in Frankfurt, Scotland fought a distinguished draw with a Brazil side which had clearly arrived equipped to cope with any attempt at intimidation such as that of 1966. Of their 1970 winning side, only Jairzinho, Rivelino and Piazza remained and the defence had a rugged European flavour to its play. Scotland had the better of the action with the occasion stimulating the adrenalin of Bremner, but Brazil gave a show of strength that proved effective, if in purist terms no way compensating for the absence of Pele and that electric attack. Overall, the holders were a disappointment.

Scotland now had to beat Yugoslavia to move into the second round; a draw would only suffice if Brazil failed to beat Zaire by three goals. With the two matches taking their courses simultaneously the drama was heightened, and at half-time Scotland were still favoured; they held Yugoslavia goalless while the shot-shy Brazilians had scored their first goal of the competition, but only one, against Zaire. The stalemate lasted another twenty minutes before Brazil scored twice, the second being an absurdly soft goalkeeping error. And then Scotland, who now needed to win, fell a goal behind, to Karasi, a substitute who had been introduced to help his country obtain the draw they needed to qualify. Jordan salvaged some pride with a late equaliser but Scotland went home unbeaten if bowed. They were to be the only country not to suffer a defeat in the final stages, a factual curiosity but of no great consolation.

Group One had been the talk of the competition since the draw had been made for it paired together East and West Germany—the East Germans supported by 3000 carefully vetted fans who were allowed across the border for the occasion. At the time they met neither side had produced their best. West Germany had only beaten Chile through a long-range shot from Breitner and outsiders Australia 3–0. East Germany, with their strong running and organisation, put two past Australia but had only drawn 1–1 with the Chileans.

The encounter, which took place in Hamburg, was the first between the two halves of a permanently divided nation. Again West Germany stumbled and stut-

Below: Argentina's Houseman and Yazalde evade the attentions of the Italian defence during a 1974 Group game which ended 1–1. With their hosting of the 1978 tournament clearly in mind, the Argentinians surprised the soccer world by playing the parts of perfect gentlemen throughout the finals. Houseman, particularly, made a considerable impression and the team's display helped quell some of the disquiet that had been expressed about the staging of the next World Cup in relatively unstable Buenos Aires.

10th WORLD CUP
West Germany, 1974

Group 1

West Germany	(1)1	Chile	(0)0
Breitner			

East Germany	(0)2	Australia	(0)0
Curran (og), Streich			

West Germany	(2)3	Australia	(0)0
Overath, Cullmann, Muller			

East Germany	(0)1	Chile	(0)1
Hoffmann		Ahumáda	

Chile	(0)0	Australia	(0)0

East Germany	(0)1	West Germany	(0)0
Sparwasser			

	P	W	D	L	F	A	Pts
East Germany	3	2	1	0	4	1	5
West Germany	3	2	0	1	4	1	4
Chile	3	0	2	1	1	2	2
Australia	3	0	1	2	0	5	1

Group 2

Brazil	(0)0	Yugoslavia	(0)0

Scotland	(2)2	Zaire	(0)0
Lorimer, Jordan			

Brazil	(0)0	Scotland	(0)0

Yugoslavia	(6)9	Zaire	(0)0
Bajevic 3, Dzajic, Surjak, Katalinski, Bogicevic, Oblak, Petkovic			

Scotland	(0)1	Yugoslavia	(0)1
Jordan		Karasi	

Brazil	(1)3	Zaire	(0)0
Jairzinho, Rivelino, Valdomiro			

	P	W	D	L	F	A	Pts
Yugoslavia	3	1	2	0	10	1	4
Brazil	3	1	2	0	3	0	4
Scotland	3	1	2	0	3	1	4
Zaire	3	0	0	3	0	14	0

Group 3

Netherlands	(1)2	Uruguay	(0)0
Rep 2			

Sweden	(0)0	Bulgaria	(0)0

Netherlands	(0)0	Sweden	(0)0

Bulgaria	(0)1	Uruguay	(0)1
Bonev		Pavoni	

Netherlands	(2)4	Bulgaria	(0)1
Neeskens 2 pens, Rep, De Jong		Krol (og)	

Sweden	(0)3	Uruguay	(0)0
Edstrom 2, Sandberg			

	P	W	D	L	F	A	Pts
Netherlands	3	2	1	0	6	1	5
Sweden	3	1	2	0	3	0	4
Bulgaria	3	0	2	1	2	5	2
Uruguay	3	0	1	2	1	6	1

Group 4

Italy	(0)3	Haiti	(0)1
Rivera, Benetti, Anastasi		Sanon	

Poland	(2)3	Argentina	(0)2
Lato 2, Szarmach		Heredia, Babington	

Argentina	(1)1	Italy	(1)1
Houseman		Perfumo (og)	

Poland	(5)7	Haiti	(0)0
Lato 2, Deyna, Szarmach 3, Gorgon			

Argentina	(2)4	Haiti	(0)1
Yazalde 2, Houseman, Ayala		Sanon	

Poland	(2)2	Italy	(0)1
Szarmach, Deyna		Capello	

	P	W	D	L	F	A	Pts
Poland	3	3	0	0	12	3	6
Argentina	3	1	1	1	7	5	3
Italy	3	1	1	1	5	4	3
Haiti	3	0	0	3	2	14	0

Group A

Brazil	(0)1	East Germany	(0)0
Rivelino			

Netherlands	(2)4	Argentina	(0)0
Cruyff 2, Krol, Rep			

Netherlands	(1)2	East Germany	(0)0
Neeskens, Rensenbrink			

Brazil	(1)2	Argentina	(1)1
Rivelino, Jairzinho		Brindisi	

Netherlands	(0)2	Brazil	(0)0
Neeskens, Cruyff			

Argentina	(0)1	East Germany	(1)1
Houseman		Streich	

	P	W	D	L	F	A	Pts
Netherlands	3	3	0	0	8	0	6
Brazil	3	2	0	1	3	3	4
East Germany	3	0	1	2	1	4	1
Argentina	3	0	1	2	2	7	1

Group B

Poland	(1)1	Sweden	(0)0
Lato			

West Germany	(1)2	Yugoslavia	(0)0
Breitner, Muller			

Poland	(1)2	Yugoslavia	(1)1
Deyna (pen), Lato		Karasi	

West Germany	(0)4	Sweden	(1)2
Overath, Bonhof, Grabowski, Hoeness (pen)		Edstroem, Sandberg	

Sweden	(1)2	Yugoslavia	(1)1
Edstroem, Torstensson		Surjak	

West Germany	(0)1	Poland	(0)0
Muller			

	P	W	D	L	F	A	Pts
West Germany	3	3	0	0	7	2	6
Poland	3	2	0	1	3	2	4
Sweden	3	1	0	2	4	6	2
Yugoslavia	3	0	0	3	2	6	0

Third place match: Munich 6.7.74
Attendance 70,000

Poland	(0)1	Brazil	(0)0
Lato			

Poland: Tomaszewski; Szymanowski, Gorgon, Zmuda, Musial, Maszczyk, Deyna, Kasperczak (Cmikiewicz), Lato, Szarmach (Kapka), Gadocha

Brazil: Leao; Ze Maria, Alfredo, Mario Marinho, Francesco Marinho, Paulo Cesar Carpegiani, Rivelino, Ademir da Guia (Mirandinha), Valdomiro, Jairzinho, Dirceu

Referee: Angonese (Italy)

Final: Munich 7.7.74
Attendance 77,833

West Germany	(2)2	Netherlands	(1)1
Breitner (pen), Muller		Neeskens (pen)	

West Germany: Maier (Bayern Munich); Vogts (Borussia Monchengladbach), Schwarzenbeck (Bayern Munich), Beckenbauer (Bayern Munich), Breitner (Bayern Munich), Bonhof (Borussia Monchengladbach), Hoeness (Bayern Munich), Overath (Cologne), Grabowski (Eintracht Frankfurt), Muller (Bayern Munich), Holzenbein (Eintracht Frankfurt)

Netherlands: Jongbloed (FC Amsterdam); Suürbier (Ajax), Rijsbergen (Feyenoord) [De Jong (Feyenoord)], Haan (Ajax), Krol (Ajax), Jansen (Feyenoord), Van Hanegem (Feyenoord), Neeskens (Ajax), Rep (Ajax), Cruyff (Barcelona), Rensenbrink (Anderlecht) [Van der Kerkhof (PSV Eindhoven)]

Referee: Jack Taylor (England)

Leading scorers: 7—Lato (Poland)
5—Szarmach (Poland), Neeskens (Netherlands)
4—Rep (Netherlands), Edstroem (Sweden), Muller (West Germany)

---

tered, so much so that Schoen summoned Netzer, out of favour since his move to Real Madrid, to substitute for Wolfgang Overath, who had regained the place he had held in the 1966 and 1970 World Cups. But the only goal of the game, a superb one at that, went to the East, scored by Sparwasser amidst stupendous joy on the pitch and disappointment among the West German crowd. But both sides qualified and students of World Cup history suspiciously recalled that West Germany had also lost a group game before winning the trophy in 1954. No other winning side has ever lost a game in the final stages of a World Cup.

Classy Holland and Sweden qualified from Group Three at the expense of Uruguay and Bulgaria, though it was by far the most open group. The Dutch were to reserve their most expressive form for the second round but, like West Germany, they enjoyed the cohesion of a nucleus of players from their club sides Ajax and Feijenoord. And in Johan Cruyff and Johan Neeskens they possessed the tournament's two outstanding individuals. Cruyff carried the label of the world's best player with dignity, at least until the final. But the Swedes had their performers, too, notably the tall Edstroem, the best header of a ball in the competition, and Sandberg, his willing ally in attack. These two shared the three goals against a disappointing Uru-

guay, a result which clinched Sweden's place in the second round.

Group Four had all the explosive potential of the meeting of a stick of dynamite and a lighted match. Uncompromising, cynical Italy against Argentina, with a track record of violence, against Poland, who had shown against Wales that they could look after themselves in a scrap, and Haiti thrown in for good measure. Happily the bomb never went off. The Argentinians defused much of the situation by arriving with the obvious intention of winning friends and influencing people—their staging of the 1978 tournament very much in mind. The ageing Italians were more in keeping with their form of 1966 than that of 1970, and the Poles eased some of the pain of England's dismissal by indicating that they were a side to be reckoned with.

Italy, who trailed to Haiti when they conceded their first goal in thirteen internationals, recovered from the brink of that embarrassment, but lost to two inspired goals from Poland and could only draw with Argentina. There were rumours that the Italians had tried to bribe the Poles on the field. Argentina sparkled in a 3–2 defeat by Poland, thrashed Haiti and their share of the spoils with Italy took them through on goal difference, along with Poland who won all three of their games. One Haitian player failed a dope test and was whisked back to the Caribbean—where

237

there were fears that he would never reappear.

The eight survivors split into two groups, a new idea with the winner of each group to contest the World Cup final. Group A developed into a contest between Holland and Brazil, a battle of paradox between the aesthetic skills of the Dutch and the tight organisation of the Brazilians. Holland savaged Argentina in a display of scintillating football which provoked no retaliation. Cruyff and Krol in the first half and Rep and Cruyff in the second finished moves of splendid incision. Brazil matched that stride with a set-piece goal from Rivelino which beat East Germany.

As the two teams swapped opponents, the form did not change. Goals from Neeskens and Rensenbrink beat East Germany and, although Brindisi put the first goal of the tournament past Brazil, the holders beat Argentina with a score from Rivelino and another from Jairzinho, the strikers of 1970. But sadly Brazil went into the decider feeling that violence was a prerequisite of beating the Dutch. Holland did not yield to intimidatory fouls from defenders Ze Maria, Luis Pereira and Mario Marinho, and when Pereira persisted he was sent off. Holland provided the right kind of riposte with thrilling goals from Neeskens and Cruyff to reach the final.

The two front runners in Group B became West Germany, now only second favourites to Holland, and Poland. A penalty save from Tomaszewski and a goal from Gregor Lato, the competition's top scorer, enabled Poland to beat Sweden, a result equalled by West Germany in one of the most thrilling games of the finals. As the rain swept down in Dusseldorf so did the Swedes and they led at half-time through an exquisite volley from Edstroem. Overath and Bonhof then scored twice in a minute before Sandberg, two further minutes on, levelled the tie again.

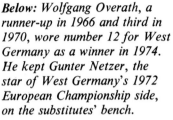

Below: Wolfgang Overath, a runner-up in 1966 and third in 1970, wore number 12 for West Germany as a winner in 1974. He kept Gunter Netzer, the star of West Germany's 1972 European Championship side, on the substitutes' bench.

Grabowski and a Hoeness penalty finally ended the challenge of Sweden who once again, with a side of veterans and amateurs, had provided a distinguished contribution.

Both West Germany and Poland beat Yugoslavia, whose players faded under the increasing pressures, and as, once again, the heavens opened the sides prepared to do battle in Frankfurt. So heavy was this cloudburst that the kick-off was delayed for mopping up operations; but for the schedule the game would surely have been postponed and eventually it began in a quagmire. Lato might have put Poland ahead but Hoeness contrived the most spectacular miss when Tomaszewski (continuing his remarkable form against England) yet again pounced on his weak penalty kick. Finally Muller, the finisher with the deadliness of a mercenary gunman, retained his balance in the bog to drive in the game's only goal.

And it was Muller again, the definitive goalscorer of the decade, who appropriately settled a final which at its very inception seemed to be going Holland's way. Hoeness made a lunging attempt to become the first German to touch the ball in the match as Cruyff carried the initial Dutch attack to the edge of the German area. The tackle was mistimed, Cruyff fell, and referee Jack Taylor awarded the first ever penalty in a World Cup final. Neeskens drove his kick into the centre of the goal as Maier, in hopeful anticipation, flung himself to his right. Following tradition, the side which was to lose the World Cup final had scored first.

Twenty-five minutes later a similar scene was re-enacted at the other end of the field. This time the tackler was Jansen and the man who fell, more doubtfully, Holzenbein. After Hoeness's miss against Poland, Breitner took the kick and sent it firmly past Jongbloed. The Dutch reacted badly to the set-back, their character not matching their fluid skills, and Cruyff received a yellow card for verbally assaulting the referee. Worse still, from their point of view, just before half-time they fell behind.

Bonhof, an outstanding newcomer, roared his way along the right-hand touch-line to the bye-line. His cross arrived slightly behind Muller who had made a sharp dash to the near post. Muller made the difficulty of his task seem inconsequential; he checked, took the pace off the cross, swivelled and placed his shot wide of Jongbloed. The prolific goalscorer had left his trademark on the majority of his senior games, and now he etched it on to a World Cup final. And Holland, though Rep and Neeskens missed chances, could never catch up. Helmut Schoen, assistant in 1954

to the victorious Sepp Herberger, had now masterminded a World Cup triumph of his own after coming second in 1966 and third in 1970. An excellent record, even if there was much talk of Beckenbauer and his Bayern colleagues having as much managerial influence as Schoen.

Managers of much less experience were faced with the challenge of rekindling the fading flame of international football in Great Britain. Apart from Don Revie, Mike Smith, an Englishman whose playing career had been in amateur football, became the Welsh manager in succession to Dave Bowen. Terry Neill relinquished the position in Northern Ireland to concentrate fully on a new job with Spurs and Dave Clements, still a player with Everton, assumed control.

But the spotlight inevitably fell on Revie, Ramsey's successor, as the 1976 European Championship became the new target. Revie contentiously altered the England strip, tried to boost support by adopting *Land of Hope and Glory* as a battle song but, of course, had basically the same players. Unlike Ramsey, he accepted the variation that substitutions could give him, and in his first international he struck a rich vein. England had struggled to break down Czechoslovakia for an hour, when Revie opted for a double substitution. Dave Thomas and Trevor Brooking, the two newcomers, immediately fashioned a free-kick from which Channon scored and in the end England won 3–0.

Yet the same ploy produced no response when Portugal visited Wembley for the next championship game. There were no goals and England's attacking play remained blunt in comparison with the sharpness that the Dutch and others had exhibited in the World Cup. Revie changed the captain, dropping Emlyn Hughes, and recalled the last survivor of 1966, Alan Ball, to lead the team. Ball began in style with a 2–0 win that brought prestige, but no championship points, in a friendly against West Germany, who put on show only five of the team which beat the Netherlands.

Malcolm Macdonald produced all five goals (equalling Steve Bloomer's seventy-nine year old record) in the European Championship tie with Cyprus, who were then beaten with some difficulty in Limassol. England also put five past Scotland at Wembley in an encouraging display —for the English. But over a year after Ramsey, Don Revie was the first to admit that not enough progress had been made towards creating a squad to challenge for the 1978 World Cup, though the short-term Ball was replaced as captain by Gerry

The new era for England; for Ramsey read Revie. The watching reporters might have welcomed the arrival of a more publicity-conscious supremo, but the former Leeds United manager experienced the same difficulties as his predecessor, and Revie's England failed to qualify for the quarter-finals of the 1976 European Championship. The length and toughness of the English season led to injuries and exhausted players at a time when Ramsey's occasional claim that '...at times there just aren't the players' seemed justified. Certainly the dominant midfield players of the First Division were all too often celtic —Mahoney of Stoke, Gemmill and Rioch of Derby, Daly of Manchester United, Bremner of Leeds and, above all, Masson of QPR. But, out of all the gloom, came a remarkable series of displays in the United States in the summer of 1976, including a 3-2 defeat of World Cup opponents Italy after being 2-0 down at half-time. Suddenly, the future seemed brighter again.

Francis. And just how little progress had been made was emphasised by the events of the first half of the 1975–76 season.

To progress into the quarter-finals of the European Championship England needed at least one good result in their two remaining games, away to Czechoslovakia and away to Portugal. They obtained neither. In Bratislava Channon sent England in front only for a sloppy goal to be conceded either side of half-time. Channon scored again in Lisbon but only to ensure a draw, and England needed the miracle of a Cypriot win over the Czechs to stay alive. The miracle did not materialise.

Scotland this time were also failures, as seemed likely after they lost their opening home tie to Spain. Moreover disgrace followed on the heels of disappointment when Billy Bremner, the captain, and other players became involved in an incident at a Copenhagen hotel after their tie with Denmark. Subsequently Bremner, Willie Young, Pat McCluskey and Arthur Graham were banned from international football by the Scottish Football Association.

Northern Ireland, too, could not clamber up the ladder from the groups, though they at least had the satisfaction of persuading the Yugoslavs to play in Belfast, the first international football at Windsor Park for three and a half years.

So it was left to Wales to provide some glory. They reached the quarter-finals and a tie against Yugoslavia on a passionate

night at Wrexham with a goal from the veteran midfield player and assistant manager Arfon Griffiths, who had discovered an appetite for international football at an age when most players contemplate retirement; and more than that discovered that he could score goals too. Wales greatest achievement lay not so much in doing the double over Hungary as in inflicting on the Magyars their first home defeat in competitive internationals since the War.

Sir Alf Ramsey watched the events of autumn 1975 from afar. He had not returned to football, devoting his time instead to interests in the building industry and sports goods. He still watched the game, but in total anonymity, buying a ticket or even standing on the terraces, hiding his identity beneath a bowler hat.

But he must have watched with avid interest. In the post-mortem of another England international failure the cries still bore the same ring. Too much football. Not enough co-operation between the League and the FA. Not enough time for preparation—Portugal's players had had a fortnight together before they played England in Lisbon. England's side had, as usual, turned out for their clubs four days prior to the game. All valid points. And all made countless times by Ramsey.

The only difference was that the words now came from another mouth. Sir Alf Ramsey was never one to show his emotions in public, but in private he must have permitted himself a smile.

APPENDICES

European Competitions

Year	European Champion Clubs Cup Finals				Fairs Cup/EUFA Cup Winners	European Cup Winners' Cup Winners	European Nations Cup/ European Championship Finals				Year
1956	Real Madrid	4	Reims	3							1956
1957	Real Madrid	2	Fiorentina	0							1957
1958	Real Madrid	3	AC Milan	2	Barcelona						1958
1959	Real Madrid	2	Reims	0							1959
1960	Real Madrid	7	Eintracht Frankfurt	3	Barcelona		USSR	2	Yugoslavia	1	1960
1961	Benfica	3	Barcelona	2	AS Roma	Fiorentina					1961
1962	Benfica	5	Real Madrid	3	Valencia	Atletico Madrid					1962
1963	AC Milan	2	Benfica	1	Valencia	Tottenham Hotspur					1963
1964	Inter Milan	3	Real Madrid	1	Real Zaragoza	Sporting Lisbon	Spain	2	USSR	1	1964
1965	Inter Milan	1	Benfica	0	Ferencvaros	West Ham United					1965
1966	Real Madrid	2	Partizan Belgrade	1	Barcelona	Borussia Dortmund					1966
1967	Glasgow Celtic	2	Inter Milan	1	Dynamo Zagreb	Bayern Munich					1967
1968	Manchester United	4	Benfica	1	Leeds United	AC Milan	Italy	2	Yugoslavia	0	1968
1969	AC Milan	4	Ajax Amsterdam	1	Newcastle United	Slovan Bratislava					1969
1970	Feijenoord	2	Glasgow Celtic	1	Arsenal	Manchester City					1970
1971	Ajax Amsterdam	2	Panathinaikos	0	Leeds United	Chelsea					1971
1972	Ajax Amsterdam	2	Inter Milan	0	Tottenham Hotspur	Glasgow Rangers	West Germany	3	USSR	0	1972
1973	Ajax Amsterdam	1	Juventus	0	Liverpool	AC Milan					1973
1974	Bayern Munich	1:4	Atletico Madrid	1:0	Feijenoord	FC Magdeburg					1974
1975	Bayern Munich	2	Leeds United	0	Borussia Monchengladbach	Dynamo Kiev					1975
1976	Bayern Munich	1	St. Etienne	0	Liverpool	Anderlecht					1976

Scottish & FA Challenge Cup finals

Year	Football Association Challenge Cup Finals				Scottish Football Association Cup Finals				Year
1872	Wanderers	1	Royal Engineers	0					1872
1873	[7]Wanderers	2	Oxford University	0					1873
1874	Oxford University	2	Royal Engineers	0	Queen's Park	2	Clydesdale	0	1874
1875	Royal Engineers	1:2	Old Etonians	1:0	Queen's Park	3	Renton	0	1875
1876	Wanderers	0:3	Old Etonians	0:0	Queen's Park	1:2	Third Lanark	1:0	1876
1877	Wanderers	2	Oxford University	0	Vale of Leven	0:1:3	Rangers	0:1:2	1877
1878	Wanderers	3	Royal Engineers	1	Vale of Leven	1	Third Lanark	0	1878
1879	Old Etonians	1	Clapham Rovers	0	[1]Vale of Leven	1	Rangers	1	1879
1880	Clapham Rovers	1	Oxford University	0	Queen's Park	3	Thornliebank	0	1880
1881	Old Carthusians	3	Old Etonians	0	[2]Queen's Park	3	Dumbarton	1	1881
1882	Old Etonians	1	Blackburn Rovers	0	Queen's Park	2:4	Dumbarton	2:1	1882
1883	Blackburn Olympic	2	Old Etonians	1	Dumbarton	2:2	Vale of Leven	2:1	1883
1884	Blackburn Rovers	2	Queen's Park	1	[3]Queen's Park		Vale of Leven		1884
1885	Blackburn Rovers	2	Queen's Park	0	Renton	0:3	Vale of Leven	0:1	1885

Year									Year
1886	Blackburn Rovers	0:2	West Bromwich Albion	0:0	Queen's Park	3	Renton	1	1886
1887	Aston Villa	2	West Bromwich Albion	0	Hibernian	2	Dumbarton	1	1887
1888	West Bromwich Albion	2	Preston North End	1	Renton	6	Cambuslang	1	1888
1889	Preston North End	3	Wolverhampton Wanderers	0	[4]Third Lanark	2	Celtic	1	1889
1890	Blackburn Rovers	6	The Wednesday	1	Queen's Park	1:2	Vale of Leven	1:1	1890
1891	Blackburn Rovers	3	Notts County	1	Hearts	1	Dumbarton	0	1891
1892	West Bromwich Albion	3	Aston Villa	0	[5]Celtic	5	Queen's Park	1	1892
1893	Wolverhampton Wanderers	1	Everton	0	Queen's Park	2	Celtic	1	1893
1894	Notts County	4	Bolton Wanderers	1	Rangers	3	Celtic	1	1894
1895	Aston Villa	1	West Bromwich Albion	0	St Bernard's	2	Renton	1	1895
1896	The Wednesday	2	Wolverhampton Wanderers	1	Hearts	3	Hibernian	1	1896
1897	Aston Villa	3	Everton	2	Rangers	5	Dumbarton	1	1897
1898	Nottingham Forest	3	Derby County	1	Rangers	2	Kilmarnock	0	1898
1899	Sheffield United	4	Derby County	1	Celtic	2	Rangers	0	1899
1900	Bury	4	Southampton	0	Celtic	4	Queen's Park	3	1900
1901	Tottenham Hotspur	2:3	Sheffield United	2:1	Hearts	4	Celtic	3	1901
1902	Sheffield United	1:2	Southampton	1:1	Hibernian	1	Celtic	0	1902
1903	Bury	6	Derby County	0	Rangers	1:0:2	Hearts	1:0:0	1903
1904	Manchester City	1	Bolton Wanderers	0	Celtic	3	Rangers	2	1904
1905	Aston Villa	2	Newcastle United	0	Third Lanark	0:3	Rangers	0:1	1905
1906	Everton	1	Newcastle United	0	Hearts	1	Third Lanark	0	1906
1907	The Wednesday	2	Everton	1	Celtic	3	Hearts	0	1907
1908	Wolverhampton Wanderers	3	Newcastle United	1	Celtic	5	St Mirren	1	1908
1909	Manchester United	1	Bristol City	0	[6]Celtic		Rangers		1909
1910	Newcastle United	1:2	Barnsley	1:0	Dundee	2:0:2	Clyde	2:0:1	1910
1911	Bradford City	0:1	Newcastle United	0:0	Celtic	0:2	Hamilton Academicals	0:0	1911
1912	Barnsley	0:1	West Bromwich Albion	0:0	Celtic	2	Clyde	0	1912
1913	Aston Villa	1	Sunderland	0	Falkirk	2	Raith Rovers	0	1913
1914	Burnley	1	Liverpool	0	Celtic	0:4	Hibernian	0:1	1914
1915	Sheffield United	3	Chelsea	0	No competition				1915
1916	No competition				No competition				1916
1917	No competition				No competition				1917
1918	No competition				No competition				1918
1919	No competition				No competition				1919
1920	Aston Villa	1	Huddersfield Town	0	Kilmarnock	3	Albion Rovers	2	1920
1921	Tottenham Hotspur	1	Wolverhampton Wanderers	0	Partick Thistle	1	Rangers	0	1921
1922	Huddersfield Town	1	Preston North End	0	Morton	1	Rangers	0	1922
1923	Bolton Wanderers	2	West Ham United	0	Celtic	1	Hibernian	0	1923
1924	Newcastle United	2	Aston Villa	0	Airdrieonians	2	Hibernian	0	1924
1925	Sheffield United	1	Cardiff City	0	Celtic	2	Dundee	1	1925
1926	Bolton Wanderers	1	Manchester City	0	St Mirren	2	Celtic	0	1926
1927	Cardiff City	1	Arsenal	0	Celtic	3	East Fife	1	1927
1928	Blackburn Rovers	3	Huddersfield Town	1	Rangers	4	Celtic	0	1928
1929	Bolton Wanderers	2	Portsmouth	0	Kilmarnock	2	Rangers	0	1929
1930	Arsenal	2	Huddersfield Town	0	Rangers	0:2	Partick Thistle	0:1	1930
1931	West Bromwich Albion	2	Birmingham	1	Celtic	2:4	Motherwell	2:2	1931
1932	Newcastle United	2	Arsenal	1	Rangers	1:3	Kilmarnock	1:0	1932
1933	Everton	3	Manchester City	0	Celtic	1	Motherwell	0	1933
1934	Manchester City	2	Portsmouth	1	Rangers	5	St Mirren	0	1934
1935	Sheffield Wednesday	4	West Bromwich Albion	2	Rangers	2	Hamilton Academicals	1	1935
1936	Arsenal	1	Sheffield United	0	Rangers	1	Third Lanark	0	1936
1937	Sunderland	3	Preston North End	1	Celtic	2	Aberdeen	1	1937
1938	Preston North End	1	Huddersfield Town	0	East Fife	1:4	Kilmarnock	1:2	1938
1939	Portsmouth	4	Wolverhampton Wanderers	1	Clyde	4	Motherwell	0	1939
1940	No competition				No competition				1940
1941	No competition				No competition				1941
1942	No competition				No competition				1942
1943	No competition				No competition				1943
1944	No competition				No competition				1944
1945	No competition				No competition				1945
1946	Derby County	4	Charlton Athletic	1	No competition				1946
1947	Charlton Athletic	1	Burnley	0	Aberdeen	2	Hibernian	1	1947
1948	Manchester United	4	Blackpool	2	Rangers	1:1	Morton	1:0	1948
1949	Wolverhampton Wanderers	3	Leicester City	1	Rangers	4	Clyde	1	1949
1950	Arsenal	2	Liverpool	0	Rangers	3	East Fife	0	1950
1951	Newcastle United	2	Blackpool	0	Celtic	1	Motherwell	0	1951
1952	Newcastle United	1	Arsenal	0	Motherwell	4	Dundee	0	1952
1953	Blackpool	4	Bolton Wanderers	3	Rangers	1:1	Aberdeen	1:0	1953
1954	West Bromwich Albion	3	Preston North End	2	Celtic	2	Aberdeen	1	1945
1955	Newcastle United	3	Manchester City	1	Clyde	1:1	Celtic	1:0	1955

Year	Winner		Runner-up						Year
1956	Manchester City	3	Birmingham City	1	Hearts	3	Celtic	1	1956
1957	Aston Villa	2	Manchester United	1	Falkirk	1:2	Kilmarnock	1:1	1957
1958	Bolton Wanderers	2	Manchester United	0	Clyde	1	Hibernian	0	1958
1959	Nottingham Forest	2	Luton Town	1	St Mirren	3	Aberdeen	1	1959
1960	Wolverhampton Wanderers	3	Blackburn Rovers	0	Rangers	2	Kilmarnock	0	1960
1961	Tottenham Hotspur	2	Leicester City	0	Dunfermline Athletic	0:2	Celtic	0:0	1961
1962	Tottenham Hotspur	3	Burnley	1	Rangers	2	St Mirren	0	1962
1963	Manchester United	3	Leicester City	1	Rangers	1:3	Celtic	1:0	1963
1964	West Ham United	3	Preston North End	2	Rangers	3	Dundee	1	1964
1965	Liverpool	2	Leeds United	1	Celtic	3	Dunfermline Athletic	2	1965
1966	Everton	3	Sheffield Wednesday	2	Rangers	0:1	Celtic	0:0	1966
1967	Tottenham Hotspur	2	Chelsea	1	Celtic	2	Aberdeen	0	1967
1968	West Bromwich Albion	1	Everton	0	Dunfermline Athletic	3	Hearts	1	1968
1969	Manchester City	1	Leicester City	0	Celtic	4	Rangers	0	1969
1970	Chelsea	2:2	Leeds United	2:1	Aberdeen	3	Celtic	1	1970
1971	Arsenal	2	Liverpool	1	Celtic	1:2	Rangers	1:1	1971
1972	Leeds United	1	Arsenal	0	Celtic	6	Hibernian	1	1972
1973	Sunderland	1	Leeds United	0	Rangers	3	Celtic	2	1973
1974	Liverpool	3	Newcastle United	0	Celtic	3	Dundee United	0	1974
1975	West Ham United	2	Fulham	0	Celtic	3	Airdrieonians	1	1975
1976	Southampton	1	Manchester United	0	Rangers	3	Hearts	1	1976

[1]Vale of Leven awarded the cup after Rangers failed to attend the replay.
[2]After Dumbarton protested the first game, which Queen's Park won 2-1.
[3]Queen's Park awarded the cup after Vale of Leven failed to attend the final.
[4]Replay ordered by Scottish FA because of the state of the pitch in the first game, won by Third Lanark 3-0.
[5]After Queen's Park protested at the first game, which Celtic won 1-0.
[6]Owing to riots the cup was withheld after two drawn games (2-2, 1-1) at Hampden.
[7]Wanderers, as holders, were exempt to the final and also had choice of ground.

Scottish League & Football League Cup finals

Season	Football League Cup Finals					Scottish League Cup Finals				Season
						Aberdeen	3	Rangers	2	1945-46
						Rangers	4	Aberdeen	0	1946-47
						East Fife	1:4	Falkirk	1:1	1947-48
						Rangers	2	Raith Rovers	0	1948-49
						East Fife	3	Dunfermline Athletic	0	1949-50
						Motherwell	3	Hibernian	0	1950-51
						Dundee	3	Rangers	2	1951-52
						Dundee	2	Kilmarnock	0	1952-53
						East Fife	3	Partick Thistle	2	1953-54
						Hearts	4	Motherwell	2	1954-55
						Aberdeen	2	St Mirren	1	1955-56
						Celtic	0:3	Partick Thistle	0:0	1956-57
						Celtic	7	Rangers	1	1957-58
						Hearts	5	Partick Thistle	1	1958-59
						Hearts	2	Third Lanark	1	1959-60
1960-61	*Aston Villa	3	Rotherham United	2		Rangers	2	Kilmarnock	0	1960-61
1961-62	*Norwich City	4	Rochdale	0		Rangers	1:3	Hearts	1:1	1961-62
1962-63	*Birmingham City	3	Aston Villa	1		Hearts	1	Kilmarnock	0	1962-63
1963-64	*Leicester City	4	Stoke City	3		Rangers	5	Morton	0	1963-64
1964-65	*Chelsea	3	Leicester City	2		Rangers	2	Celtic	1	1964-65
1965-66	*West Bromwich Albion	5	West Ham United	3		Celtic	2	Rangers	1	1965-66
1966-67	Queen's Park Rangers	3	West Bromwich Albion	2		Celtic	1	Rangers	0	1966-67
1967-68	Leeds United	1	Arsenal	0		Celtic	5	Dundee	3	1967-68
1968-69	Swindon Town	3	Arsenal	1		Celtic	6	Hibernian	2	1968-69
1969-70	Manchester City	2	West Bromwich Albion	1		Celtic	1	St Johnstone	0	1969-70
1970-71	Tottenham Hotspur	2	Aston Villa	0		Rangers	1	Celtic	0	1970-71
1971-72	Stoke City	2	Chelsea	1		Partick Thistle	4	Celtic	1	1971-72
1972-73	Tottenham Hotspur	1	Norwich City	0		Hibernian	2	Celtic	1	1972-73
1973-74	Wolverhampton Wanderers	2	Manchester City	1		Dundee	1	Celtic	0	1973-74
1974-75	Aston Villa	1	Norwich City	0		Celtic	6	Hibernian	3	1974-75
1975-76	Manchester City	2	Newcastle United	1		Rangers	1	Celtic	0	1975-76

*Aggregate scores.

Football & Scottish League Champions

Season	Football League Championship	Scottish League Championship	Season	Football League Championship	Scottish League Championship
1888-89	Preston North End		1929-30	Sheffield Wednesday	Rangers
1889-90	Preston North End		1930-31	Arsenal	Rangers
1890-91	Everton	Dumbarton/Rangers (shared)	1931-32	Everton	Motherwell
1891-92	Sunderland	Dumbarton	1932-33	Arsenal	Rangers
1892-93	Sunderland	Celtic	1933-34	Arsenal	Rangers
1893-94	Aston Villa	Celtic	1934-35	Arsenal	Rangers
1894-95	Sunderland	Hearts	1935-36	Sunderland	Celtic
1895-96	Aston Villa	Celtic	1936-37	Manchester City	Rangers
1896-97	Aston Villa	Hearts	1937-38	Arsenal	Celtic
1897-98	Sheffield United	Celtic	1938-39	Everton	Rangers
1898-99	Aston Villa	Rangers	1939-46	No competition	No competition
1899-1900	Aston Villa	Rangers	1946-47	Liverpool	Rangers
1900-01	Liverpool	Rangers	1947-48	Arsenal	Hibernian
1901-02	Sunderland	Rangers	1948-49	Portsmouth	Rangers
1902-03	The Wednesday	Hibernian	1949-50	Portsmouth	Rangers
1903-04	The Wednesday	Third Lanark	1950-51	Tottenham Hotspur	Hibernian
1904-05	Newcastle United	Celtic	1951-52	Manchester United	Hibernian
1905-06	Liverpool	Celtic	1952-53	Arsenal	Rangers
1906-07	Newcastle United	Celtic	1953-54	Wolverhampton Wanderers	Celtic
1907-08	Manchester United	Celtic	1954-55	Chelsea	Aberdeen
1908-09	Newcastle United	Celtic	1955-56	Manchester United	Rangers
1909-10	Aston Villa	Celtic	1956-57	Manchester United	Rangers
1910-11	Manchester United	Rangers	1957-58	Wolverhampton Wanderers	Hearts
1911-12	Blackburn Rovers	Rangers	1958-59	Wolverhampton Wanderers	Rangers
1912-13	Sunderland	Rangers	1959-60	Burnley	Hearts
1913-14	Blackburn Rovers	Celtic	1960-61	Tottenham Hotspur	Rangers
1914-15	Everton	Celtic	1961-62	Ipswich Town	Dundee
1915-16	No competition	Celtic	1962-63	Everton	Rangers
1916-17	No competition	Celtic	1963-64	Liverpool	Rangers
1917-18	No competition	Rangers	1964-65	Manchester United	Kilmarnock
1918-19	No competition	Celtic	1965-66	Liverpool	Celtic
1919-20	West Bromwich Albion	Rangers	1966-67	Manchester United	Celtic
1920-21	Burnley	Rangers	1967-68	Manchester City	Celtic
1921-22	Liverpool	Celtic	1968-69	Leeds United	Celtic
1922-23	Liverpool	Rangers	1969-70	Everton	Celtic
1923-24	Huddersfield Town	Rangers	1970-71	Arsenal	Celtic
1924-25	Huddersfield Town	Rangers	1971-72	Derby County	Celtic
1925-26	Huddersfield Town	Celtic	1972-73	Liverpool	Celtic
1926-27	Newcastle United	Rangers	1973-74	Leeds United	Celtic
1927-28	Everton	Rangers	1974-75	Derby County	Rangers
1928-29	The Wednesday	Rangers	1975-76	Liverpool	Rangers

BIBLIOGRAPHY

Football as a subject area has long suffered from a surfeit of poor books and a lack of good ones. No bibliography can pretend to be completely comprehensive, but this is a selection of those publications which were used to provide some of the background for *The Story of Football*, and can be recommended in their own right. Most are available at the time of going to press or are likely to be reprinted in the near future.

The two most comprehensive works on football are the partworks 'The Game' and 'Book of Football' (Marshall Cavendish 1969–1973) but these are now difficult to obtain in complete form. From a historical point of view, the definitive work is undoubtedly Percy Young's *The History of British Football* (Stanley Paul first printed in 1968) which covers the pre-1863 period far better than any other title. *Football!* by Nicholas Mason (Maurice Temple Smith 1974) also provides an excellent description of the origins and early years of soccer as well as the development of the various other forms of football. John Rafferty's *One Hundred Years of Scottish Football* (Pan 1973) is invaluable reading for historians north of the border. Similarly Tony Pawson's *100 Years of the FA Cup* (Pan/ Heinemann 1972) is a comprehensive treatment of its subject.

For the connoisseur, the best source of material on the nineteenth century is *Association Football and the Men who made it* (Caxton 1905) by Alfred Gibson and William Pickford, originally published in four volumes and the earliest known general history cum reference book on the game. In 1960 Caxton published another four-volume set edited by Geoffrey Green and titled *Association Football*. Both can occasionally be discovered in second-hand bookshops.

For detailed, factual information, the annual *Rothmans' Football Yearbook* (Queen Anne Press, first published 1970 and edited by Jack Rollin and Leslie Vernon) is an incomparable source and the fan's bible. For a detailed history of all the major competitions in the British Isles, including final placings in all English and Scottish Leagues since 1888, plus the results of Cup games from the early rounds back to 1872, the *Encyclopedia of British Football* (Collins 1974 revised 1976) is a unique source and provides the only available reference for pre-First World War Scottish Cup and League. Maurice Golesworthy's *The Encyclopedia of Association Football* (Robert Hale, first published 1956 and updated most years since) is the 'Guinness Book of Records' of the game—full of detail, minutae and records. *The Sportsman's World of Soccer* (Marshall Cavendish 1975) also provides a fully illustrated record of the world's major competitions.

For anyone wanting a coaching and tactical guide, there is a large selection, the best illustrated title probably being *The Professionals' Book of Skills and Tactics* (Marshall Cavendish 1973) by Ken Jones and Pat Welton.

On the international scene, Maurice Golesworthy and Roger Macdonald's *AB-Z of World Football* (Pelham 1966 and since updated) is the best source of detailed information along with *World Soccer from A to Z* (Pan 1973) edited by Norman Barrett. Brian Glanville updates his *World Football Handbook* (Mayflower) annually and has also published *Football—a Panorama* (Eyre Methuen) which provides a good grounding in the world game at both club and international level. On individual tournaments, the *World Cup* series by Hugh McIlvanney, Arthur Hopcraft and Ronald Atkin (Eyre Methuen), published after each of the recent World Cups provides excellent entertainment, while for sheer enjoyment little can beat Arthur Hopcraft's *The Football Man* (Penguin).

PICTURE CREDITS